God's Blessings
John 15:5-8

Breaking the Peanut Butter Habit...

Following God's Recipe for a Better Life

By Larry Davies

Breaking the Peanut Butter Habit...

Following God's Recipe for a Better Life

By Larry Davies

Copyright © 2001
Larry Davies
Lynchburg, Virginia

ISBN # 0-9656688-3-5
Published by
ABM Enterprises, Inc.
T/A The Amelia Bulletin Monitor
Amelia Court House, Virginia
Cover Artwork by Sandra Mick
Editing by Ann B. Salster
"How Should We Live" a story by Ree Cathey
"One Nation Under God" by Kirsten Porter

Table of Contents

Breaking the Peanut Butter Habit…
Following God's Recipe for a Better Life

3. Breaking the Peanut Butter Habit
Examining Some Old Recipes

4. Breaking the Peanut Butter Habit
Snapshots in Time

5. Breaking the Peanut Butter Habit
Surfing through the Obstacles of our Faith

6. Breaking the Peanut Butter Habit
For Those Who Like their Food Hot!

7. Breaking the Peanut Butter Habit
Seasonal Food: Fall, Christmas and Winter

8. Breaking the Peanut Butter Habit
Seasonal Food: Spring, Easter and Summer

9. Breaking the Peanut Butter Habit
A Little Desert Never Hurt

Breaking The Peanut Butter Habit…
Following God's Recipe for a Better Life

My son, Stephen, loved peanut butter sandwiches. Actually love is too mild. He… **LOVED** peanut butter sandwiches. Every meal… he wanted a peanut butter sandwich: not a peanut butter sandwich with jelly… just a (well you get the picture.) We traveled to restaurants having to carry a paper bag that contained… you guessed it: a peanut butter sandwich.

Can you imagine the looks we received from waiters? *"We would like two shrimp dinners. By the way, my son brought his own food. Nothing personal! Do you mind?"*

Stephen was also very stubborn. Especially when it came to his eating habits. When he set his little mind to something…it was like trying to stop a freight train. I don't know where he picked up that trait? (You can stop laughing now.)

"Would you like a hot dog?"	***"No!"*** You could see his look of determination.
"How about some spaghetti?"	***"No!"*** A tear was beginning to form in one *eye.*
"Please eat the broccoli?"	***"No! I want my peanut butter sandwich!!"***

Something had to be done! (I know better now but Stephen was my first child. I hadn't read the training manual.) My son could end up in college still eating those same peanut butter sandwiches. Can you imagine his first job interview… over lunch? Oh, the shame of it all! Somehow… someway, Stephen needed to broaden his eating habits and I was determined to help him change. A showdown was brewing!

The day of the big battle started innocently enough. *"I have to run a few errands. Why don't you come with me, Stephen?"* We pulled into the restaurant before the lunch crowd arrived. *"Let's get something to eat."* I ordered the food and began setting it on the table. The inevitable question beginning the first skirmish soon came: *"Where is my peanut butter sandwich?"*

"I didn't bring a peanut butter sandwich, son. Why don't you eat this hamburger?" (Can you imagine having to force someone to eat a hamburger? Is the world out of alignment?)

That determined look appeared on his face and the tears began. *"No! I want my peanut butter sandwich!"*

"Son, there will be no peanut butter sandwich today. You are going to eat this hamburger!" As father and son squared off in a quiet restaurant, I recalled an old sales lesson. In a battle of stares the one who looks away first, loses. This time, I would not, could not and dared not lose!

Slowly, with a tear trickling down his cheek, he picked up the hamburger and took his first bite… His face slowly changed from a frown to a slight smile. Then he took a second bite and a third. Then Stephen actually reached for a French fry. Wow! As Mikey would say: *"He liked it! He liked it!"*

Larry is there a point to this story? Of course there is. My son settled for the security of peanut butter and overlooked a smorgasbord of delectable food to savor.

In many ways, don't we all?

We seek security and pass on new choices, which although involving risks, also lead to golden opportunities.

He complains about his job but never goes back to school to acquire new skills.

She says: "I'm lonely" and stays home watching TV.

Many of our churches cry out, "We want to be alive! We want to grow in our faith! We want to receive new families! We want a youth ministry! We want to make a difference in the world!" Yet so few churches are willing to venture beyond what they already know is safe.

It's time to break the Peanut Butter habit!

Now you know why I wrote this book. For the last fifteen years, I've served as a pastor of small, medium and large churches. At times, just like my son, we stubbornly clung to our peanut butter habits. At times we took risks and God blessed us. Sometimes our ideas worked… sometimes they didn't. But in the end, we grew stronger as we sampled God's amazing menu.

If you are looking for a textbook on theology or how to grow the church in ten easy steps… this is not it.

But if you are looking for spiritual nourishment from stories carefully designed as loving encouragement to break your peanut butter habits and at the same time teach a lesson from Scripture then you will enjoy reading this book.

Jesus said this about food. *"I have food you don't know about... My nourishment comes from doing the will of God... Look around you! Vast fields are ripening all around us and are ready now for the harvest. The harvesters are paid good wages, and the fruit they harvest is people brought to eternal life. What joy awaits both the planter and the harvester alike!"*   (John 4:31-36)

Jesus has a great menu waiting for us...
We receive nourishment doing the will of God...
Vast Fields are ripening all around you...
You will be paid good wages...
The fruit will be people brought to eternal life...
What joy awaits the planter and harvester alike...

Look at all those promises of good food!

This has never been truer then now. I write this within days of the September 11, 2001 terrorist attack on the World Trade Center, the Pentagon and the plane crash in Pennsylvania. The horror we have witnessed and the renewed search for faith throughout the world has convinced me more than ever that we need God in our lives... now!

Are you settling for a peanut butter sandwich when God offers so much more? Maybe it's time to take a hard look at your relationship with God and with your church? Venture out and sign up for a Bible study. Join a small group to pray and offer godly encouragement. Suggest starting a prayer group at work. Volunteer to help a neighbor in need. Serve on a mission project. Set aside a quiet time for prayer.

Why settle for peanut butter when God offers... steak, lobster, salads, chocolate cake, pizza... well, you get the picture. (And I'm getting so hungry!)

There is only one problem. My son still won't eat broccoli!

Loaves and Fishes and the World Wide Web

By Darrell Laurant – *Lynchburg News and Advance*

Dear Pastor Davies: You won't believe how I stumbled on your site. I did a Google.com search for the "best mulch" and your experience about buying a bag of mulch and witnessing to the clerk came up. Since I'm here, I would appreciate a prayer for my sister-in-law's husband. He goes for major surgery at the University of Maryland tomorrow. – Esther Sue

It is indeed, a brave new world, and the Rev. Larry Davies of Timberlake United Methodist is taking full advantage of it.

Of course, Davies has never been your average pastor. For one thing, he used to sell Honda automobiles in Tidewater, Virginia. For anther, his first marriage ended in divorce. Recently, he planned a service in which congregation members were encouraged to dress in beach wear and the choir filled the sanctuary with Beach Boys tunes.

"I really think too many ministers worry way too much about their dignity." Davies said on a recent morning at the Koffee Kup restaurant, his "alternate Sunday school."

Dignity never sold Hondas, he discovered, and it doesn't do a very good job of selling the gospel. Nor does Davies agree with the religious point of view that regards "the world" as something to be avoided at all costs.

There are bad things out in that world, he knows. He's experienced some of them. But there are also good things.

So while others may fear the Internet as a seething Sodom and Gomorrah, filled with porn sites and rip-off schemes and lurking child molesters, Davies and an increasing number of other ministers prefer to embrace it as an opportunity.

The advantages are obvious. If you preach a sermon on Sunday, your audience is limited to the members in the pews. Put it on television and that audience increases exponentially but it's still dependent upon people switching on their sets at the time of your program. With the Internet, a sermon can be e-mailed to thousands and they can experience it any time they choose.

Put another way, the Web is to words what the miracle on the Mount was to loaves and fishes.

"It (the Internet) scared me a little bit at first," Davies said of the new

11

medium, "but I'm getting more and more comfortable."

His Web site, *www.SowingSeedsofFaith.com* offers a literal helping hand. The first thing you see when you click on it is an almost-as-large-as-life hand reaching onto the screen and dropping a seed. The seed disappears, only to explode upward into a flower with a family of three cupped in its petals. Another seed brings forth an older man standing all alone, still another a mother and child. This symbolizes Davies' belief that a church has to reach people in all sorts of situations, not just the hallowed "nuclear family."

Once you get past the special effects, you find a weekly devotional, some of Davies' thoughts (he is an excellent writer), some "hot issues" and "Biblical turning points," and a link to prayer requests.

This, of course, has transcended Timberlake United Methodist and turned Sowing Seeds Ministry into a nationwide – and maybe even world wide - - - ministry.

"The last time I checked, we had a list of over 6,000 Sowing Seeds subscribers," Davies said, "and over 2,000 people on our prayer team."

He's also accumulating a list of success stories. There was, for example, a woman named Janice who sent Davies an e-mail about her impending suicide. She sounded definite about taking her life, but concerned about the effect it might have on her family.

"That sent chills down me," said Davies, who had experienced the suicide of a close family member.

He tried offering Janice some pastoral wisdom. It didn't take.

"I'm not afraid to die," she wrote back. "I'm afraid to live."

He was stumped, he recalled. And scared.

"So I finally slowed down and began to pray… and listen," he later wrote. "During those quiet peaceful moments, I finally realized God's answer. Share Janice's story and allow a community of faith to pray and be used by God to reach out to her.

"Within minutes, copies of Janice's letter were forwarded over the Internet to hundreds of people who had promised to pray for anyone in need. The response was rapid and incredible. Many began to pray immediately. Soon, Janice received dozens of e-mail letters and a few phone calls from people who shared their own struggle with pain and depression and how God guided their recovery."

In this case, the 'success story was not Janice' – not yet, anyway. She emailed Davies that she felt depressed, but was encouraged by the outpouring of support "to try and remain alive one minute at a time, day by day."

What stunned and energized Davies was the speed at which his unseen "cyber-congregation" leaped to a stranger's aid.

Ministers, like all authority figures are stalked by their egos. It's so tempting to believe that you have all the answers, or that you can produce them by simply turning to an appropriate page in the Bible.

"A lot of times, though," said Davies, "other people who have had the same experience are far more effective in helping than any minister. Your greatest pain, in many cases, is your greatest ministry."

And there's always more to learn. In Davies' case, he soon realized that the Internet was useless to him unless he could find out how to negotiate the labyrinth of search engines.

"I was so naïve, I though all the sites on search engines were ranked in order of importance," he said. "I soon found out that a lot of it involves money."

Armed with that knowledge, he hooked the "Sowing Seeds Ministry" up with some entrepreneurs who promised to give it good placement in return for a small fee per "hit."

"One of them charged five cents a hit," Davies said with a chuckle, "and I got so many responses that I had to quit using them. It was too expensive."

Acknowledgments

This is my chance to say thank-you to the people who have meant so much in my life. There have been many. Whether you have been named or not, please know that I thank God for your influence in my life.

Thank you!

Mell — Thank you for being the best wife and friend anyone could ever ask for. Thank you for loving me unconditionally.

To Stephen & Lisa. You've grown up with me writing about you and survived. This father is very proud of both of you.

Timberlake UMC – You've been more than a church. You've become a family and living proof what a great church can do.

Keysville UMC – You were my inspiration and the source of much of my writing. Thank you for encouraging the best in me.

Aldersgate, Centenary, North Amelia Churches — Thank you for helping me get started in my ministry.

The Amelia Bulletin Monitor – All this writing is your fault! You got me started. Thanks for making this book possible.

To C.B. King – Thanks for being my encourager, my cheerleader and my friend when I needed it most.

To Tom Riddle - Thanks for being a friend and teacher and showing the true meaning of breaking my comfort zone.

There are many more that have helped along the way. Thank you for loving and supporting me when I needed it the most.

To the survivors of the September 11, 2001 terrorist attack. I forget you or your loved ones. I dedicate a portion of the proceeds of this book to you. May God be with you.

Thank you God for Your amazing grace. May the power of your Holy Spirit use this book to show others how very special they are in your eyes.

14

Breaking The Peanut Butter Habit . . .

Following God's Recipe For A Better Life.

Chapter 1

Every Good Meal Begins With An Appetizer

All I Want Is A Bag of Mulch…

All I wanted to do was purchase some mulch at the discount store and go home but the checkout cashier discovered a hole in the bag so someone was sent to bring us another bag of mulch. Meanwhile, we waited. Then, another item was missing a price tag so once again someone was sent to find the correct price. We waited some more. While we waited the cashier talked… boy did he talk.

While filling out the check, I asked: *"What is today's date?"*

"I don't know. I don't care. All I know is that today is Friday!" he said with emphasis and a grin.

In a feeble attempt to be polite, I replied: *"So, you like Fridays?"*

"Oh yeah," he said with obvious enthusiasm. *"I love Fridays… because it's party time and I love to party! I live to party!"*

Before I could respond… he continued: *"I drink and party all night long! Yep! My friends and me love to have a good time. We try to do it every night. That's what I live for: friends, drinking and partying."*

I thought to myself: *"Why is he saying this to me? Should I respond? Should I tell this young man he's making a big mistake? Should I tell him there is another way to enjoy life? Should I talk about God in a crowded department store to a stranger? I really don't want to be a witness right now Lord. I just want to make my purchase and go home. Is there anything wrong with that?"*

Yet, if I say nothing it looks as if I approve or at least condone his outrageous behavior. But if I say something… how do I say it without sounding judgmental and arrogant? In essence, I was in a fix.

There is a great verse in the Bible that seems appropriate: *"And now dear children, continue to live in fellowship with Christ so that when he returns, you will be full of courage and not shrink back from him in shame."* (1 John 2:28) I needed a dose of Godly courage and wisdom to say something appropriate to this young man and let him know I did not approve his actions but loved him as a child of God.

After a pause, I looked at the young cashier and flashed my biggest smile. *"I want to thank you for telling me about your parties. You just made my day!"*

This time, it was his turn to pause. *"What do you mean?"* he asked with a look of confusion.

"Well, I'm a preacher looking for someone who needs prayer… and my friend, you are the one!"

His mouth opened in astonishment and he stared at me for a long moment

16

before a smile began to appear. Then he laughed and said: *"You won't believe this but my preacher said the same thing!"*

For the next few moments my new young friend talked about his minister and church. Recently, He had left home to make it on his own. You could see a trace of loneliness in his eyes as he said: *"My pastor is a great guy. He writes me occasionally and the church still sends newsletters."*

I left the discount store with a bag of mulch, a smile on my face and a new perspective on the importance of creatively communicating God's message to each other. What we say, how we choose our words and our attitude behind those words can literally spell the difference between healing and hurting. *"Evil words destroy one's friends; wise discernment rescues the godly."* (Proverbs 11:9)

Whether you are standing in line at a department store or participating in a church committee meeting, God is continually offering opportunities to witness your faith. What will you say? How will you say it? Take a deep breath, pause, say a short prayer and remember God's promise, *"...continue to live in fellowship with Christ and you will be full of courage..."* As for me, I have a new friend to pray for and a valuable lesson to remember and practice. Now, if I could only find someone to spread this mulch!

'Myst' & Our Journey of Faith

There are two types of people who play computer games. One uses the computer and occasionally plays a game (that's me... so far). The other type lives to play games and only occasionally realizes there is a real world outside the computer screen. "Why do they do that?"

Being an enterprising and curious kind of guy, I decided to investigate the strange world of computer games and see if there would be any good lessons for a pastor and writer. (In other words, I wanted to check out the latest toys and call it work!) My research led me to "Myst," a top selling computer game where the creators wanted no violence but plenty of entertainment.

"Myst" sounded like the right kind of game for a pastor to check out... (Besides, it was on sale!) Of course, the last time I attempted to understand a video game, it was made by Atari and involved bouncing a little ball back and forth. Boy, have computer games dramatically changed...

"You have just stumbled upon a most intriguing book, a book titled Myst. You have no idea where it came from, who wrote it, or how old it is.

Reading through its pages provides you with only a superbly crafted description of an island world. But it's just a book, isn't it?" (Introduction)

Amidst eerie music, you open the book on the computer screen and find yourself on "Myst" island, which is deserted. "Why? What happened?" As you wander amidst beautiful surroundings, you begin looking for clues to help you find out where everyone went. All of it is intertwined in a story full of mystery and intrigue. "Who are these two mysterious brothers? Which one is evil? Why do I care? Why is the music so weird?" I have to admit... "Myst" is fascinating and addicting fun.

The secret to successfully playing the game is to pay close attention to the details and take careful notes. What do you see? What do you hear? You must be patient and never give up. The instructions add, *"But most importantly — think of what you would do if you were really there."*

Maybe I could learn from this...

"You have just stumbled upon a most intriguing book, a book titled The Holy Bible. You have very little idea where it came from, who wrote it, or how old it is. Reading its pages provides you with only a superbly crafted description of the real world. But it's just a book, isn't it?"

In many ways, exploring the Bible is similar to "Myst." You open the book and find yourself in a different world. You begin looking for clues to help you find answers. All of it is intertwined in a story full of mystery and intrigue. "Who are these mystifying people of God? How do they grow from 'mistake prone' followers to mature disciples of faith? How can their lessons help me?"

The secret to a successful journey through the scriptures is to pay close attention to the details. What do you see? What do you hear? What do you feel as you read? You must be patient and never give up. But most importantly — think of what you would do if you were really there.

All Scripture is inspired by God and is useful to teach us what is true and to make us realize what is wrong in our lives. It straightens us out and teaches us to do what is right. It is God's way of preparing us in everyway, fully equipped for every good thing God wants us to do.

(2 Timothy 3:16-17)

Playing "Myst" is challenging and can be an interesting way to occupy your free time. Reading the Bible is also challenging but more than simply occupying your free time... Bible study can change your life. Try it... you'll like it!

A Tale of Two Restaurants

Mell (my wife) and I were attending a conference in Florida. It was only 11:00 AM but we were hungry and wanted lunch. *"Would you like a seat for breakfast?"* The greeter at the hotel restaurant asked.

"No thank you, we would like to eat lunch." I replied.

"I'm so sorry, but this restaurant will not serve lunch for another half-hour. However, another restaurant in this hotel is serving lunch now. Let me show you where it is." Immediately she left her workstation and walked with us down the corridor until we came in sight of a sandwich shop. She then smiled and said, *"I hope you enjoy your meal..."* and returned to her station. We were impressed but not for long.

The sandwich shop was quiet and empty. We saw only one employee at the other end of the restaurant who seemed to be busy adjusting a big screen TV. He was making no attempt to notice us so we walked over and I asked him, *"Where do we go to order lunch?"* He slowly turned around and gave us one of those, *"why are you bothering me?"* looks and pointed to the counter across the room.

Humph! So, we turned and walked to where he pointed and then kept on walking through the door and back down the corridor to the other restaurant. Why?

a) We didn't like the station he chose on TV.

b) Sandwiches just aren't for me.

c) The wallpaper colors clashed with our clothes.

d) We wanted a restaurant that sincerely wanted to serve us.

Of course the answer is d) unless you happen to be a gourmet chef or a fashion designer. Then choose e) all of the above.

We felt welcome in the first restaurant and decided it was worth waiting a few extra minutes. But the best is yet to come. During the meal, the waitress tripped and spilled a tray filled with glasses of ice water all over our table, barely missing us. It could have been a disaster, but she was so embarrassed and apologetic we all ended up laughing. Later, the manager offered her own apology and free desert.

We were impressed enough to eat most of our meals there and told others at the conference about the good food and extraordinary service of this restaurant. Often we waited in line to receive a seat but we always found the experience worth the wait.

Occasionally we would pass by the sandwich shop and see the same guy, still watching TV… alone.

Why am I telling you this? The story of the two restaurants illustrates the difference between "magic moments" where you feel appreciated or "tragic moments" that leave you feeling neglected. The secret to offering "magic moments" is to understand what someone needs and then try to exceed his/her expectations. One restaurant succeeded because it specialized in "magic moments."

We have the same opportunity to specialize in "magic moments" by offering a loving relationship with God and with fellow Christians. In other words, we work as the church to understand someone's needs and through our best efforts combined with God's grace strive to exceed their expectations. The last thing Jesus said to his disciples was, *"go and make disciples of all the nations."* (Matthew 28:19) It's a great challenge for individuals and churches to offer "magic moments" through the power of God.

Question: If someone encounters you on the street or enters your church will they be offered…

    a) Tragic Moment? *"What are you doing here? Why are you bothering me?"*

    b) No Moment? *"Maybe if I don't speak, he/she will go away."*

    c) Magic Moment? *"I'm so glad to see you? Tell me how you have been doing…"*

Can you imagine the difference this attitude would make in your church, in your home… in your life? All this talk of "magic moments" has made me hungry. Anyone know where I can get a sandwich?

The Harvest is Great: The Workers Few

My Uncle was the head of Parks and Recreation for one of the largest cities in the country. It's a demanding job managing thousands of employees. Several years ago, he asked the leaders of his local church how he could become more involved. They immediately asked him to serve on the Pastor-Parish Relations committee, one of the most important tasks in any church. He also served on the building committee and even became a trustee. But as he talked, I noticed that the church never seemed very interested in the job my Uncle managed most every day of his life: A job, which often impacted several million people. **My Uncle was asking for a ministry and the church put him on a committee.**

I also heard of a grocery store checkout cashier who could read people's moods by their body language while standing in line. After interpreting their mood, she felt called by God to offer encouragement if they were down or praise if their mood was upbeat. She did all of this while bagging groceries. Remarkable! When is the last time you were offered a word of encouragement at a grocery store check out line?

What about you? God has called you for a ministry. Do you know what it is? How should the church help? Committee work is important but there is so much more. As a minister, I emphasize two themes:

1. Provide an atmosphere of encouragement and love for you to improve your relationship with God through prayer, Bible study and church participation.
2. Help you discover your unique gifts and talents and use them toward a ministry of serving and helping others within your family, at work, at church, in your community and around the world.

"The Lord now chose seventy-two other disciples and sent them ahead in pairs to all the towns and villages he planned to visit. These were his instructions to them: *'The harvest is so great and the workers are so few. Pray to the Lord who is in charge of the harvest and ask Him to send out more workers for his fields. Go now and remember that I am sending you out as lambs among wolves. Don't take along any money or a traveler's bag or even an extra pair of sandals.'"* (Luke 10:1-4)

I found at least five major lessons in this passage:

1. *The Lord chose:* You don't just decide to serve God. You were chosen long before you were born. The questions you should ask: "What task were you chosen for? Are you doing it?"
2. *Travel in pairs:* God knows it is very difficult to work alone. We all need encouragement either from a friend, a pastor, a church group or family. Ministry always needs a partner.
3. *Pray for more workers:* Your life of prayer is just as important as your willingness to work. Praying and asking for God's help is an important part of your ministry.
4. *Lambs among wolves:* You are receiving a divine warning to be careful. Remember wolves see lambs as only one thing… supper. Serving God always involves risk. Be prepared.
5. *Travel lite:* The ad says, "less filling… tastes great!" Too much stuff, no matter how good can become a burden and weigh down your ministry. Keep your message and your faith simple.

How are most churches doing with following these basic lessons:

Actually, not very good. A survey was taken among active Christians.

What they found was startling:

➤70% never or rarely encouraged someone to believe in God.

➤45% never or seldom talked about their faith.

➤64% infrequently pray.

➤77% seldom read the Bible.

Why? There are many reasons. We are afraid of controversy. Churches tend to seek members rather than disciples. We're busy and preoccupied. We fear rejection. We face too many choices for our time.

What can we do about it? Several months ago, a minister friend suggested I read a little book by Bruce Wilkinson called *The Prayer of Jabez* about a virtually unknown Bible character named Jabez hidden in First Chronicles 4:9-10. *"It's one of the best books I've ever read,"* he declared.

He may be right. Using the prayer of Jabez on a regular basis can change your life: *"Oh, that you would bless me indeed and enlarge my territory that your hand would be with me and that you would keep me from evil."* And God granted him his request._Next, I'll try using this prayer to answer the question: What should we be doing as disciples in God's church? Until then… pray the "Prayer of Jabez" faithfully and watch what God does with you.

Spiritual Gifts, The Prayer of Jabez and 'Mousetrap'

Just as our bodies have many parts and each part has a special function, so it is with Christ's body. We are all parts of his one body and each of us has different work to do. And since we are all one body in Christ, we belong to each other and each of us needs all the others. (Romans 12:4-5)

If you walk by my office this week, you may be concerned about my sanity or at least my work habits. Why would a preacher take time out from a hectic schedule to play, "Mousetrap?" But it's so exciting! Watch. *"This is the crank… that turns the shoe… that kicks the marble back and forth down the stairs… then rolls down the chute… that moves the hand… that drops the marble through the thing-a-mi-jig into the tub… that flips the diver… into the pool… that triggers the cage… that traps the mouse!"*

Isn't this fun? No, I'm not crazy! (Well, maybe a little.) "Mousetrap" is an interesting way to explain how a church functions. (You are crazy!) No, I'm serious. The game is a fascinating mixture of cranks, marbles, stairs, chutes, tubs, divers and pools all designed to trigger a cage that traps a mouse? But if you remove even one piece from the formula... the trap no longer works and the mouse goes free.

How is that like a church? Well... A church is an interesting mixture of preachers, teachers, musicians, secretaries, youth, children, single adults, families, new Christians, old Christians, laborers and sales people all designed to trigger an atmosphere of encouragement that will help you deepen your relationship with God, discover your spiritual gifts and use them to reach out to others. But if you remove even one piece from the formula... the church weakens and others remain unreached.

But pieces have been removed from the formula... As I wrote earlier, the church is not doing well. A survey taken among active Christians discovered that most of us never or rarely encourage someone to believe in God, seldom talk about our faith and rarely pray or read the Bible. If this is true then how can the church change? A friend recommended that I read, *The Prayer of Jabez* by Bruce Wilkinson.

There is a virtually unknown Bible character hidden in First Chronicles named Jabez, whose name means, "pain." What a name! After giving birth, his mother names him "pain." Yet, Jabez apparently overcame his "painful" background because he alone is singled out as being blessed by God. Why? Because Jabez said a prayer and God granted his request. Obviously, this is a very special prayer.

So, let's examine this prayer more carefully:

1. ***Oh, that you would bless me indeed...*** sounds selfish at first but Bruce Wilkinson describes blessings as supernatural favors from God. Asking for a blessing is seeking the power of God to flow through you. You are requesting miracles so don't be surprised when God provides.

2. ***And enlarge my territory...*** challenges you to go beyond what is comfortable. Today as you begin your day ask God to look for someone or something new in your life. Take risks for God.

3. ***That your hand would be with me...*** Stepping beyond what is comfortable can be dangerous. You are in uncharted territory. Ask for God's Hand to look after you.

4. ***And that you would keep me from evil...*** is simple recognition that you will be tempted in many ways. Your very success with this prayer can cause feelings of no longer needing God. There are more distractions and more temptations. This is a reminder that you always need God.

23

Take the *Prayer of Jabez* challenge: Every day for thirty days, use this prayer as often as possible. Paste copies wherever you can easily see it. *Oh, that you would bless me indeed and enlarge my territory that your hand would be with me and that you would keep me from evil.* Then simply be alert for what opportunities God sends your way. Will you take the challenge with me?

Now, I'm excited! I anticipate a "Mousetrap" church coming together. As you and your church begin to pray, God starts the miracle: The crank is turning and the shoe kicks the marble down the stairs then rolls down the chute that moves the hand that drops another marble through the thing-a-mi-jig into the tub that flips the diver into the pool that triggers the cage that traps the... well, that's the exciting part!

Just as our bodies have many parts and each part has a special function, so it is with Christ's body...

Trust, Faith & "The Dentist Office"

Name three scenes from movies that were so scary, you still have occasional flashbacks.

➤ To this day, I cringe upon seeing a flock of birds sitting, watching, and waiting. Do you remember hundreds of them attacking school children in Alfred Hitchcock's, "The Birds?"

➤ Whenever I hit the beach and enter the water... something in me looks for a telltale fin and the familiar musical cadence begins... dum-dum, dum-dum. You guessed it: "Jaws."

➤ Do you remember "The Marathon Man?" Dustin Hoffman is strapped in a dentist's chair while Sir Lawrence Olivier, the villain, stands over his open mouth with a drill and says, *"Tell me every thing..."* You hear the whirring sound as Dustin Hoffman... *"screams!"*

I had a chance to relive all three scenes recently while waiting in the dentist office. The birds were perched on the chairs watching, waiting and the familiar musical cadence began... dum-dum, dum-dum as I heard the nurse call my name. Suddenly I was strapped in the chair, looking up helplessly as the "mad" dentist held a whirring drill over my mouth and said, *"Tell me everything!"*

I'm kidding but I did go to the local dentist for root canal surgery. I couldn't stop my overactive imagination. Every time he placed that drill near my mouth, I wanted to… *"scream! Oh that hurts!"*

"Come on Larry, you're being a wimp!" Yes, I know. He was an excellent dentist who took great pains (poor *word choice*) to do everything just right… so far! But he could make a mistake! After all, he's only human. Something could distract him. The drill could slip! Couldn't it? *Ouch!!*

Actually, the surgery went well with no complications but for two long hours the future of my mouth was dependent upon someone else's skills. I had no choice but to place my teeth and my trust in the hands of another. I hate to admit this, but trust does not come easily for me.

A dictionary defines trust as: *"a confident reliance on the integrity, honesty or justice of another; faith."* Trust for me is a confident reliance on the skills of my dentist. Trust for you may be…

> ➢ … beginning a new relationship after a messy break-up.
> ➢ … preparing yourself for needed surgery.
> ➢ … allowing your children appropriate freedoms and responsibilities.
> ➢ … giving God more control over your life.

Trust would best describe Jesus' attitude while approaching the end of his earthly life and ministry. Shortly after a last meal with disciples and friends, Jesus went to the garden of Gethsemane to pray. *"Father, if you are willing, please take this cup of suffering away from me. Yet I want your will, not mine."* Jesus knew about the suffering to come yet in the end placed his confident reliance on the integrity, honesty and justice of God. There can be no greater trust.

Jesus' prayer was answered, not by having the suffering removed but by receiving strength. *"An angel from heaven came down and strengthened him."* (Luke 22:43) It was enough. Even on the cross Jesus' last sentence was from Psalm 31:5: *"I entrust my spirit into your hand…"* in other words, I place my total trust and confident reliance in God.

Some other Biblical examples of trust:

✝ *"That is why we have a great High Priest who has gone to heaven, Jesus the Son or God. Let us cling to him and never stop trusting him."* (Hebrews 4:14)

✝ *"Without wavering, let us hold tightly to the hope we say we have, for God can be trusted to keep his promise."* (Hebrews 10:23)

✝ *"For every child of God defeats this evil world by trusting Christ to give the victory."* (1 John 5:4)

In other words: "We have Jesus to cling too. God can be trusted to keep His promise. We defeat evil by trusting Christ to give the victory." What about you? Are you learning to trust others? How much do you trust God? Learning to trust is a critical part of faith. So, the next time I go to the dentist office, I may still relive a few horror movie scenes but I'll do my best not to… *"scream!"*

Hang In There; Bad Habit but Good Theology!

"Have mercy on me, O God, because of your unfailing love. Because of your great compassion, blot out the stain of my sins. Wash me clean from my guilt. Purify me from my sin." (Psalm 51)

Confession time: I mean well, but I have a bad habit. People come for spiritual guidance and pastoral counseling. (Well, Larry you are a pastor.) I try to listen carefully and offer sound practical and Biblical advice. But at one point during the session I will inevitably blurt out to someone…

    "Hang in there!"

- ☹ A couple with marital problems… *"Hang in there? What is that supposed to mean?"*
- ☹ An alcoholic struggling with addiction… *"Hang in there? Is he really listening to me?"*
- ☹ A friend just told he has cancer… *"Hang in there? Does he think I'm a bat or what?"*
- ☹ Our soldiers are fighting a war with terrorists… *"Hang in there? Have you lost your mind?"*

People, who come looking for hope during a time of crisis, instead receive a canned answer… *"Hang in there!"* They could watch a talk show and get better advice. I have a tendency to say, *"Hang in there,"* when my brain is on automatic pilot. To someone else it could be interpreted: *"I don't care enough about you to give a more meaningful answer, so 'hang in there!'"* Ouch! I am so sorry, Lord!

"Have mercy on me God…" I confess my shortcomings to you, Lord. Help me become a better listener. Help me to more thoughtfully and prayerfully answer the deep concerns of others. *"…purify me from my sin."* Confession and a desire to change is part of what being a Christian is all about.

Larry… what do you really mean when you say, *"Hang in there?"*

I thought you would never ask. The Bible calls it among other things: **persistence.**

✝ **Romans 2:7** - He will give eternal life to those who persist in doing what is good…

✝ **Ephesians 6:10 & 18** - Be strong with the Lord's mighty power. Put on all of God's armor so that you will be able to stand firm… Stay alert and be persistent in your prayers...

✝ **Matthew 24:13-14** - But those who endure to the end will be saved. And the Good News about the Kingdom will be preached throughout the whole world…

First: *If you will persist in doing what is good… Be strong… Stay alert… Be persistent in your prayers… But those who endure…* In other words, God understands your trouble, your disappointments and pain. You are not alone. **"Be persistent!"**

Second: There is a promise of reward for persistence. *He will give eternal life… you will be able to stand firm… you will be saved… the Good News will be preached throughout the world…* God's assurance for persistence amidst the obstacles is eternal life and a heavenly reward.

Have you heard the story about an old mule that fell into a dry well? The farmer didn't think the mule or the dry well was worth saving. So, he decided to bury the mule in the well and put him out of his misery. Initially, the poor old mule was in a panic! But as the shovelfuls of dirt struck his back…the mule began to… *"shake it off and step up!"* Each time the dirt hit he would shake it off and step up. It wasn't long before the old mule, battered and exhausted, shook off that last shovel full of dirt and stepped triumphantly out of the well!

What seemed to bury the old donkey, actually blessed him…all because of his persistence amidst the dirt. He was able to *"shake it off and step up!"* Maybe this is what it really means to "hang in there." If we endure despite our difficulties and refuse to allow panic, bitterness, or self-pity control us… The obstacles that appear to bury us could actually become part of God's richest blessings!

This is especially true during today's uncertain and dangerous times. Yet God consistently promises that if we persist, be strong and endure through our trials, we will be able to stand firm. It may be a bad habit, but it is certainly sound theology when I sincerely say to you… "hang in there!"

Prayer

"Does God answer prayers?" I asked a class.

"Of course... yes... always," were the quick and enthusiastic replies followed by stirring examples.

"Then, why don't we pray more frequently?" A long uncomfortable silence filled the room.

Finally, the excuses began pouring out: *"I'm too busy... No time... God's too busy to listen to me... I don't know what to say... I'm not worthy... I don't know how..."*

Our individual excuses may sound different but our predicament is basically the same. We (*confession time: including me*) do not fully appreciate the importance and power of prayer. Prayer should be as critical and functional as the steering wheel on your car. *"Without you, O Lord, I can go nowhere!"* Yet, for most of us, prayer is more like the spare tire. In other words: *"Don't call us... we'll call when we need You!"*

Prayer is supposed to be an ongoing relationship with almighty God more than an opportunity to present a wish list to a heavenly Santa Claus. But any good relationship needs commitment and a willingness to invest time... lots of time.

For example: Suppose you told a trusted spouse or friend the reason you couldn't be with them is: *"I'm too busy... No time... You're probably too busy to listen to me... I don't know what to say... I'm not worthy... I don't know how...?"* How long would your friendship or intimacy last? Ouch, that hurts!

Here is God's promise on the subject of prayer: *"Don't worry about anything; instead, pray about everything. Tell God what you need and thank him for all he has done. If you do this you will experience God's peace, which is far more wonderful than the human mind can understand. His peace will guard your hearts and minds as you live in Christ Jesus."*

(Philippians 4:6-7)

Our tendency is to worry isn't it? Yet we know worry solves nothing and more often causes emotional, physical and spiritual harm. Prayer offers a means to give our worries to God, who in return promises a supernatural peace... a peace *far more wonderful than the human mind can understand.* Could it be as simple as that? Yes, but it requires a commitment to pray regularly.

Here is a basic formula for prayer that has helped me over the years:

1. **Praise**: Praise sets the tone and reminds you who God really is. Try looking at some of the Psalms and reading them out loud to get you started: Psalm 8, 19 & 148.
2. **Confession**: A good relationship strengthens with honesty. No sane doctor would offer a cure without hearing what hurts. Admitting your faults promotes spiritual healing.
3. **Listen**: Sometimes, it's easier to talk than to really listen. Easy but not smart. Quiet times are often where you will find direction. Listening allows God to speak to your soul.
4. **Ask for Help**: This part becomes more meaningful when you take the time to praise, confess and listen. At this point, you learn to stop worrying and keep praying.
5. **Keep a Journal**: It may be the most important part of my prayer ministry. The journal is where disappointments, struggles, joys and miracles are recorded and remembered.

"Does God answer our prayers?" Yes, but are we doing our part?

Two people with similar difficulties pray. One expects results and finishes his prayer frustrated and confused. Months later, the problem and the prayer are forgotten. Another prays looking to spend a few quiet moments with her Lord and completes her prayer feeling content and at peace. Over the next few months while recording her thoughts in a journal, she notices progress with the problem and especially in her ability to cope. She thanks God.

Think about it. You have a unique opportunity to be in a relationship with God: One that can make an authentic difference in your life and the life of anyone who comes in contact with you. So, what are you waiting for? God? He's been waiting patiently for you a long, long time.

A Prayer Ministry

✟ A two-year old girl is struggling with cancer and a friend requests prayer over the Internet.

✟ Thirty-eight men attend a "Walk to Emmaus" weekend while hundreds more pray.

✟ At 6:00 every morning a bell rings calling members of one family to devotions and prayer.

Earlier, I described prayer as a unique opportunity to be in relationship with God: One that can make an authentic difference in your life and the life of anyone who comes in contact with you. But this is only the first step among many towards an exhilarating prayer ministry.

Prayer Ministry begins with you and then spreads outward in ever-wider circles.

"At 6:00 AM, Mom rings the bell to summon us to the prayer room. At 6:15 we better be there," laughs one of the children. *"We've been gathering every morning for over ten years. I hated getting up so early but now Morning Prayer time is a regular habit. Our family has held together through good times and bad and what I cherish the most is our morning prayers."*

The first circle begins with family: It can start with grace at mealtime. We can pray with our spouse or friend. Parents should pray regularly with their children. *"Listen to my voice in the morning, Lord. Each morning I bring my requests to you and wait expectantly."* (Psalm 5:3) Prayer can be the glue that holds your family together in a world that seems to be falling apart.

"Every Sunday morning at 7:30 our group meets at church to offer encouragement and prayers. It's the only time all of us can make it. We've helped each other through marriage problems, deaths and serious illness. Each week, we challenge each other to be a better Christian then we were the week before. It hasn't always been easy but this group has helped me become a better person."

The second prayer circle involves a small group: Two key features of this ministry are accountability and encouragement. Accountability represents the desire to improve while warm, loving encouragement keeps you going when accountability is difficult. *"Devote yourselves to prayer with an alert mind and a thankful heart."* (Col. 4:2) Prayer sustains and challenges us.

"During worship I asked for prayer on behalf of a man in another state facing surgery. A candle was lit reminding us to pray and a card of encouragement was mailed. He called me later in tears. That prayer card was the first thing he saw when he woke up in the recovery room."

The third prayer circle is your local church: Prayer should be an integral part of any worship service. There should also be prayer gatherings and occasional healing services. Many churches post lists where someone can pray at any hour of every day. There are prayer chains so that urgent prayer needs can get out quickly. "They… devoted themselves to… prayer." (Acts 2:42)

Thirty-eight men recently attended a "Walk to Emmaus" weekend while others worked behind the scenes and hundreds more prayed: Some at a certain hour for the success of the weekend, while others prayed for a particular individual. When the 'walk' was over, thirty-eight men spoke of having life-changing experiences. Why? There were many reasons, but mainly it was prayer."

The fourth prayer circle is within the wider community: Following a tragedy many communities traditionally gather to pray for those involved and to search for solutions. But why wait for a tragedy? "I urge you first of all, to pray for all people." (1 Tim. 2:1) A wider community of prayer can be expanded to include your neighborhood and even the entire world. For example:

A two-year old girl named Becky is struggling with cancer and a family friend goes home to her computer and begins searching the Internet for prayer groups. To each group, she sends an urgent email message asking them to pray for Becky. Within hours, thousands of people around the world are praying and sending emails to her family offering words of love and encouragement.

Prayer Ministry begins with you and spreads outward in ever-wider circles. The possibilities are endless and the potential is awe-inspiring. Question: *How is your prayer ministry doing?*

Be a Tough Encourager

Despite my best efforts, sales were off and I was perilously close to being fired.

My new job began with such promise. Three short months ago, I moved the family from Richmond to Virginia Beach for what seemed to be the opportunity of a lifetime. I was in charge of a thriving metropolitan automobile dealership. At first, everything seemed fine and our sales were beginning to improve. But it wasn't long before old problems reappeared and sales began to drop. Yet, I was working harder than ever. What was going wrong?

Tom Riddle, the owner would have been justified in finding someone else to run the dealership but instead chose to have a meeting with me. Our talk became one of those turning points that changed my philosophy of leadership and helped me understand the importance of becoming a tough encourager.

At one point, Mr. Riddle said: *"I notice you are usually on the sales floor talking to customers."*

"Yes, sir." I answered, thinking he would be pleased. *"I try to meet everyone personally."*

Mr. Riddle paused for a moment and then said something, I will never forget. ***"That's fine but tell me why I pay the salaries twelve sales people when you are doing all of the work? Unless something changes, I will either have to fire twelve sales people or I'm going to have to fire you!"***

What could I say? Mr. Riddle had found my critical weakness. By insisting on doing most of the selling I was limiting our sales efforts to my capabilities and energy. One individual no matter how talented can only do so much. However, one person leading a team can accomplish miracles! A critical point that is true in business, family relationships, sports and especially our walk with God.

The writer of Hebrews sums up the whole purpose of being in God's church: *Without wavering, let us hold tightly to the hope we say we have, for God can be trusted to keep his promise. Think of ways to encourage one another to outbursts of love and good deeds. And let us not neglect our meeting together, as some people do, but encourage and warn each other, especially now that the day of his coming back again is drawing near.*
(Hebrews 10:23-25)

In other words, our calling as Christians is to **hold tightly to our faith and encourage others to outbursts of love and good deeds!** But how do we do that?

Encouragement is more than merely giving a compliment. Funk and Wagnall defines encourage: *"To inspire with courage, hope or resolution."* What I received from Mr. Riddle was definitely not a compliment (The compliments came later.) but what he said inspired me with courage, hope and resolution. I call it tough encouragement. I left his office that day determined to be a team builder and a tough encourager. A valuable lesson I would never forget.

As a manager, more time was spent encouraging sales people to treat people honestly and fairly. I still enjoyed meeting the customers, but selling became a team effort utilizing the best of all our gifts and talents for the good of the business. Being an encourager also helped me stay employed.

As a pastor, it is still important for me to foster teamwork and offer tough encouragement. Like most organizations, churches have plenty of

32

hard workers, but need more people who are willing to encourage others to outbursts of love and good deeds. Only then will we begin to act as a team filled with the power of God's Holy Spirit. We are all called to be tough encouragers.

I still enjoy working with others, but my ministry has become a team effort utilizing the best of many gifts and talents for God. Paul said it clearly: *"If your gift is to encourage others, do it!"* (Romans 12:8) By the way, being a tough encourager still helps me stay employed.

Comfort by Computer?

I was a little slow entering the computer age, so when my sister gave me her old machine, I was delighted, but fearful. To be better equipped, I bought the book, "Computers for Dummies". As a reasonably intelligent person, I figured with a little reading and practice, a book for "dummies" could certainly help me figure out anything, even a computer. Right? Wrong!

It took many long hours and several days with numerous intelligent, very patient friends to help me do the simplest tasks with this "brain in a box." My self-esteem was completely shattered. After all, if I couldn't learn from a book for "dummies: *"What does that make me? Less than a dummy?"* Don't answer that, please. I feel low enough already.

I did eventually learn how to perform some simple everyday jobs on this machine. One was learning how to use a computer Bible study program. At the time, I happened to be teaching a lesson on "comfort" which called for looking up examples. So I turned on the computer and asked: *"How often does the word "comfort" appear in scripture?"*

The machine hummed for a few seconds and out came the number 69. *"Wow, this is great!"* I said. *"Sixty-nine verses in the Bible offer the comfort of God."* Next, I hit the print button and received five full pages of scripture. That night at the Bible study, each student was given a copy and asked to pick their favorite verse and tell why.

✞ *"Even though I walk through the valley of the shadow of death, I will fear no evil, for you are with me; your rod and your staff, they comfort me."* (Psalm 23:4) She talked of her father dying and how hearing those words at the funeral reminded her of Dad's loving protection and discipline.

✞ *"I have seen his ways, but I will heal him; I will guide him and restore comfort to him..."* (Isaiah 57:18) He laughed and said, "God knows what kind of rascal I am and still offers healing and comfort!"

✠ Two women spoke of Ruth 2:13: *"May I continue to find favor in your eyes, my Lord. You have given me comfort and have spoken kindly to your servant — though I do not have the standing of one of your servant girls."* They spoke of the love in their families and in their church family during difficult times.

✠ One man became excited when he found this one. *"My comfort in my suffering is this: Your promise preserves my life."* (Psalm 119:50) He had been going through a painful marital separation and was looking for direction in his life. He found the comfort of God and the strength to begin putting his life back together.

✠ Another student added: *"May your unfailing love be my comfort, according to your promise to your servant." (*Psalm 119:76) Her children had been difficult that day as she began to cry. Across the table someone quietly read another verse to her. *"As a mother comforts her child, so I will comfort you..."* (Isaiah 66:13)

You could feel God's Holy Spirit in the room offering reassurance as scripture began to soothe troubled hearts and quiet frayed nerves. Tears of sorrow were replaced by sighs of relief as our class members experienced the compassion and the love of a God who never fails to offer comfort, even in the most difficult of circumstances.

What kind of crisis have you been experiencing lately? Have you lost a loved one? Are you worried over your children? Maybe you are experiencing marital difficulties? Have you lost a job? Maybe you are facing some medical problems? There are verses of comfort for you and it doesn't take a computer to find it. Just open your Bible and begin to read. Before long you will feel the power of God and the words of comfort will flood the very depths of your soul.

The lesson ended with a reminder from Isaiah: *"Comfort, comfort my people, says your God."* (40:1) It doesn't get any clearer. May God bless you and give comfort. *Now, please pray that I receive comfort and learn how to work this %$&*##$@ computer. (OOPS!)*

Ship of Fools or Lifeboat to Heaven?

Did you hear about the man traveling from New York to Atlanta on a business trip? Upon arrival, he sent an e-mail message to his wife but it went to the wrong address. Instead the note was delivered to a pastor's wife whose husband recently died. She read the message and promptly fainted. *"Honey, I made it okay, but it sure is hot down here!"*

When the funeral is over and dirt is being shoveled onto your fresh grave... where will your soul be? Will you be in heavenly bliss or will it be a little hot? I know, I know. I've gone from story telling to meddling. People cringe when talking about spiritual matters of any kind, but mention heaven or hell and most of us start looking for a polite way to exit the room.

On the other hand, people are also becoming fascinated with the topic. Like Job we are asking: *"If mortals die, can they live again?"* (Job 14:14) Movies and books about death and the afterlife are increasingly reaching the best-seller lists. One TV series mom, worried that her son would ask about the meaning of death remembered a statement from her father: *"If you pull the plug on a refrigerator, does it keep running?"*

I'll never forget her next comment: *"Between the ages of five and seven, I thought when you died the Goodwill truck hauled you away."*

Is that all there is to life and death? Absolutely not!

Lee Strobel, an award-winning journalist at the Chicago Tribune made the journey from spiritual skeptic to teaching pastor at Willow Creek Community Church. He investigated the truth of Heaven or Hell in his book: *"God's Outrageous Claims."* His central point is that if you can believe Christ rose from the dead... you can have faith in the existence of heaven and hell.

Lee investigated the resurrection as an experienced reporter. He questioned leading authorities of history, the Bible, medicine, law and psychology. Lee researched historical sources and even checked the reliability of eyewitness accounts. His conclusion:

"But we can proceed with bold assurance, thanks to the evidence of history that establishes with convincing clarity how Jesus not only preceded us in death but also came back from the dead and blazed the trail to heaven."

John said it best: *"I write this to you who believe in the Son of God, so that you may know you have eternal life."* (1 John 5:13) Christ rose from the dead so you can confidently believe in your own eternity secure in the knowledge that God loved you enough to sacrifice it all on the cross.

Paul promised in a letter to the Romans: *"And I am convinced that nothing can ever separate us from God's love. Death can't and life can't. The angels can't and the demons can't. Our fears for today, our worries about tomorrow and even the powers of hell can't keep God's love away. Whether we are high above the sky or in the deepest ocean, nothing in all creation will ever be able to separate us from the love of God..."* (8:38-39)

Don't take my word for it; investigate the claims for yourself. Once accepted, you are faced with some significant choices. Do you pursue heaven or hell?

I bought a necktie recently to match a new suit. Later, I noticed the late Jerry Garcia of the Grateful Dead designed and named the tie: *"The Ship of Fools."* According to newspaper accounts written shortly after his death, Jerry Garcia due to his exploits with women and drugs was often described as a wild and crazy party animal who knew no sensible boundaries. If true, than Jerry Garcia may have been on his own *"Ship of Fools."*

What about you? Are you on a *"ship of fools"* with no happy ending in sight or have you chosen *"Christ's lifeboat to eternity"* full of promises that our fears for today and our worries about tomorrow will never keep God's love away? **Make the choice today and I'll look forward to seeing you on the lifeboat!**

Jerks & the Secret of Sturdy Faith

Imagine driving to work on a busy highway, minding your own business. Suddenly, to your right, someone runs a stop sign and with squealing tires, zips in front of your car, forcing you to slam on the brakes and pull off to the side of the road. As you try to calm your nerves, the jerk in the other car never seems to acknowledge his mistake and speeds merrily down the highway.

How would you react? Would you scream, cry, shake your fist, curse him and all of his ancestry? Would you spend the rest of the morning, describing what happened to your coworkers? Would your day be ruined, all because of the senseless, irrational, act of a stupid jerk who thinks the open road is paved for him? And another thing... I am sick and tired of being everyone's patsy?!! (Calm down, Larry.)

(Okay... I'm calm now.) Yet, the other driver... the jerk who caused all of your suffering is merrily going on with his life having no knowledge of what he did to you. Think about it. The other driver was responsible for the near-accident but your reaction was not his fault. It was yours. The real damage was entirely self-inflicted. In a word, it is called: resentment.

One definition of resentment is to re-feel the pain. Resentment is like accidentally cutting your hand with a knife and then deciding to avenge yourself by stabbing the other hand. Ouch, that hurts!

The disciples were asking Jesus how to strengthen their faith. *Jesus said: "If your brother (or sister) sins, rebuke him and if he repents, forgive him. If he sins against you seven times in a day and seven times comes back to you and says, 'I repent,' forgive him."* (Luke 17:3,4)

Does this mean we have to forgive the jerk that tried to run over us? No way! Anyway, what does this have to do with faith? This is exactly what those listening to Jesus asked and He responded:

"If you have faith as small as a mustard seed, you can say to this mulberry tree, 'Be uprooted and planted in the sea,' and it will obey you." (Luke 17:6) What? What does that mean?

The mulberry tree has extensive roots that run deep into the soil. It's nearly impossible to uproot. Resentment has extensive roots that run deep within our soul and is nearly impossible to overcome. Forgiveness is a process that begins as a tiny mustard seed. As the mustard seed of forgiveness grows the roots of resentment, like the mulberry tree are loosened and our faith is strengthened.

Do you want to strengthen your faith? Then, learn to forgive…

- A spouse or former spouse who hurt you deeply.
- Maybe a boss or fellow worker who stepped all over you.
- A trusted friend who violated your confidence.
- A parent or relative who abused you.
- And usually… you need to forgive yourself.

Does this kind of forgiveness sound impossible? Sure it is… without God. Yet, one psychiatrist wrote that 75% of his patients could walk out of the hospital if they could truly understand what it means to forgive and be forgiven. Such is the power of grace. Let me give you an example:

In 1660, John Bunyan was thrown into prison just for being a Christian. He could have let the experience ruin him but instead chose to forgive everyone involved and used the isolation as an opportunity to write *Pilgrim's Progress*, one of the most influential Christian books ever written. The power of learning to forgive can produce that kind of sturdy faith within you.

Does an attitude of forgiveness ever come easy? Never! It's a process that we must work at continually but God makes a clear promise that your willingness to forgive will give you a faith that will move mountains and change your life. Great! *Now if I can only forgive that jerk on the highway that almost killed me!*

A Lighthouse…

A few years ago, I created a children's story called, "Christians and Lighthouses." The kids were asked to imagine themselves on a ship, lost just offshore in a fierce squall. To make the story more realistic, I added a few special effects. In my best storyteller voice, I said:

It is a dark and stormy night…	(All the lights are turned off.)
Lightning flashes…	(Various lights begin blinking.)
The wind is howling…	(Sounds of a storm fill the room.)
The ship is tossed about…	(The children start swaying from side to side.)

Here is the best part:

Huge waves crash overhead…	(I whip out a spray bottle and commence squirting.) ☺

Can you imagine what's happening now? The children are squealing and laughing. There's total chaos in the room as the storm continues to rage. *"We're lost! Help! Who will save us? Help!!"*

Look… Up ahead! What's that?	(In the corner of the room a light begins to shine.)

It's a light… from a lighthouse! We're saved! We were lost and now we are found!

Could anything in all creation offer more hope and direction to a ship lost in the grip of a fierce thunderstorm than the bright, steady beam of light coming from a lighthouse?

Ships are not the only ones needing a lighthouse as recent newspaper headlines attest:

It is a dark and stormy night…	(Romania finds new mass graves…)

38

Lightning flashes...	(Kayla Rowland, a first grader was shot...)
The wind is howling...	(Over a million people Worldwide commit suicide..)
The ship is tossed about...	(Divorce rates at all-time high...)
Huge waves crash overhead...	(South Africa struck with unprecedented drought...)

Sometimes it seems that we have more questions than answers. The world we love is total chaos as the storms of life continue to rage. *"We're lost! Help! Who will save us? Help!!"*

Here is the best part: *Look... Up ahead! What's that?* (In the far corner of the world a light begins to shine.) *It's a light... from a lighthouse! We're saved! We were lost and now we are found!*

☦ Lord, you have brought *light* to my life; my God, you *light* up my darkness. (Psalm 18:28) Like a lighthouse... God offers the light of direction to lead me out of the darkness.

☦ The Lord is my *light* and my salvation – so why should I be afraid? (Psalm 27:1) Like a lighthouse... God offers the light of salvation to rescue you from the storms of life.

☦ Jesus said, *"I am the **light** of the world. If you follow me, you won't be stumbling through the darkness, because you will have the **light** that leads to life."* (John 8:12) Like a lighthouse... God offers the whole world a strong steady beam of light to follow that will lead to life.

Have you been experiencing a few dark and stormy nights complete with lightning flashes and howling winds? Does the world around you resemble a helpless ship tossed about with huge waves crashing overhead? Maybe now is the time to... *"Look! Up ahead! What's that?* (In the far corner of your soul a light begins to shine.) *It's a light... from a lighthouse! We're saved! We were lost and now we are found!*

Could anything in all creation offer more hope and direction to a world lost in the grip of a fierce thunderstorm than the bright, steady beam of light coming from God's lighthouse?

From Ordinary to Extraordinary:
The Influence of a...

Recently, I became a lighthouse... Before you think I've lost my mind, maybe I should explain.

The Lighthouse Movement is a coalition of Christians representing churches around the world. Our goal is to **pray** for and **care** for our neighbors while looking for opportunities to sensitively **share** our beliefs. Dr. Reccord writes, *"I am convinced that if we Christians can mobilize and equip our people to get out of the church walls and into their neighborhoods, schools and offices and establish Lighthouses for their neighbors, we can witness an amazing movement of God..."*

Jesus said to the people: *"I am the light of the world. If you follow me, you won't be stumbling through the darkness because you will have the light that leads to life."* (John 8:12) In other words, we are called to be lighthouses while remembering that Jesus is the source of all light.

It's such a simple idea: Choose three to four people in your neighborhood, school or workplace.

1. **Prayer:** Pray for them regularly by name and ask God to use you as an influence.
2. **Care:** Look for opportunities to demonstrate God's love with simple acts of caring.
3. **Share:** At this point, trust God to provide an opportunity to share your faith.

Just before facing the cross, Jesus said to his disciples: *"Yes, I am the vine; you are the branches. Those who remain in me and I in them will produce much fruit."* (John 15:5) In other words, *"Jesus is the light; we are simply the lighthouse."*

After hearing this, I wondered: "Who has been a lighthouse for me? Who influenced you? Sometimes we overlook the obvious. The influence of those we see on a regular basis."

Of course, it begins with family. Mell, my wife loves me even when I'm not always loveable. As a gifted schoolteacher, she manages to subtly offer Godly influence to her first graders. My children, Stephen and Lisa, allowed me to learn and grow on the job as dad. My sister and parents provided an atmosphere of love and support. What about you? How has family influenced you?

"Come, people of Israel, let us walk in the light of the Lord!"

(Isaiah 2:5)

There are lighthouses who appear suddenly and burn brightest when you need them most. What would we do without them? Who were the lighthouses that burned for you? For me there was...

✝ A boss who believed in me and taught the meaning of, *"you can do anything if you try."*

✝ An author and motivational speaker who strengthened my commitment to serving Christ.

✝ An unknown missionary who warned me: *"Larry, keep your nose buried in God's Word."*

✝ An elderly lady who opened her home and heart while I was a struggling seminary student.

✝ A neighbor who stayed awake all night and helped me through a devastating divorce.

"You are the light of the world – like a city on a mountain, glowing in the night for all to see. Don't hide your light under a basket! Instead, put it on a stand and let it shine for all." (Mat. 5:14)

For eighty years, Pearl Gough was a lighthouse for all to see. Confined to a motorized wheel chair for the past several years, she refused to slow down. Every day you might see her either out among her flowers or wheeling down a steep driveway at breakneck speed to retrieve the mail. Recently, Pearl was buried before her ten children, twenty-six grandchildren and seventeen great-grandchildren, neighbors and friends who were all inspired by her dazzling light.

What about you? Truthfully, you have always been a lighthouse... the question is: ***"How bright is your light?"*** You can check out the Lighthouse Movement at *www. LighthouseMovement.com*

The Miraculous Influence of a...

Drayton Hawthorn, a good friend recently wrote describing tense moments they experienced while waiting for his wife's surgery: *Ten o'clock at night and she was outside looking at the stars! I thought it was settled and done. Robin's surgery was a few short days away and although the doctors assured her this was a routine procedure, she was still looking as if they were going to amputate something! As her husband, I assumed my duty was to hide concern while showing a strong front. Like most men, I substituted statistics and reason for assurance and thought it was enough. Now she was worrying again. I walked toward her ready to offer more of my male logic.*

That's when the miracle happened...

Everything I was going to say vanished. Unknown words came from my lips, as I silently wrapped my arms around her waist and kissed her cheek. "God loves you. Everything will be all right. You will see a shooting star as my promise that you will be ok." In an instant the most spectacular shooting star we have ever seen blazed across the sky from horizon to horizon. A surprised and delighted, "Ooh!" came from Robin! For a long moment neither of us spoke. What could we say?

Moments before, I was an insensitive, scolding husband walking towards a fearful, anxious wife. Somehow, God miraculously intervened and changed us both into vessels of His gracious love.

Most of the time, our influence as a lighthouse is seen through a steady, consistent beam of light. People know and remember us by our day-to-day actions among our family and friends. There is the mother or father who continuously offers love and acceptance. It can be an employer who offers encouragement when you need it most or a friend who telephones when you're at a low point.

Occasionally, there are life-changing moments when God's extraordinary light shines where it's needed most and the only word that adequately describes what happens is... miracle.

What started, as a normal day at our local high school became a tragedy for Van Lee, a young boy full of enthusiasm and friendly mischief. One afternoon during tennis practice he suddenly dropped to the ground clutching his chest. Within minutes Van Lee was gone.

Lighthouses quickly appeared from all over the county. School officials opened up the high school auditorium and encouraged the students to gather there. A minister's wife got word to fellow pastors. The students themselves began to gather in small groups sharing memories, tears and prayers.

But, just as we were starting to leave, Russell Yancey, a father of one of the students quietly stood and said: *"Before we go, I think we should pray. Let's form a circle and hold hands. I'll start and the rest of you please join me."* Hundreds of crying parents, students, pastors and school officials formed a giant circle, bowed their heads and earnestly began to pray. For a few moments, we could all feel the Holy Spirit of God in our circle of mourners: Russell was a lighthouse that day: A miracle amidst tragic grief.

Drayton Hawthorne went on to write: *Being an instrument of God's will, at times may not be voluntary or even expected. I always believed God would use me as a prophet only if I asked and was spiritually clean. Sometimes, this is undeniably true but not in my case. God abruptly interrupted my mission and lovingly substituted His own. I wanted to comfort Robin with common sense and almost interrupted a miraculous moment of faith. No matter the reason for why it happens, when God, uses you for whatever purpose, you will feel blessed because of it.*

Thinking of that wonderful moment Robin and I shared with God is very emotional for me. Several times in telling our shooting star story Robin would need to finish because I would become too "choked up" so I will let her once again finish... After we stood there a few moments just soaking in what had just happened. I turned to Drayton and whispered, **"Do it again!"**

Things Change: It's not the Fruit!

As we get older things change... have you noticed?
- We still wear cool shades... only they're prescription.
- I still occasionally browse in the record department... but my music is easy listening.
- You may still play softball... for just a few innings then you're disabled for two weeks.
- We can still party with the best of them... as long as we're home by 10:00 PM.

As I get older, I seem to have lost control over life's sudden changes. Over the last few weeks, my father died, which is devastating in any family. My daughter moved back home to seek a fresh start, which is good news but requires a lot of adjustments. My son graduated from college and began a new career, which is great news but there are emotional adjustments. Whew... that's a lot of change.

When I was young... I felt totally in control of everything. I wanted to change the world and make it a better place. I imagined a career path that would lead to the top. I wanted a perfect marriage to match my perfect children. God would be so proud. What happened? Actually, we seldom control what happens around us. Most of us will not dramatically change the world. Our career path is far from perfect. Marriages falter and flounder. Children struggle and even fail. As we get older we even lose the ability to control our bodies as we become ever more dependent on those who care for us.

What a bummer! Why are you so depressing, Larry? Don't give up on me yet. There is hope but first we must understand how suddenly things can change and how easily our lives can spin out of control.

Even the Bible changes… (What?) No, not the words themselves but how it affects our lives. For example: When I first committed myself to becoming a serious Christian, Zig Ziglar a famous motivational speaker and author, signed the book he wrote that changed my life "Confessions of a Happy Christian" and then added John 15:1-7. I couldn't wait to look it up in the Bible. Here is a portion of the Scripture:

Jesus said: *"I am the true vine, and my Father is the gardener. He cuts off every branch that doesn't produce fruit, and he prunes the branches that do bear fruit so they will produce even more… Remain in me, and I will remain in you. For a branch cannot produce fruit if it is severed from the vine, and you cannot be fruitful apart from me… Those who remain in me, and I in them, will produce much fruit."*

I loved these verses then and love them now. One word beckoned to me as if it were my own… fruit. *"You will produce much fruit."* I can do that. This is what I should do with my life. Be fruitful for God. I was a professional motivator, so nobody could bear more fruit than me. (No self-esteem problem here.) I rushed back to work determined to bear a lot of fruit… and I failed miserably! Why?

Zig Ziglar gave me a pin to wear that displayed a fish with the number seven. The idea is that someone would notice the fish and ask: *"I know that the fish stands for Christian but what does the seven mean?"* There is the opportunity to talk about my relationship with Jesus Christ. I was prepared to say, *"You are right. The fish means that I am a Christian and the seven is a reminder that I should serve God all seven days of the week."* Wow! I knew this was a great way to share my faith.

There was just one problem… no one asked about the pin! I was ready. I had a plan. I was in control. All I needed was an opportunity. Yet, nothing happened! What was wrong? How can an excited new Christian be ready to witness and have no one give them a chance? After a fruitless few weeks, I was sitting alone at my desk wondering if my experience with

God was a delusion.

Do you see any similarities between my difficulties over the past few weeks and my struggles as a new Christian? The answers mean changing the way we look at the scripture reading. I was focusing on the wrong word. For me to understand what was happening, I needed to listen more carefully to what Jesus was teaching. It's not the fruit that makes this verse special. The right word is…

Oops! Not yet! Read John 15:1-7 before reading on.

Things Change: Vines and MOPS

"Martha, I have a marvelous opportunity for you," said my mother's pastor. "Our church has been looking to expand its ministry to families with small children so we joined a national organization called M.O.P.S. (Mothers of Pre-Schoolers). We want you to be an older adult mentor and speak to the group as well as offer individual counseling to those mothers who need it."

"I thought my pastor had completely lost his mind," mother said. "I was busy with other church projects. My children were grown up and gone. My grandchildren were near adult age. My marriage was certainly not perfect and I wasn't that great a mother. Why me?" I didn't know what to say because I never thought of her helping young mothers either. This strange job offer didn't make sense.

The pastor however smiled serenely and said, "Martha, your situation is exactly what these struggling mothers need to hear. You are perfect for this job and I believe God is calling you to do it."

As I wrote last week… When you least expect it, things change. Whether it's an unexpected job, a tragedy or a sudden illness, events can spin out of control. Like it or not, things do change… The best question to ask is, "How can we learn to deal with the change?" The answer may surprise you.

I just wrote how Zig Ziglar shared his favorite Bible verses from John 1:1-7. *"I am the true vine, and my Father is the gardener. He cuts off every branch that doesn't produce fruit, and he prunes the branches that do bear fruit so that they will produce even more… Remain in me and I will remain in you. For a branch cannot produce fruit if it is severed from the vine and you cannot be fruitful apart from me… Those who remain in me and I in them will produce much fruit."*

45

The word that stood out for me was fruit. "You will produce much fruit." As an experienced salesperson, I expected to go out and produce fruit for God but instead I failed miserably. After a fruitless few weeks, I was alone in my office wondering if everything God promised was a delusion.

But I was missing the point. The key word was never meant to be fruit. Fruit is the end product. There can be no fruit without another word. It's not fruit... it's the vine. I was trying to produce fruit with a weak link to the vine. I needed to strengthen my relationship with God and let the fruit grow naturally.

- **The vine provides life-sustaining nutrients.** I started listening to Bible tapes on the way to work.
- **The vine provides a link to the gardener.** I set the alarm clock earlier to allow time for prayer.
- **The vine prevents the fruit from falling to the ground.** I became more active at my local church.
- **Without the vine... there is no fruit.** I began to listen compassionately and genuinely care.

Learning to focus on the vine gave God the opportunity to change me. Only then would I begin to bear fruit.

But what about my mother? She took the job and nervously stood up to talk to her first group of MOPS mothers. She cleared her throat and slowly began to tell her story. "I'm not the best example of an ideal marriage or a good mother. At times the tragedies I faced nearly destroyed me but I survived and learned a valuable lesson: **God seldom changes circumstances... God changes you!**"

She went on to say, "God seldom changes circumstances... even though we desperately want them changed. I know many of you are suffering with troubled children or a bad marriage or a messy divorce. Some of you are struggling financially and most of you are praying that God will make your circumstances better. Like you, I prayed for relief from all the misery and pain but I was looking for the wrong answer."

"...God changes you! At first, this may not sound like what you want to hear but allowing God to change me was what got me through. In addition, I found hope and love I never knew. I found peace in the midst of my pain. God began to change me. As I changed... everything changed."

Do you get it yet? It's not the fruit... it's the vine. When dad died, my mother received a precious gift. Those same women from MOPS surrounded her, fixed meals, cleaned the house and helped her recover. Why? Because through her loving witness as a mentor, they began looking for the vine... and found a closer relationship with God.

A Witness in the Real World!

What is the first thought that comes to mind when you hear the word...*witness*: a murder trial, an automobile accident or someone in a long orange robe trying to sell you flowers? For Christians, *witness* is a word preachers use frequently to make everyone feel guilty. But Jesus says: "*...you will receive power when the Holy Spirit comes on you; and you will be my witnesses...*" (Acts 1:8) But what does it really mean to be a witness? Maybe this story will help:

One of my first jobs after college was selling automobiles at a local dealership. A fellow salesman talked me into visiting a nearby church. So, one Sunday morning, just before time for worship, I took a seat in the back of the sanctuary. Just then, two men I immediately recognized entered through another door directly across from me. *"At that moment, I knew there was going to be trouble."*

Both men had purchased used cars through me recently. Both cars had mechanical problems and the dealership I represented did not fix them satisfactorily. Both men left my office upset.

Have you ever wished the floor would open up and swallow you whole? I tried to scrunch my body behind the pew so they couldn't see me, but it did no good. They both with startled looks, recognized me and started walking my way. Knowing this could be embarrassing; I frantically looked for an exit.

"You've got a lot of guts showing up here after what you did!" No! No! That's not what they said, but it is what I expected and probably deserved. Instead they each enthusiastically shook my hand and said: *"Larry Davies, what a wonderful surprise. We're so glad to see you."*

- ✝ They offered no judgment or even mentioned what happened to their automobiles.
- ✝ They sat and talked to me as if we had been friends for years.
- ✝ They enthusiastically talked about their church and how God changed their lives.

✝ They introduced me to others in the congregation as their friend.

✝ They involved me in a small group with people my own age.

In just a few short weeks, I felt right at home in a brand new church. All because two people, who should have been angry with me, reached out the hand of friendship and offered the forgiving love of God. Looking back, I realize this was a life-changing moment in my young life and I will always be grateful for their enthusiasm and especially for their loving example of forgiveness. For me… they represented the best possible illustration of what it means to be a witness.

What about you?

✝ Who were the witnesses who helped you along the way?

✝ What did they do or say to make a difference in your life?

✝ How can you learn from their example as you seek to become a witness to others?

You don't need to go to an airport or a busy street corner. You are already a witness to relatives, coworkers and friends who see you nearly every day. Becoming a witness means a willingness to stop what you are doing and listen to someone who is lonely, confused or hurting. Becoming a witness means a willingness to get involved… not to judge but to offer love as others have done for you.

This is never easy, but real world witnessing often means getting our hands and our hearts a little dirty as we reach out in Godly love to someone who is in need of a friend... not a speech. Your witness can make a difference. It sure worked for me.

Why not start today. Share this story with someone. Who knows! You may find yourself becoming a witness for God. Remember, Jesus never sends us out to witness alone: *"...you will receive power when the Holy Spirit comes on you; and you will be my witnesses..."* So, what are you waiting for?

Under the Cross: A Divine Warning

Why was I becoming angry? I was in the mountains attending a meeting with other church leaders. The speaker was comparing two common church attitudes. One attitude focused first on prayer, Bible study and community service. This one was desirable. Another emphasized cafeteria-style, pick and choose programming. "This attitude," said the speaker, "was undesirable." At this point, I was angry!

I stood up and insisted that today's church really needs both philosophies. "Yes," the speaker answered, "to some extent that may be true but what is important is where do you place your priorities?" His point was to urge churches to seek an ongoing relationship with God first before blindly creating programs just because people asked for them. He was right so why was I upset?

After the meeting, I took a walk to clear my head and get some fresh air. It was cold but I was too preoccupied to notice. After a few minutes, I saw a bright light in the shape of a cross. It took a few minutes of climbing and walking to get there but finally I stood below a beautiful cross that could be seen for miles. Despite the temperature, I somehow felt warm and secure beneath the shining beacon of light. It was as if Jesus himself was with me offering comfort and reassurance.

After a few minutes of standing quietly, I began to understand my anger. It wasn't over church attitudes or programs. It wasn't even the speaker. The problem was with me. Underneath the glow of the cross, the words of the speaker became a divine warning. I was the one focusing on creative programming ideas while neglecting my own relationship with God. My priorities were focused on people rather than God: programs rather than relationships. It was so simple, yet I almost missed it.

In the Bible, a young man named Timothy was also struggling and faced many pressures and challenges but an experienced pastor named Paul wrote several letters filled with Godly wisdom.

✝ *Cling tightly to your faith in Christ and always keep your conscience clear.* (1 Timothy 1:19)

✝ *I urge you, first of all, to pray for all people. As you make your requests, plead for God's mercy and give thanks.* (2:1)

✝ *Do not waste time arguing over godless ideas and old wives tales. Spend your time and energy in training yourself for spiritual fitness.* (4:7)

✝ *Until I get there, focus on reading the Scriptures to the church, encouraging the believers and teaching them.* (4:13)

✝ *Keep a close watch on yourself and on your teaching. Stay true to what is right and God will save you and those who hear you.* (4:16)

The lessons are abundant and clear:

1. *Cling tightly to your faith...* Always put God first in everything we do.
2. *Pray for all people...* Prayer should be the foundation of our life and ministry.

49

3. *Train yourself for spiritual fitness…* Spiritual discipline is an all-important part of faith.
4. *Reading the Scriptures…* Still the best way I know to discover God's love and grace.
5. *Encouraging and teaching others…* Emphasis is on relationships not activities or programs.
6. *Stay true to what is right and God will save you…* Putting our ultimate trust in God.

What about you? Maintaining a Christian lifestyle is about so much more than attending church, singing in the choir or serving on a committee. A Christian lifestyle is more about who you are, how you act and whom you serve. Question: What priorities are you neglecting in your relationship with God? What needs to change in your life? How can the church encourage you? When can you start?

One cold dark night beneath a brightly lit cross, I received a divine warning and a priceless lesson. Yet at the same time, I felt the love and comfort only a loving Christ can give. I walked back to the hotel with a bounce in my step and a fire in my heart. *But you, Timothy, belong to God; so run from all these evil things and follow what is right and good. Pursue a godly life along with faith, love, perseverance and gentleness… May God's grace be with you all.* (1 Timothy 6:11 & 21) Amen! Thank you, God!

Power of The Word

After two long days and nights of fruitless searching, a weary volunteer passing a wooded area for the umpteenth time spotted a tiny bare foot protruding from the underbrush. Gently, she cleared the leaves from the motionless three-year old boy. *"Billy… Billy, wake up. Are you okay?"*

Slowly, one eye began to open, then another. *"Where's my mommy?"* he hoarsely whispered. The shout *"Come quick, little Billy's alive!"* could be heard clear across the county. Hundreds of neighbors, rescue personnel and family came running to see the most precious sight in the world. **A precious child was lost, feared dead but now he was found, hungry but alive.**

What's going on? Who is Billy? Were you involved in the story? It's interesting how words can affect you. Good writing can move you from laughter to tears: expose painful memories or provide the motivation to accept a new challenge. Have you ever read a story or book and couldn't stop? Such is the power of the word.

But what about God's Word? Can a two to five thousand year old collection of words still have the power to change lives even as we approach the 21st century?

For the eighth straight year, I participated in the graduation of a Disciple Bible Study class. For nine months, students committed to reading the Bible 30 minutes per day plus attend a two-hour class each week. Why did they do it? Here is what the Bible says:

✟ Your word is a lamp for my feet and a light for my path.

(Psalm 119:105)

✟ Every word of God proves true.   (Proverbs 30:5)

✟ The grass withers, and the flowers fade, but the word of our God stands forever.   (Isaiah 40:8)

✟ In the beginning the Word already existed. He was with God, and he was God.   (John 1:1)

✟ For the word of God is full of living power. It is sharper than the sharpest knife, cutting deep into our innermost thoughts and desires. It exposes us for what we really are.   (Hebrews 4:12)

Wow! "A lamp to light my path." "The truth, which has always been, that will stand forever." "The living power that cuts deep into our innermost thoughts and desires." Can God's Word really do all that? Yes it can and more.

Shortly before deciding to leave the automobile business and become a minister, I was invited to a breakfast honoring a missionary on vacation from Uganda. Just like everyone else, I went forward to meet her and offer prayers. She was politely thanking people and talking until she came to me. She paused and took my hand, held it for what seemed like hours and then looked deep into my eyes. Finally, she asked: *"Are you going into the ministry?"*

Now it was my turn to pause and look into her eyes. *"Yes, I am, but how did you know?"*

"Never mind that," she said. *"What is important is that God wants me to say something to you!"*

I was stunned. Nervous already about my dramatic career change, I desperately needed to hear something from God. But she didn't know me. What could a missionary possibly say that would resolve my fear and confusion?

What she said next, I will never forget. *"God says that you are to keep your nose buried in the Bible and let your first priority always be to teach God's Word. If you do that you will succeed! I will be praying for you."* Having said what needed to be said, she turned away from me and began talking once again to the others.

Over the years, I have discovered how right she was. God's Word has all the power anyone could possibly need or use. My responsibility as a pastor is simply to enable you to experience it. Paul emphasized to a young pastor named Timothy: *"Until I get there, focus on reading the Scriptures to the church, encouraging the believers, and teaching them."*

(1 Timothy 4:13)

After years of fruitless wandering your weary eyes scan a passage of Scripture for the umpteenth time. Suddenly you spot a tiny nugget of truth amidst the words. A soft voice whispers, *"Wake up! Are you okay?"* Slowly, one eye begins to open, then another. *"My God... My Lord!"* you say and all heaven shouts as they witness the most precious sight in the world.

"Come quick, she is alive! A precious child was lost, feared dead but now he is found, hungry but alive."

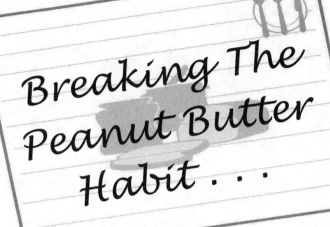

Breaking The Peanut Butter Habit . . .

Following God's Recipe For A Better Life.

Chapter 2

A Look Inside . . . The Kitchen: The Church

"What's Wrong with my Parrot?"

Chuck Swindol wrote about a lonely lady who went to the pet store to buy a parrot for companionship. She was assured that once the bird began to feel at home, she would have a friend for years. A week later she returned to complain that her bird was not talking. "Did you buy a mirror?" asked the owner. "When parrots look at themselves, words flow." Hoping that would help she bought a mirror.

A few days later, she returned and complained that the bird still hadn't uttered a peep. "Well, did you get a ladder? Parrots love to climb and need to feel comfortable." She bought a ladder. The end of the next week, she returned grim and disappointed: Same complaint – no parrot talk. "Well, have you bought a swing?" She attached a swing.

Three days later she came storming in, slammed the door of the shop and demanded to speak to the owner. "He died this afternoon!" she blurted out.

"Died! Died? Did he ever talk?" asked the owner.

"Yes," she responded. "He said just a few words as he breathed his last. 'Don't they sell any food at that store?'"

Swindol added, "We live in a day of religious mirrors, ladders and swings, where the majority of hungry souls are given empty promises and sold a bill of goods. There are lots of trinkets and gimmicks but no food... no solid substance to sustain life." It's like the once-famous commercial featuring a sweet little old lady standing at a fast food counter holding two buns and asking: "Where's the beef?"

As this chapter begins it may be time to ask of yourself and the church you serve: "Where's the beef?"

The Bible says it even better: *"How sweet are your words to my taste; they are sweeter than honey. Your commandments give me understanding; no wonder I hate every false way of life. Your word is a lamp for my feet and a light for my path."* (Psalm 119: 103-105) Look at the promises:

1. *How sweet are your words*... God's Word offers hope and for giveness.
2. *They are sweeter than honey*... God's Word adds purpose and importance to our lives.
3. *Your commandments give me understanding*... God's word teaches right from wrong.
4. *I hate every false way*... God's Word gives you the desire to do what is right.

5.   *Your word is a lamp for my feet...* God's Word provides a sense of direction.
6.   *A light for my path...* God's Word is a source of encouragement during tough times.

Recently, I had the honor of attending a Bible study graduation for a group of high school students. The best part was watching each student stand up and participate in the service. You could positively feel their excitement. Over the past nine months these young people met every Wednesday evening and together they studied nearly eighty per cent of the Bible. Isn't that amazing? Seeing their enthusiasm and energy inspired me to renew my own commitment as a pastor and writer. How are you doing?

✠   Have you been feeding the "parrot?" What are you doing to strengthen your spiritual life? When is the last time you participat ed in a good Bible study?

✠   "Where is the beef?" Is your spiritual life challenging? Does your church strive to teach God's Word? What can you do to help? Are you praying for your church?

✠   Are you sharing your food? Do you serve a ministry that is reach ing out to the community? Here is a good question: If someone had a problem, would they come to you for help?

Somewhere... maybe just down the street, there is a heavenly "store" waiting to serve you. You will find a few mirrors. They may offer you a ladder or a swing but you don't notice them right away because they are off to the side. What you immediately discover is the main aisle. Like a magnet, you are drawn to the bright lights and colorful displays but once you enter you can't help but notice the mouth-watering variety of delicious food: appetizers, vegetables, grains and yes: "beef... lots of beef."

Ten Questions of Faith and Ministry

People often ask: "Larry am I doing what God wants me to do?" Shucks! I don't know but I do know what helps me.

I use ten questions to regularly guide my ministry and spiritual life. Recently, I shared them in church and several people asked me for a copy. (Well, actually it was just mom but she seemed genuinely interested.) So maybe you will find the questions helpful too. Warning: Don't think you have to check off everything or feel guilty about what you are not doing. These questions are simply meant to be a practical guide for you and your church.

1. **Do I pray regularly?** It sounds so simple yet nothing happens without prayer. When I am struggling it is often because my prayer life is not what it should be. Does your church emphasize prayer as a regular and critical part of their ministry? Prayer is always step one.

2. **Do you have a vision?** It is difficult to shoot an arrow if there is no target. So how can you function without a vision from God and goals to help you fulfill the vision? What talents and resources are available to you... to your church? What is needed in your community?

3. **Are we growing in faith?** Spiritual formation is a continuous journey of learning, experiencing and sharing the Word of God. Young and old are discovering a passion for God's Word but don't always know where to begin. Bible studies and small groups play a key role in spiritual development. Take a class, participate in Sunday school or join a prayer group.

4. **Are you caring for others?** What are you doing to maintain loving contact with friends and family? Do you regularly offer encouragement? What is your church doing to care for each other? Most offer shepherd groups, support ministries or prayer chains. Perhaps you can help. The simple gesture of sending a card is a ministry that often works miracles.

5. **Do you cultivate friendships beyond your own comfortable group?** If you don't... why not? Maybe you need to get a life! Just kidding but it's important that you reach beyond your comfort level and seek to understand other age groups and cultures. You will learn a lot and enjoy an exciting new experience. Young and old, Spanish or Korean, black or white alike have so much to offer but they all need our love and respect.

6. **Am I involved in a community ministry?** Is there a Habitat for Humanity near by? Am I doing anything for children at Christmas? Are groups fixing broken down houses for people too poor or sickly to make their own repairs? Is there a "Meals on Wheels?" Every community has needs? To meet those needs God has given us all unique talents. What am I doing with mine? It's usually not that hard to discover what's needed and ask: "How can I help?"

7. **Are you a witness?** Do people really know what you believe? How can you talk about God without others feeling intimidated or offended? Do coworkers look upon you as someone they can trust? Will you listen to

their concerns with respect and love? Are you praying for opportunities to share your faith? My favorite definition for witness: "is the willingness to make a sincere and honest attempt to be a friend in the name of God."

8. **What about men?** 61% of those not attending church are men. The most successful ministries that reach men are: mission trips, building projects and sports. Many men that participate in these ministries become more involved with their church.

9. **Are we reaching single adults?** More than 56% of the unchurched population is single. Surveys indicate that many single adults believe in God but feel isolated from the church. We can start recognizing their needs by changing our language. Family night supper implies that you must be married to attend. Instead call it a "Fellowship and Fun" supper. Ministry ideas could include divorce and grief recovery workshops or single parent programs.

10. **What about children?** Parents are struggling to provide a wholesome environment for their children. How are you helping? It starts at Sunday school but there are other ideas such as: After-School Ministry, Parent's Day Out or M.O.P.S. (Mothers of Pre-Schoolers)

I can't possibly do all that! True but you can do something. My prayer is for these questions to stimulate your thinking. Then, let God guide you. We face a challenge to reach out in ministry in creative ways. The main thing is to be open-minded, be in prayer and celebrate the victories.

In the last few years, I have witnessed many people inspired by God to become involved in ministry. It has been the biggest joy of my life. The excitement of doing something worthwhile for God is more contagious than a flu epidemic and the results are far more lasting and satisfying. So, what are you waiting for? Find your ministry today and may God be with you!

"Why Do We Use Big Church Words?"

Have you heard the old seminary joke about a professor explaining the difference between exegesis and eisegesis? Exegesis, she said is a careful analytical study of scripture. Eisegesis is interpreting and applying the exegesis, as a preacher would do in a sermon. While the class discussion was continuing someone mumbled in the back of the room: *"I don't know nothin' about exegesis and I don't understand eisegesis. I came here to learn about Jesus!"*

I asked folks to send me "frustrating favorites" of big church words heard recently. Here are some of their responses:

- *Modality: I used the word in a sentence one time and a lady laughed and said: "You come up with the funniest words some times!" She almost suggested I made it up!*
- *Propitiation: It's a big word in the King James Bible but what does it mean?*
- *Sanctification: Do the Methodists still use this word a lot?*
- *Any word with millennialism that seems to be used more frequently after finishing with Y2K, oh yeah… that one too!*

But… the all-time "frustrating favorite" big church word mentioned by more than half of our survey belonged to (Drum roll please!) …*eschatology*. Use this fancy word in a sentence and watch the *modality* of your listener grow strangely quiet as he or she mentally questions your *sanctification* and prays for *propitiation* that would end any further conversations with you… you *postmillennialist* crumb cake!

Come on Larry, what does Eschatology mean? I thought you would never ask. Let's break it down:

Escha… short for escargot, a fancy word for snail... eat it and strange things happen.

…tol… is pronounced "tall" as in telling a "tall tale."

…ogy… pronounced: "Oh Gee!" Short for… "Do you take me for an idiot?"

Escha-tol-ogy is your reaction to eating escargot, which causes you to spin endless millennial tall tales as the poor listener can only reply… *"Oh Gee!"* It sounds silly but this definition may be closer to the truth than you think. One frustrated survey response asked: *"Why can't people just say end-times?"*

Question: *"Why do church leaders feel the need to use those big church words?"*

Actually, the problem is not as much with the words themselves as with the attitude of those using them as one survey response astutely pointed out: *"It doesn't hurt to stretch the mind – especially with spiritual vocabulary. All one has to do is define these words for others rather than throwing them out with spiritual arrogance."*

The key word is arrogance: Jesus warns: *"And how they love to sit at the head table at banquets and in the most prominent seats in the synagogue! They enjoy the attention they get on the streets, and they enjoy being called 'rabbi.' Don't ever let anyone call you 'rabbi,' for you have only one teacher, and all of you are on the same level as brothers and sisters."*

(Matthew 23:6-8)

Then Jesus shouts: *"Blind Guides! How terrible it will be for you. Hypocrites!"* Why is he so livid? He goes on to say: *"You are careful to clean the outside of the cup and the dish, but inside you are filthy – full of greed and self-indulgence!"* (25) Jesus' concern is not so much with what we say but with the sincerity of our attitude and the humbleness of our spirit. *"For I tell you this,"* Jesus continues, *"you will never see me again until you say, 'Bless the one who comes in the name of the Lord!"* (39)

Big church words can be meaningful teaching tools enabling others to deepen their spirituality or those very same words can also represent arrogant symbols of your sinful pride. In effect, you can become coldly proficient at *exegesis* but when you lack a humble spirituality you fail to display a meaningful *eisegesis* and in the end you say very little about *Jesus* and without *Jesus* you end up with nothing and fool no one!

Oh… As far as eschatology is concerned, I would like to quote a famous entertainer who summed up the future with this insightful statement: *"Chances are, we ain't seen nothin' yet!"*

A $5 Challenge: Random Acts of Kindness

At the end of a worship service, forty families were handed an envelope. Enclosed was a five-dollar bill and instructions:

Take this $5 combined with whatever gifts or talents God has given you and use it for one act or several random acts of kindness toward someone you would not normally help or even know. Give a gift. Bake a cake. Buy several cards and mail them. Put gas in your car and drive someone to a doctor's appointment. In four weeks, we will share stories of how we have helped others in the name of Christ. Let's practice what we preach by simply performing a random act of kindness for another.

What would you do with the $5?

The Bible certainly supports acts of kindness. Here are some examples:

✝ There was a believer… she was always doing kind things for others and helping the poor. (Acts 9:36)

✝ (The voice of God… angry!) "There is no faithfulness, no kindness, no knowledge of God in your land." (Hosea 4:1)

✝ (Jesus) "If you are kind only to your friends, how are you different from anyone else?" (Matthew 5:48)

In other words, acts of kindness tell the world what kind of people we can be. Would you like another example? Think of two people who deeply influenced your life in a positive way. Why do you remember them? Was it something they said? Probably not! More than likely it was their attitude of kindness and generosity toward you.

When I was a student returning to college, my car overheated near a small town on the way. It was Sunday and everything was closed. I was stranded, hungry and broke. I had no choice but to knock on a nearby door and ask for help. An elderly couple answered the knock, graciously invited me inside for dinner and then called a neighbor to fix the car. This simple act of kindness and generosity by two strangers had a lasting impact on me. Can we do no less?

Four weeks after receiving the $5 we met again to hear the results of the challenge:

✞ A schoolteacher bought special paper and ribbon, then used her computer to make beautiful Bible verse bookmarks to give to every resident of a local nursing home.

✞ One woman made homemade loaves of bread and distributed them to neighbors.

✞ A visitor from another state went home and filled a box with paper towels, trash bags, tea and coffee and gave it to a friend preparing to move to a new house.

✞ Another created beautiful floral wreaths and distributed them in another local nursing home.

✞ Someone bought a book and mailed it to a sick friend.

Everyone had a story to tell during the worship service as we celebrated and learned a valuable lesson. In addition to helping others, we felt better about ourselves. God blessed us with a challenge that will not soon be forgotten. All for just $5.

What about you? What could you do with $5 combined with a little creativity to give a stranger a gift of kindness? Challenge yourself, your family or your church. Think of the possibilities!

Will you accept the challenge? If you do, please let me know. Visit our website at *www.SowingSeedsofFaith.com* and send me an email. I'm getting excited already... aren't you?

Our Youth: Eight Success Stories

Eight high school seniors in our area recently received a $1,000 scholarship. In addition to being intelligent these seniors were chosen because they would be the very first in their family to attend college. Their stories are inspiring examples of courage and faith. It wasn't always easy...

> ➤ My life got off to a very bumpy start: literally. I was born in transit to the delivery room, somewhere between the back seat of a 1979 baby blue Volkswagen Rabbit and the fourth floor of the hospital... My father was sent to prison a few years ago...

> ➤ I was four when my parents divorced. I can truly say that it was one of the worst experiences that I have had yet...

> ➤ I was raised in a house full of people... so I always had to fight for everything I wanted, including attention...

> ➤ These seventeen years of my life have been filled with heartache, joy, compassion, love, and devotion.

If there is a recipe for college preparation, these youth started with many of the wrong ingredients. Yet they succeeded beyond all expectations. How?

First, I noticed that each of them had a clear idea of what they wanted to do for a living: Doctor, Prosecuting Attorney, United States Army Officer, Special Education Teacher, Certified Public Accountant, Child Counselor, Social worker. Setting clear goals is important.

Peter explains goal setting in his letter to a struggling church: *"God has given gifts to each of you from his great variety of spiritual gifts. Manage them well so that God's generosity can flow through you. Are you called to be a speaker? Then speak as though God himself were speaking through you. Are you called to help others? Do it with all the strength and energy that God supplies. Then God will be given glory in everything through Jesus Christ."* (1 Peter 4:10-11)

Goal setting is the process of learning to understand and appreciate your God-given gifts and then managing them well so that God's generosity can flow through you. Is your goal to help others? Do it with all the strength and energy that God supplies. These eight seniors are doing that. Here are some other valuable lessons from the comments of these remarkable youth:

☺ Desire: *...despite the emotional distress that loomed due to those*

61

circumstances, I maintained my "A" average in school... I attribute this to my strong, independent character.

☺ Perspective: *...I had a better understanding of how to pray... Throughout my entire life, religion and school seem to be the meaningful topics in my life.*

☺ A Mentor: *I will be eternally grateful for my mother's instruction. ...my academic success can be traced back to her taking the time to teach me, when others left it up to the schools.*

☺ Appreciation: *I believe that there is no greater place on this earth than the United States of America. I want to put my life on the line for the country that has been so good to me.*

☺ Service: *I will strive to help students with disabilities... "The best thing that a person can do in life is to help someone else."*

☺ Influence: *In my opinion, the difference between a child that sells drugs and a child that makes the honor roll is the encouragement and faith that adults instill in them.*

☺ Faith: *I thank God every night for blessing me in so many ways and ask him to keep giving me the strength and knowledge to live a prosperous and positive long life.*

Most of us will never receive a scholarship or attend a major university, but we have been given remarkable abilities and talents by God. Yes, for all of us there are also obstacles to overcome. Success is defined as our ability to use those God given gifts and talents to defeat whatever obstacles stand in the way. That is what makes these eight high school seniors so extraordinary. May God continue to bless and inspire them. They have already inspired me.

Help, I'm Blind...

"Pick a partner. One of you will be blind and the other will be a guide," the teacher said. All went black as I slipped on the blindfold and allowed my partner to nudge me forward and lead me by the hand. A once-familiar classroom was now a breeding ground of desks and chairs to bump into or trip over. No longer self-secure, I was utterly dependent on my guide for directions and safety. The worst was yet to come.

Leaving the classroom, we staggered down the hall. Other senses, once ignored, began to provide clues where we were. Laughter and talking meant other students were nearby. We must be in the hall. Ouch! There's a doorway. The hard surface under my feet meant a sidewalk. Automobile sounds fading in and out, suggested nearness to a road. Wait a minute! We're on a road... with cars? Isn't that dangerous?!

"You are stepping off the curb and onto the highway," said the teacher. Suddenly, my body lurched out of balance as the ground under my feet dropped eight inches. Imagine eight tiny inches with the power to disrupt everything that was secure in my life. Knowing exactly where I was never seemed to matter before, but now it was crucial. How could I take the next step if I didn't know where it would lead?

"Stop and listen," commanded the teacher. I heard the familiar sound of an automobile engine only this time it was getting louder. Alarms in my brain screamed, *"You idiot, run. That car is heading straight toward you!"* But the sound went safely by only to be quickly followed by a similar sound from the opposite direction. Again, the voice inside me screamed, *"Run!"* But again, nothing happened. We removed the blindfolds and found ourselves standing in the middle of a busy road: A terrifying lesson.

I never before apprehended the fear and helplessness that accompanies blindness.

Could this lesson also illustrate our spiritual blindness? At first, you manage okay as other senses provide clues but suddenly something shifts and you are thrown off balance. Alarms in your brain scream out as you sense approaching danger. Your spiritual eyesight now becomes crucial but you seem to be blindfolded. How can you take the next step in life if you cannot see where to place your feet?

Spiritual blindness can also produce feelings of helplessness and fear?

God always offers hope to the blind. *Oh, the joys of those who do not follow the advice of the wicked... But they delight in doing everything the Lord wants...* (Psalm 1) Not an everyday promise of joy as in eating ice cream. This is indescribable joy that only comes from God. How do we obtain it? We begin to open our spiritual eyes and carefully watch where we place our feet. No shortcuts but look at the benefits.

There are two opposing principles within Psalm One. First is the promise: *They are like trees planted along the riverbank, bearing fruit each season without fail. Their leaves never wither, and in all they do, they prosper.* The storms still exist but God gives strength to withstand and continue bearing fruit?

Second is the warning: *But this is not true of the wicked. They are like*

63

worthless chaff, scattered by the wind. They will be condemned at the time of judgment. Most of us would not quickly claim to be spiritual trees but none of us want to be chaff. So, what do we do? How can we improve our eyesight?

The experience of being blindfolded and Psalm one yields four valuable lessons:

1. Appreciate what you already possess. *Oh the joys of those...*
2. Learn to develop other senses. *They are like trees... bearing fruit...*
3. Avoid crowded highways. *Do not follow the advice of the wicked...*
4. Know and trust your guide. *The Lord watches over your path...*

Psalm One ends with a promise and a warning: *For the Lord watches over the path of the godly, but the path of the wicked leads to destruction.* Are you struggling with spiritual blindness? Has your equilibrium been knocked around lately? Are you sensing approaching danger? Maybe it's time for a new Guide: One who knows exactly where you need to go and can be depended upon to lead you safely. What are you waiting for? Open your eyes and pray for God to guide your next steps. It sure beats an oncoming car.

Worship: Annoying Sounds or Vital Communication?

Tap-tap...tap-tap-tap...tap-tap-tap-tap...tap-tap-tap... annoying sounds?

Captain Eugene 'Red' McDaniel tapped on the walls of his cell in the Vietnamese Prisoner of War camp commonly known as the Hanoi Hilton. The taping was a secret code prisoners used to communicate with each other. The number one rule at the Hilton was... *"No communication with other prisoners at anytime."* Anyone caught in the attempt would be tortured.

Isolation was the prime weapon of the communist captors. As the hours slowly turned into days and weeks, Captain McDaniel came to fear the loneliness and the silence far more than any threats of physical harm. The highlight of each day was being taken to the washroom where he occasionally managed to whisper briefly with two other Americans brought in at the same time. They told him about the camp code, a series of taps (or other signals) to spell out letters. McDaniel in his book, "Scars and Stripes" came to recognize the code as his lifeline and only link with sanity.

If a new prisoner couldn't learn the code and communicate with fellow prisoners within thirty days of arrival, he would gradually begin to draw inward and deteriorate. Captain McDaniel saw nearly fifty of America's best trained enter isolation never to be heard from again. As the days dragged on, a prisoner would slowly lose any will to live. "Little by little," McDaniel wrote, "he would deteriorate as that strange predator... isolation, would suck the very life out of him."

Tap-tap...tap-tap-tap...tap-tap-tap-tap...tap-tap-tap ... just annoying sounds or vital communication?

How do secret codes and POW's help us understand worship? One word: communication. Worship represents one of our best opportunities to communicate with God. Without it, the spiritual part of our being will begin to draw inward, deteriorate and die. More than just a hymn, a sermon and a prayer, worship is the camp code that becomes our lifeline and can at times be our only link with sanity.

Come let us sing to the Lord! Let us give a joyous shout to the rock or our salvation! Let us come before Him with thanksgiving. Let us sing Him psalms of praise.

For the Lord is a great God, the great King above all gods.

He owns the depths of the earth, and even the mightiest mountains are His. The sea belongs to Him, for he made it. His hands formed the dry land, too.

Come, let us worship and bow down. Let us kneel before the Lord our maker. For He is our God. We are the people He watches over, the sheep under His care. Oh, that you would listen to His Voice today!

(Psalm 95:1-7)

I found at least seven vital lessons in Psalm 95 that teach the value and meaning of worship.

1. *Sing and Shout* – Worship is active. Don't just sit there... join in.
2. *Give Thanks and Praise* – Worship is our way of saying, "Thank you, God!"
3. *God is Great* – Worship is recognizing the awesome nature of God.
4. *God Made It All* — Worship is remembering creation and our unique role.
5. *Let us Bow Down* – Worship is the humility of accepting God's authority.
6. *For He is our God* – Worship is hearing the promise that God tenderly shepherds us.
7. *Listen to His Voice* – Worship is the bold call to follow God's voice wherever it leads.

Worship — *Tap-tap...tap-tap-tap...tap-tap-tap-tap...* annoying sounds or vital communication?

Dr. Charles Swindoll, author and preacher writes, "Worship is a human response to a divine revelation." God speaks and we respond. *Tap-tap...* through the quietness of a prayer. Tap-tap-tap... through singing a hymn. *Tap-tap-tap-tap...* through the prophetic words of a sermon. Worship is the camp code for vital communication with God. Without it there is only spiritual isolation and... death.

Worship: Contemporary or Traditional?
Wrong Question!

Hundreds of ministers throughout Virginia gathered together for a conference about worship. We came with more questions than answers. What is good worship? What is our role as ministers? Should worship be contemporary with modern music and drama or should we focus on preserving the traditions of our past? With so many churches declining... it's critical that we discover new answers.

The conference fittingly opened with worship and Bishop Joe E. Pennel, Jr., our main speaker read scripture before beginning his message. Here is an excerpt:

Just then there was in their synagogue a man with an unclean spirit, and he cried out, "What have you to do with us, Jesus of Nazareth?" But Jesus rebuked him, saying, "Be silent, and come out of him!" And the unclean spirit, convulsing him and crying with a loud voice, came out of him. They were all amazed, and they kept on asking one another, "What is this? A new teaching—with authority! He commands even the unclean spirits, and they obey him." (Parts of Mark 1:23-27)

After a pause, Bishop Pennel said, "The presence of Christ always stirs up unclean spirits. Worship centered in Christ will bother the unclean spirit. Worship will condemn the unclean spirit." In other words, worship encompasses so much more than the words contemporary or traditional can adequately describe. Worship is about stirring up unclean spirits... What does that mean?

To stir up unclean spirits, worship should emphasize:

✝ **Teaching:** Worship should always revolve around and teach God's Word.
✝ **Commitment**: Worship should ask for a renewed commitment of our faith.

✝ **Leadership:** Worship should offer us direction and a plan of action.
✝ **Variety:** Worship should respect the needs and cultural distinctness of everyone, young and old.
✝ **Consistency:** Worship should at the same time remember and build on our traditions.
✝ **Passion:** Worship should express the passion that comes from a healthy relationship with God.
✝ **Creativity:** Worship should make the best possible use of our God-given talents.
✝ **Judgment:** Worship should warn of God's impending judgment.
✝ **Grace:** Worship should always offer the forgiving gift of Jesus Christ.

Throughout the conference leaders admitted that the debate over worship is not as much about contemporary versus traditional styles as it is about leadership and passion. All too often churches settle for what is easy and predictable and lose their opportunity to stir up the unclean spirits.

Bishop Pennel ended with his message with a story of an all-white church he served in Memphis, Tennessee from 1964 to 1968, a time of heightened racial tension. One Sunday a group of black students came to attend worship services. The ushers didn't deny entrance but in silence brought the students down to the front pew of the church. Later that night the room was full for the monthly board meeting... people anticipating trouble. Nothing was said at first but the anxiety mounted. It was just a matter of time.

Finally, the chairman of the board, a very influential member of the church stood up. Many who came to cause trouble assumed he would be on their side. The chairman paused for a moment, cleared his throat and said, *"What a great worship service today. Isn't it wonderful that we can worship together as God's church? May it happen over and over. Is there any other business?"*

No one responded... Such is the passion and power of Godly worship. Even unclean spirits are afraid.

Worship: We're Only Human

Sometimes... things don't always work out as planned. Worship services are no exception.

Rev. Ronna L. Swartz from Kenbridge, Virginia was preparing to lead a communion service for the leadership team of an upcoming Emmaus Walk. Holy Communion is always an important part of Emmaus and she wanted to do her part as a minister to make the service meaningful and inspiring. Several people on the team experienced some particularly difficult situations so Rev. Swartz wanted to offer God's hope in the midst of their hardship. Her Scripture reading came from Psalm 56:

You keep track of all my sorrows. You have collected all my tears in your bottle. You have recorded each one in your book. (Verse 8) Ronna said, "For me, this verse is a comforting reminder of God's love during the tears. God feels my pain… knows your struggles… understands our sorrows."

Ronna then picked up the chalice holding the grape juice, symbolizing the atoning blood of Christ and served each person on the team. After setting it back on the table, she turned to face the group and brushed her hand against the chalice, knocking it to the carpeted floor where it shattered spattering grape juice everywhere. "Every preacher's worst nightmare!" said Ronna. The worship service was momentarily forgotten. "I felt as though I could cry my own bottle of tears!"

The team members were stunned. For several long seconds, nobody moved; nobody spoke.

Despite our best efforts, worship is still an all too human response to God's impact on our lives. Musicians occasionally make mistakes. Preachers sometimes babble on and on. Babies cry at inopportune times. We could stay at home and watch a better performance on television. Why should we commit ourselves to worship at a local church? What difference does it make?

For the answer as Radio Host Paul Harvey would say, we turn to the rest of the story.

Team members were stunned. For several long seconds, nobody moved; nobody spoke. But suddenly, like a scripted play… everyone sprang into action. Three or four people cleaned the carpet while another collected the broken chalice pieces. Someone else went for the container of grape juice while another cleaned the white-lace tablecloth. Soon the rug and the tablecloth were spot free and the embarrassing moment forgotten… or was it?

Worship was never meant to be polished entertainment but rather a vehicle giving you the opportunity to respond to God's desire to be in an intimate relationship. At anytime, God can and will reach out to touch someone within a worship service maybe during a quiet time of prayer, through a song or a sermon. Even a flawed worship service can be used by God to teach a life-changing lesson. The story continues.

The next time the Emmaus team met, there was clearly no stain on the carpet or the tablecloth but rather than forget Rev. Swartz's embarrassing moment, the group decided to honor the memory of how everyone pulled together to help their minister and friend. On the table beside the new chalice were the broken pieces of the old. A group that once struggled now gloried in their newfound confidence of knowing God loved them and would see them through any struggle… any tragedy.

Later one member of the group collected the broken pieces of pottery and had them made into jewelry. One piece of the chalice was given to each member of the group as a distinctive reminder of what God can do with the broken pieces of our lives.

Ronna Swartz concluded by saying, "I am wearing that chalice fragment today. I learned that the very brokenness our group shared actually turned out to be the glue, which spiritually bonded us together. Is it not the brokenness of Jesus Christ on a cross that not only brings us to our knees but also enables us to feel loved, forgiven and whole?"

Sometimes… things don't always work out as planned. Sometimes God makes them better!

Worship: Creative Fishing and Breaking Bricks

"You can do almost anything and catch a few fish but to do more you have to experiment, to be creative, in other words be willing to listen to the voice and fish on the other side of the boat."

The brochure featured a picture of a guy's head crashing through a pile of bricks and read: *"Team Impact: Revolutionize Your City One Heart At A Time! Crowd-Drawing Entertainment… A ministry of world-class athletes who are also world-class preachers using feats of strength to convey a world-class message. An event so spectacular; people will stand in line, waiting for the church doors to open. This is how you reach the masses. A proven bait to fill your sanctuary with the lost…"*

Breaking baseball bats? Chopping bricks? Ripping telephone books? Bending steel bars? I thought it was funny at first but something enticed me to keep this particular brochure. For several years, I had been looking for something that would help me reach out to people who would not normally come to a church service… but how? Could a "Team Impact" worship event be what I was looking for? No way!

The disciples had been fishing all night long and caught nothing. At dawn, a voice on the beach called out, "Friends, have you caught any fish?" They replied, "No."

Then he said, "Throw out your net on the other side of the boat..."

(From John 21:4-6)

"You can do almost anything and catch a few fish but to do more you have to experiment, to be creative, in other words be willing to listen to the voice and fish on the other side of the boat."

At first the advice of the mysterious voice on the beach makes no sense. The distance from one side of the fishing boat to the other is only six feet. Six feet! How can moving the nets six measly feet catch more fish? It doesn't make sense unless you are willing to trust the voice... The disciples trusted. They threw the nets on the other side and couldn't draw them in because there were so many fish.

A voice was urging to throw my nets on the other side of the boat. So, our church invited "Team Impact" to Virginia and for five days, four of the most powerful men in the world performed amazing feats of strength. One guy took a steel horseshoe and bent it into a heart. Another danced through fire breaking pile after pile of bricks. Another broke out of regulation police handcuffs behind his back. Crowds came from all over to watch them perform but the performance was simply bait...

Each man spoke of his faith in God. One served aboard the aircraft carrier, USS Saratoga and told of a sailor who fell overboard. He described the helplessness of struggling to stay afloat and watching his safe haven and his home sail away. The total darkness and the thought of creatures lurking beneath the surface was terrifying. After a few hours, a rescue chopper appeared and dangled a lifeline. But the sailor couldn't reach it. As the light shined down from the chopper he could see the fin of a nearby shark circling closer and closer. Salvation was so close yet so far away. He desperately needed help.

At times we all feel lost and alone in a darkness filled with fear and foreboding. Unknown creatures seem to lurk just below the surface. God feels so close yet so far away. Our own efforts to reach the lifeline come up short. We desperately need help. The sailor received his help when a search and rescue expert shimmied down the rope, attached a special harness to him and together they were pulled upward to the safety of the chopper.

Jesus is our search and rescue expert who shimmies down the rope and attaches a special harness to you and together we are pulled to the safety of God.

Each night people came forward to accept Jesus Christ as his or her Savior. Over one hundred and fifty lives were changed thanks to the unique ministry of "Team Impact." Just as important, hundreds more of us felt our faith renewed and strengthened by the testimony of these mighty representatives of God. We listened to the voice, fished from the other side and our nets were filled to overflowing.

"You can do almost anything and catch a few fish but to do more you have to experiment, to be creative, in other words be willing to listen to the voice and fish on the other side of the boat."

Youth and the Curse of the Pink Flamingos

Please note that I am writing this column while being held captive by insidious members of our church youth group. As the esteemed writer Dave Berry would say: "I am not making this up!" Also, my humble apologies to the Flamingo Lawn Ornament Preservation Society, commonly referred to as F.L.O.P.S. I realize there are wonderful, wholesome benefits to having flamingo lawn ornaments in your yard and any remarks that they are tacky, ugly, and serve no benefit to mankind except to scare away salesmen were made under duress. Please, I beg you... no letters!

It all started weeks earlier when I read the following announcement given to me by this same ruthless youth group now holding me hostage:

"Alas! There is an affliction in our church! At any time... at any hour... at any moment... your yard is in jeopardy of being saturated with tacky, ugly, pink flamingos. Think about your usual morning routine; comfortable and relaxed. You calmly go to pick-up the morning paper and there out in your front yard are those bright, plastic, pink flamingos! Oh, the shame! What will the neighbors think? *"But don't despair! There is hope in the air!"* Our brave youth group has taken on another name. "Flamingo Busters!" Quick as a flash, before you can say, *"Help! Get these *%^$#*@% pink flamingo's out of my yard!"* our "flamingo busters" are ready to respond... for a small donation of course. Quickly and efficiently they will remove the tacky and distasteful affliction from your yard. Better yet, buy our new *"no pink flamingo's in my yard please!"* insurance policy and receive a 24-hour watch to protect your property for one full year from these awful pink destroyers of "good taste." In other words… pay a little now… or pay more later! Proceeds naturally go to charity."

In an effort to keep our congregation duly informed, I read the announcement. But then I paused and added, *These pink flamingo threats don't intimidate me. I refuse to buy insurance or give-in to these cheap theatrical tricks.* While speaking, I noticed two people running over to the youth to buy insurance.

The next morning, the following email message was on my computer: *"The Pink Flamingo reign of terror has begun!"* "Oh no," I screamed and ran outside. There were fifteen pink flamingos in all their glory perched in my front yard. I dialed "Flamingo Busters" and did the only noble thing a poor preacher could do. I begged them to come immediately and remove those pink, ugly birds from my yard! They came but before removing the pink terror, they tied me up and forced me write this story so everyone will know of the Pink Flamingo Affliction.

I know what you're thinking! Larry, what in the world does this have to do with religion, serving God or the church? Maybe more than you think.

Psalm 95 begins: *Come, let us sing to the Lord! Let us give a joyous shout to the rock of our salvation! Let us come before him with thanksgiving. Let us sing him psalms of praise. For the Lord is a great God… (1-3)* Be honest, when was the last time you heard a joyous shout in your home, in your office, at your school or in your church?

Expressing joy with creativity and imagination is part of our service to God. No group expresses joy in more creative ways than our youth. (Remember, I'm still tied up.) Recently, the youth led one of our worship services. There was creative dancing, flags, amusing but thought-provoking drama, music and lots of participation. Everyone left the church with a smile on their face and a new appreciation of God's awesome love.

I learned two things from this story:
1. Creatively, look for joy in serving God. If your home or church seems lacking then look for innovative ways to add your own style of joy.
2. Don't overlook the contribution of our youth. They can restore the joy in us all.

Oh, one more thing. If someone offers to sell you "no pink flamingos in my yard, please" Insurance… buy it, immediately… before it's too late!

Turning Points: Accepting God's Miracle of Healing!

"Come on Larry, I'm taking you to a 'real' church! We're going to a healing service!" Those words, served as my introduction to Dot, an energetic 75-year-young woman who felt led by God to provide a room for me during seminary studies at Duke Divinity School. Before I could set down my suitcase she steered me back outside to her car and forcefully exclaimed, *"I'll drive! Get in!"*

"As Jesus was walking along, he saw a man who had been blind from birth." (John 9:1)

As we entered the crowded church everyone was on their feet exuberantly singing and clapping. We were ushered to the only seats available… on the first row, directly in front of the speakers. Boy, was I feeling intimidated. It had only been a few short weeks since I left the business world to become a preacher and here I was on the front row of a crowded healing service having no idea what was going to happen next. Truthfully, I didn't even know what a healing service was? I would soon find out.

"'Teacher,' his disciples asked him, 'why was this man born blind?' … Jesus answered. 'He was born blind so the power of God could be seen in him.' " (2-3)

Dot, looked my way and gave me a knowing look that implied, *"Trust me!"* The music was catchy and easy to sing so I found myself beginning to relax and enjoy the service. The speaker gave an excellent message on the importance of fasting and prayer. *"We cannot be an example for others unless we are willing to practice what we believe!"* he said. Nothing unusual so far, but then…

"Then he (Jesus) spit on the ground, made mud with the saliva and smoothed the mud over the blind man's eyes. He told him, 'Go and wash in the pool of Siloam' (Siloam means Sent). So the man went and washed and came back seeing!" (6-7)

The preacher paused for a moment as if in prayer. Then he pointed to a young woman and mentioned a recent divorce and how God would help her cope as a single mother. He then turned looked at a young man and spoke of his struggle with alcoholism and how God could overcome it. Then, the minister looked directly at me and asked me to stand. He told everyone that I was a new minister (that much he already knew) but then he shared personal details about my life that he could not have known. He asked everyone to pray for my ministry and told me to sit down. Now I was

73

extremely uncomfortable and my head was spinning with questions.

"His neighbors and others who knew him as a blind beggar asked each other, 'Is this the same man - that beggar?' Some said he was and others said, 'No, but he surely looks like him.' And the beggar kept saying, 'I am the same man!'" (8-9)

As if guided by an unspoken command people began slowly moving to the front. The minister approached one woman standing directly in front of me, gazed into her eyes and mentioned a severe blood disorder. *"In the name of Jesus, heal her!"* he screamed. Then the woman seemed to swoon as she spread her arms straight into the air, screamed and fell backwards right into my arms. Two women seeing my confusion immediately grabbed her and gently eased her to the floor while discreetly covering her with a sheet.

"So for the second time they called in the man who had been blind and told him, 'Give glory to God by telling the truth, because we know Jesus is a sinner.' The man replied, 'I don't know whether he is a sinner but I know this: I was blind and now I can see!'" (24-25)

I left the service that night with more questions than answers. Are special healing services necessary for God to respond? How did the preacher know so much about me? Was the woman really healed of her blood disorder? What about people who are not healed? Do all healing services require this sort of drama? Are there other ways we can be involved in a healing ministry?

For years I have struggled with the questions presented by this story. I pray that my answers based on scripture and personal experience as a pastor will help you clearly understand and appreciate how we as the church can be actively involved in God's miracle of healing?

Turning Points: Accepting God's Miracle of Healing 2

For years, I struggled with feelings of inadequacy as a pastor and Christian. Should our church offer healing services? Could God heal others through a special service? What if we had a healing service and no one was healed? Does this mean we are doing something wrong? So recently, along with several leaders of our church, I began to study God's teaching on healing.

Our first Step was to study scripture. Here is what we found:

1. God heals. *"He forgives all my sins and heals all my diseases..."*

(Psalm 103.3)

2. Jesus heals. *"...and he* (Jesus) *healed all the sick."*

(Matthew 8:17)

3. The disciples heal. *"Then he* (Jesus) *sent them out... to heal the sick."*

(Luke 9:2)

4. We can heal. *"Are any among you sick? They should call for the elders of the church and have them pray... and their prayer offered in faith will heal the sick."* (James 5:14-15)

Step two: We invited leaders from a nearby church to talk about their healing ministry. Two of the leaders joined us for an evening of study and prayer. They emphasized that as Christians we are already deeply involved in God's miracle of healing. Every time we visit someone in need, send a card, deliver a basket of food, bake a cake, offer a prayer or simply share a conversation over a soothing cup of coffee we are offering God's miracle of healing. We could stop feeling inadequate and start learning how to improve our healing ministry. They described healing as:

- ✝ *Healing is...* a loving act of God's compassion and mercy... not a performance or circus act.
- ✝ *Healing involves...* spiritual, emotional and physical wholeness... as much as a physical deed.
- ✝ *Healing occurs...* in God's way and in God's time... not simply because of what we say or do.
- ✝ *Healing can include...* human responses such as nursing care, counseling and acts of friendship.
- ✝ *Healing may...* mean courage to endure suffering and hardship rather than instant reprieve.
- ✝ *Healing ultimately...* trumpets our earthly death as a victory ensuring eternal life in heaven.

"Jesus went to the blind man and asked, 'Do you believe in the Son of Man?' The man answered, 'Who is he, sir, because I would like to.' Jesus said, 'You have seen him and he is speaking to you!' The blind man responded, 'Yes, Lord, I believe!' And he worshiped Jesus."

(John 9:35-39)

After months of preparation and prayer we reached a critical turning point. We agreed to share our findings with the church during a Sunday worship service. At the conclusion of the service we decided to offer a period of time for others to come forward and ask for healing prayers.

On Healing Sunday, I shared what our leadership had discovered and how we hoped to expand our healing ministry in several spiritual and practical directions. I also explained our intent to offer prayers for healing on a regular basis at the conclusion of worship. After we sang the final hymn, several leaders stood with me near the altar as we offered the opportunity for anyone who needed healing to come forward. For the longest moment, nothing happened…

Then the miracle of God's healing began. First one woman slowly and painfully stood up and came forward. She told me that she needed help with Osteoporosis. Right behind her stood another person suffering from chronic back problems. One man came forward confessed an addiction to alcohol and asked for help. The line grew as we gathered around each person, heard his/her request and took turns offering prayers to God. The recorded music stopped and for several minutes, all you heard were sounds of people sobbing and praying. In thirteen years of ministry, I never before witnessed such a spiritual and emotional outpouring.

Over the next few days, several who came forward told me of dramatic changes and yes… even miracles! Understanding and believing the miracle of God's healing was a critical turning point in my life and the ministry of our church.

Have I successfully answered all the questions and concerns about healing? Of course not! But like the healed blind man, I can now emphatically say to Jesus and to you… *"Yes Lord, I believe! I was blind and now I can see!"*

Church Quilts & People Squares

Mell and I were once surprised at Christmas with a beautiful hand-made quilt. The contributors, some experienced, others just wanting to help, each made squares and signed their name. The individual piece was then carefully sewn together to form a lively mixture of patterns and colors. The result was a quilt of lasting beauty, which will always remind me of a special church and the love they shared with our family.

Like my quilt, churches are a lively mixture of people-squares with varying degrees of challenges, joys and sorrows. The list below highlights some good and flawed examples of people-squares who have helped form a church-quilt of beauty and color, pleasing to God.

✟   Seven children, with nervous giggles begin a Bible study. Their enthusiasm is contagious and questions are penetrating. Upon hearing the story of Abraham and the miracle birth of Isaac, which means "laughter," there are visible reactions of snickers and joy.

✞   Fifty-some folks hop into pick-up trucks after worship to drive through mud and debris to a near-by creek bank. Singing, "Shall we gather at the river," they have come to witness the baptism of three dedicated men who have given their lives to God in the cold frigid waters near their home.

✞   The church board debates whether to buy curtains or stained-glass windows with their $3000 surplus. One member asks for $300 to purchase Christmas gifts for several needy children. After a long silence, no surplus money is offered, but they do agree to take up an offering. The children receive bicycles and the church gets a new carpet.

✞   A man in the local community has a heart attack and nearly dies. While in the hospital, he makes a commitment to serve God by attending a small-struggling church. Within a few months he is motivating and encouraging others through his enthusiastic witness. Both are blessed.

✞   One thirty-something member feels led to start a new Sunday school class for younger adults. Another wants to reach-out to single adults. Soon, with encouragement, help and prayer the two new groups combine and become one of the largest classes in the church.

✞   A nurse asks a nearby church to build a handicap ramp for an elderly patient in the county. The men's group sends a team of volunteers who spend their Saturday building the ramp and making a few minor repairs to the house as well.

✞   A new member attending her first leadership meeting suggests the church occasionally sing more upbeat music, younger people can relate too. Another member stands and makes it clear she is not interested in learning new songs. The subject is dropped. The new member no longer attends.

✞   A young man asks if he can play softball with the church team. Before the season is over, God touches his life. The team however, still finishes in last place.

✞   On two warm spring evenings, 24 students of all ages gather to celebrate completing a demanding nine-month Bible study. During the worship service class members talk of receiving life-changing support from God and the group.

Just as squares are stitched together to form a colorful quilt, the church is made up of various individuals looking for an ongoing relationship with God. There are a few mistakes made and sins committed but there are also wonderful acts of love and courage. The result is a church-quilt of lasting beauty, which will always remind me of a special community and God's gracious love.

Oops! I almost forgot. There is something missing. One square is deliberately blank and waiting for you because without you and the unique contribution and gifts God has given you, our quilt is incomplete. God's church-quilt has plenty of space available for people-squares just like you and me. Come join us but don't forget your needle and thread.

Do you have a great church story? Please send it to me at our website: *www.SowingSeedsofFaith.com*

The Church in Cyberspace

"You Christians are all alike! Holier than thou narrow-minded people who think that your way is the only way and you look down on those that have a different opinion...

"I'm trying to contact as many churches as possible. I am thinking about suicide and this is the only way I know to work through the pain!"

"I have been facing many challenges recently, one of which involved signs and symptoms of cancer. I was in so much pain..."

All three people approached me within a few days. All were suffering and needed to be reassured in a way only God can offer. One was probably deeply hurt by a church or minister and was looking to vent his frustration. Another suffered with emotional and physical disabilities. Discouraged by the constant obstacles thrown in her way, she was considering the worst. The third had been told of having a life threatening illness and was seeking healing comfort.

Their problems are not unique. How they found me to share those problems is very unique. I've never actually met any of them. All three approached me through my new website (*www.SowingSeedsofFaith.com*) by e-mail. Strange? Not anymore!

It is truly a different world! Surveys show heightened interest in spiritual issues. The phenomenal popularity of "Touched By An Angel" on television and the "Left Behind" book series illustrate the general public's newfound interest in God. Religious websites offering devotions, Bible study, chat rooms and prayers are the fastest growing segment on the Internet. Yet the typical mainline church is still declining and hundreds are even closing. In other words, many people seeking God are going someplace other than their local church.

In Matthew 25, Jesus tells the story of a business owner going on a journey and entrusting various sums of money with three employees. After a time the owner returns and asks the three for a report. The first two employees give glowing accounts of how they doubled their boss's original investment. The owner is very pleased and invites them to join the company as full partners. The third employee, however, afraid of failure, did nothing. The reaction of the owner was righteous anger as he took the money away, gave it to the other two and sent the timid one into darkness.

Jesus has gone on a journey and has entrusted the church to act as His holy messenger. The lesson clearly favors those churches that respond to today's needs by creatively applying and teaching the active and penetrating Word of God. Churches that do not adapt, like our timid employee, will face a dismal future of too many funerals and too few baptisms.

Why are so many people becoming tuned in to God yet being turned off by God's church?

➤ *They don't understand my situation:* The church is considered to be out of touch with typical career and family concerns. For example: More than fifty percent of unchurched adults are single. Yet few churches support any kind of singles ministry.

➤ *All they want is my money:* A group of men were asked to describe what the church expected of them. They said: *Attend worship, write a check and don't make waves.*

➤ *Worship is dull:* Television, movies and sporting events offer exciting entertainment so worship services can easily be perceived as dull by comparison.

➤ *Church members are eager to judge and slow to help:* Most of us find God in the midst of great struggle or tragedy, yet the church often seems ill equipped to provide real aid.

If most folks think we are dull, badger them for money and offer criticism rather than understanding is it any wonder why they stay away? Yet, God's church offers the reassuring message of God's continuing love and grace to a world desperately seeking hope! But we must be willing to adapt the methods used to present that message to a changing world. Three people sharing their concerns through email and the Bible story of three employees investing their boss's money vividly remind us that we as the church can and must do better.

Parking Lots & The Church in Cyberspace

After a long, tiring week at school, I just needed to walk to my parking place and begin the two-hour journey home. Only… something was wrong. My car was missing! "Can you believe this?" I thought. "Some dirty rotten, no-good… stole my car. Now what?" Furious, I stomped to the campus police station and demanded action. After filing a report the car's description was broadcast over the radio. Within five minutes an officer called back saying, "I think I've found it!"

"What happened?" I wondered. "Did the thief take a joyride and then abandon the car? Would there be any damage?" A few minutes later, I was driven to a parking lot less than 200 yards from where my car was stolen…. Or was it stolen? Oops! With a sickening feeling in the pit of my stomach, I suddenly remembered that this particular week, I had parked my car in a different parking lot and out of habit simply expected it to be where it never was. "How embarrassing!"

Many church leaders could be accused of the same problem "…out of habit, I expected our congregation to be where they never were." As a pastor I need to be careful to guide our church to the right parking lot. In other words… As a church are we merely comfortable with doing what worked forty or fifty years ago or are we truly reaching out to serve God and meet the real needs of the world as it is today?

The last words of Jesus were: "I have been given complete authority in heaven and on earth. Therefore, go and make disciples of all nations, baptizing them in the name of the Father and the Son and the Holy Spirit. Teach these new disciples to obey all the commands I have given you. And be sure of this: I am with you always, even to the end of the age."

(Matthew 28:18-20)

I see three lessons and a promise:

✞ **Vision:** *I have been given complete authority…* Jesus has been given complete authority from God. Does your church have a vision that reflects God's authority? It's hard to know what path to travel without an eventual destination. Where does your church want to go?

✞ **Teach:** *Teach these new disciples…* Are you teaching disciples? People are hungry to grow stronger in their faith. Is your church offering a good Bible Study that will allow them to ask tough questions? Do you offer small groups for prayer and support?

✣ **Empower:** *...baptize them in the name of the Father and the Son and the Holy Spirit.* As a church, are you in the business of empowering disciples? The church could be described as matchmaker: matching community needs with the unique talents of people. New disciples are encouraged to join existing ministries or form new ones which in turn, attract more new disciples to teach and empower. It is an endless spiral of growth and renewal.

Here is the promise: *I am with you always, even to the end of the age.* This wonderful assurance gives us wisdom to pray, patience to wait, discipline to prepare, humility to encourage and ultimately courage to take risks knowing God lovingly protects us. Some examples:

✣ A dying church participates in a special Bible study. During one class, they decide to start an after-school program. Three years later the church is back on it's feet and growing.

✣ A coat salesman in Sunday school hears of school children with no winter coats. The resulting coat project now provides new coats for more than 500 children every year.

✣ A struggling church sends a discouraged widow to a singles retreat. She comes back with a vision to start a singles ministry. Thanks to her ministry, the church is thriving.

Larry, what about the future? It took a lost automobile to help me realize that looking towards the future first means asking if I am in the right parking lot. If our church has a vision and is faithfully teaching and empowering disciples then ultimately God will give us a unique ministry suitable for our community and us. Meanwhile, I'm working on improving my memory.

God's Power, The Church and Cyberspace

The hospital informed June, a young single mother that her nine-year-old daughter, Melissa contracted a rare virus that affects the heart. Usual treatments would not be effective. Without a miracle her precious child could die within the next few days. Later that night, alone and feeling especially vulnerable, June gave in to her fears and began to sob uncontrollably. What would she do? Where would she go? The closest relatives were over 500 miles away and she had few friends.

Kathy, a nurse at the same hospital heard about June's situation and after returning home, turned on her computer and went online. First she contacted a regular chat group and asked for prayers. Within minutes a reply appeared suggesting that she take the request to a national prayer web site that would literally reach thousands. Over the next few hours, nearly a hundred emails offering prayer and support arrived. Kathy printed each letter to bring back to the hospital.

John, a pastor in the same community came home and checked his email. One message was from the same web site asking prayers for the same little girl. Noticing the location, he called a church leader and asked her to contact other members of the church prayer chain. Then he slipped on his coat and rushed to the hospital to be with the little girl and her mother.

Sharon, a virile disease specialist stationed at a hospital in Venezuela also saw the prayer request and had a hunch that she could help the little girl. She emailed her reply to the message: *"Please send the phone number of her doctor. An experimental drug just released for testing may be helpful."* Within minutes she received the phone number and was talking to the doctor. Within an hour the hospital received her fax including detailed treatment instructions.

Early the next day, it was evident that the treatment was beginning to work. Melissa was now in a regular room and was sleeping peacefully. Her mother, June was sitting nearby reading the stack of email notes offering support and prayer. Also in the room were John and several members of the church prayer chain. The atmosphere as if by magic was now full of the healing spirit of God.

This amazing story describes God's power at work in a new medium called cyberspace.

The business world has been mesmerized by the profit potential of the Internet, but few people realize how much the digital world is also transforming the nature of the church and how we do ministry. Andrew Careaga, author of "E-vangelism: Sharing the Gospel in Cyberspace" writes: "On the 'Net,' any Christian with a home computer, a modem and access to one of many available online services can be a missionary to thousands of people without ever leaving home."

Here are some common examples of Christian Cyberspace Ministry:
  ◆ A pastor continues to keep up with those in her church who have moved through email.
  ◆ A Bible Study web site gives thousands a chance to understand God's Word.
  ◆ A student beginning to explore her faith finds love and acceptance in a

cyber chat room.

- ♦Our own Sowing Seeds of Faith devotions reach thousands instantly yet at the same time we offer individual feedback and counseling support around the world.
- ♦A Single Adult uses a Christian based Singles Ministry Website to meet new friends.

In the early days of the church, the book of Acts reports: *" 'They devoted themselves to the apostles' teaching and to the fellowship, to the breaking of bread and to prayer. Everyone was filled with awe, and many wonders and miraculous signs were done by the apostles."* (2:42) The reminder is that our mission as the church should never change: only our method of transmission.

Can a Christian web site or email prayer chain ever replace the intimacy of personal contact? Of course not! What the Internet represents is a powerful tool that allows our church to teach, offer fellowship and be in prayer in creative new ways. Just as in the book of Acts we can be filled with awe at the many wonders and miraculous signs being done in the name of Christ. A single mother and her healthy child can certainly attest to that and are no doubt… very grateful.

Bathrooms and Literacy!

Recently, at a nearby restaurant, I left my family to go to the bathroom. Looking back, I remember thinking this particular bathroom looked, somehow… well, different. I soon found out why. While washing my hands, the door opened and a woman stood there looking at me with an inane smirk. *"What is she grinning about and what's she doing in the men's room?"* I thought, but politely smiled and then gasped as she pointed a finger to a sign which clearly said… WOMEN.

"Can't you read?" she asked and started laughing, hysterically. After a mumbled apology, I hurried back to the table and hustled my family out of the restaurant before she could come out of the restroom and tell the whole world about this bizarre man who visits women's bathrooms.

Okay, you can stop laughing now! It was a silly mistake but suppose I really couldn't read?

How would I know which bathroom to enter, drive a car, fill out an employment application, read a newspaper or study a Bible? How would you hold a job, shop for groceries or order a meal? Is there anything more traumatic than being unable to read in our information-driven society?

Yet, 21% to 23% of our population or one of every five adults in America are functionally illiterate which means an inability to read in most everyday life situations. Why? There's no single reason. One non-reader dropped out of school early. Another has an emotional or physical disability. Another grew up with non-reading parents. English is a foreign language for some non-readers.

Regardless of the cause, illiteracy hurts us all. 60% of prison inmates are illiterate and 85% of all juvenile offenders have reading problems. Many illiterates are unemployed and dependent upon public support. Even, employed, non-readers have more accidents and require more training. One statistic estimates the cost of illiteracy in low productivity and higher training expenses to be billions of dollars every year. Illiteracy costs our society financially, emotionally and spiritually.

Proverbs is clear: *"Happy is the person who finds wisdom and gains understanding. For the profit of wisdom is better than silver and her wages are better than gold. Wisdom is more precious than rubies; nothing you desire can compare with her. She offers you life in her right hand and riches and honor in her left. She will guide you down delightful paths; all her ways are satisfying. Wisdom is a tree of life to those who embrace her…"* (3:13-18)

So, Larry, what can I do?

You can volunteer to help someone read by volunteering or supporting a literacy group in your community. Volunteers in a typical group meet individually with students and help nonreaders learn basic skills. Tutoring is usually offered free of charge to anyone with the desire to learn. Your donations provide training for the tutors plus books and other materials for the student.

One student dictated this letter to a tutor after only a few months: *"I started school when I was seven. I liked going through the fourth grade. When I got in the fifth grade, I started having problems— I got in trouble that summer. I was sent to reform school when I was thirteen…I never went back to school. I can read a whole lot better now since I've been coming here (to reading class). I enjoy reading more too. I want to get my GED so I can get a good job… My 'tutor' is really helping me."*

Would you like to "really help" someone in need? Contact your library and ask about a local literacy group. Most organizations desperately need donations and volunteers. Nationally, you can contact Literacy Volunteers of America or *www.literacy volunteers.org* and Laubach Volunteers at *www.laubach.org*. You really can make a difference.

Meanwhile, please pray that I learn to visit the right bathroom. This could be embarrassing!

A Church Fire and A Miracle of Rebirth!

One early Friday morning, several years ago, I received a telephone call informing me that Tabernacle United Methodist, a beautiful old church in Amelia County, Virginia burned to the ground. When I arrived, all that remained were cement steps leading to nothing more than charred posts and black soot. Church members and bystanders could only stare in shock and disbelief.

For me, it was like being a witness to death because in many ways a church building represents a community full of life and shared memories. Think about it: baptisms celebrating life, funerals remembering our after-life, worship services giving glory to the God we love and serve, covered-dish suppers providing good food and joyous fellowship, meetings agonizing over how best to serve God, children's Christmas specials and youth activities offering fun and spiritual opportunities.

All I could do at the time was stand and stare in shock. Like many who were there, I wanted to help but how? How could we as Christian's respond to such a horrifying tragedy?

We decided to take action. Our church canceled services on the first Sunday after the fire and we all drove to Tabernacle to be with friends and fellow Christians. We came to grieve and bring gifts of love.

We came expecting a funeral, but there was none to be found. Instead, we witnessed the miracle of a church being reborn!

A colorful banner was propped over the front steps proclaiming proudly: *Worship, Sunday 9:45 AM.* Two greeters were there to welcome us, hand out bulletins and attach yellow ribbons. Chairs were placed on the lawn, donated by a local funeral home. A makeshift pulpit with a cross and pictures of the church were placed in front of the burned-out building. A pick-up truck held a makeshift sound system and the choir was seated off to one side. *The miracle for God's church was just beginning!*

The pastor began the service describing the events leading up to the fire, including a church meeting that actually discussed building an addition, which would include a fellowship hall and a kitchen. Then he described the total shock of the fire and how he had to keep returning to the scene just to make sure it wasn't all a nightmare. Finally, he paused and announced to the congregation and to us: *"We are going to build a new church and it will have a fellowship hall and a kitchen."*

He went on to describe a stranger driving by and seeing what happened. He immediately took all the money out of his wallet and gave it to the pastor to help rebuild and vowed to come back with more. A cabinetmaker promised to build new cabinets and donate them all to the church. A carpenter volunteered his labor. A local church offered their mission team to assist in the work. Another church offered free use of their building. Other churches donated hymnbooks and office equipment.

During the service, the children and choir sang. Prayers were offered to the sick, and we worshipped God, just as the church has done for over two thousand years. In the midst of the smoking ruins, a resurrected church began to dream and build toward the future. A miracle was quietly taking place.

Jesus asked the disciples, "Who do you say I am?" Simon Peter answered, "You are the Messiah, the Son of the living God." Jesus replied, "You are blessed, Simon son of John, because my Father in heaven has revealed this to you...Now I say to you that you are Peter (the rock) and upon this rock I will build my church and all the powers of hell will not conquer it." (Matthew 16:16-18)

Let's face it… most of us take the existence of our church for granted. Sometimes, it takes a fire to remind us of the vital role of God's "rock" the church. During the service a minister spoke of courage and faith of Christians forced underground in the Soviet Union only to be reborn stronger than ever.

One short year later, I was invited to another worship service at Tabernacle United Methodist. This time we were celebrating our own miracle of rebirth. In twelve months, money was raised, contractors secured and a new church was built on the ashes of the old. As word got around, more people were caught up in the enthusiasm. Worship attendance and membership nearly doubled. All I could say was, "Wow!"

On the day of the fire, two white lilies appeared as symbols of Easter and rebirth. Now a new church in Virginia serves as a vivid reminder of how God creates life amidst ruins whether it is buildings or souls.

Turning Points:
Asking for Help and A Prayer Ministry

- Alice (Alabama) We are the custodial parents of a seven-year-old granddaughter. Now her unfit biological mother is going to file to regain custody and we are devastated.
- Stephanie (California) I am a single mother raising a teenage daughter. My church is not offering much support. It's scary and very lonely sometimes.

Some say problems have the potential to become opportunities for growth. Well, I had a problem. Recently, I encouraged visitors to our Sowing Seeds of Faith Website to share their concerns through an interactive web page, entitled "Prayer Needs." Over the next few weeks, I received nearly one hundred requests for prayer from around the world. Here are a few examples (Names were changed)

- Larry (Canada) I would like to change but I have a hard time obeying God's Word. I would like to serve him and find happiness. I don't want to fall back to the world.
- Allison (Maryland) We have been trying to have a child for almost five years. We have been through many doctors and procedures. We conceived once and lost the baby ten weeks later. We were both devastated.

I personally answered each request with encouragement and prayer but every day three to four more letters would arrive. Soon the requests for prayer became overwhelming. I was beginning to feel inadequate to meet the needs.

- Nicole (California) I lost my Mom and have a broken heart. She is with Jesus and I should be rejoicing but some days I hurt so much inside. I want to feel joy again.
- (No name) I am thirty-three and mother of a twelve-year-old son. My husband was unfaithful and I must file for a divorce. He has no desire to continue being married to me. I am really struggling with why this happened to me. I don't run around. I've been a good wife.
- Patricia (South Carolina) My son is serving a fifteen-year sentence for something he is innocent of. Please ask God to turn his heart. Pray God's blessings upon him.
- Colleen (Colorado) My friend was badly injured in a terrible car

accident. He looks well on the outside now but he's still having memory loss, fatigue, mood swings, etc. He desperately needs help.

I wanted desperately to suggest words of hope that would movingly articulate God's love and grace but at this point the person needing help and solid scriptural guidance was me.

Several respected leaders asked Jesus to come and heal the slave of a Roman officer who was near death. Before they arrived, however, the officer sent friends to meet Jesus who said, *"Lord, don't trouble yourself by coming to my home, for I am not worthy. Just say the word from where you are, and my servant will be healed. I know because I am under the authority of my superior officers, and I have authority over my soldiers. I only need to say, 'Go,' and they go." When Jesus heard this, he was amazed. Turning to the crowd, he said, "I tell you, I haven't seen faith like this in all the land of Israel!" And when they returned the slave was healed.*

(Parts of Luke 7:6-10)

On the surface, Jesus using a Roman officer as the main character in a lesson about faith makes no sense. Unless that is the lesson… For you see, it was the Roman Officer, not the religious leaders who grasped exactly Who Jesus was. *"Just say the word from where you are and my servant will be healed."* While the religious experts, the insiders were conducting debates, a religious outsider; a Roman officer went from debates to faith to action.

✝ **The Bad News:** I am the religious insider who neglected to trust in God's authority.

✝ **The Good News:** It's never too late to ask for help. For me, that was a turning point.

The Roman Officer's example helped me learn that it's never too late to ask for help. Faith is my willingness to trust in God's answer. Meanwhile, prayer needs continued to arrive by email.

- Marsha (Minnesota) My 20-year-old twin daughters are leaving home. They both suffer with learning disabilities. I pray their co-workers will be patient and help them succeed.

- Holly (Kentucky) My boyfriend has decided to go into the ministry. We are both seeking God's will for our lives and hope to stay close together.

- Sharon (California) My son and his wife and five children. Their house caught fire and they still have no home, as they are low income. Nearly everything was lost.

- Alex (Virginia) Granddaughter has non-Hodgkin's, T-cell lymphoma cancer. She has a growth in her chest, near her heart and has spots and holes in her kidneys...

First: I needed to kick myself, hard. These prayer requests weren't burdens... far from it. God is giving me a breathtaking opportunity to provide ministry for the needs of others around the world. I clearly must learn how to replace worry over what "I" will do with faith in what "God" can do. After all, people are seeking guidance from God, not me. I am simply being asked to pray.

God was giving me an opportunity to learn and grow. The question is: "What would I do with it?"

With renewed enthusiasm, I began to pray... really pray. When prayer needs flash across the computer screen, I'm learning to bow my head and pray for their situation now not later. On the Sowing Seeds Ministry website *www.SowingSeedsofFaith.com,* I asked volunteers to pray with me. Thousands have responded. Several times each week, I email them a list of "prayer needs.

One thought kept nagging me. *"What about the church I serve? Shouldn't they be involved?"*

One Sunday, our church devoted a worship service to healing and prayer. Copies of the nearly 100 e-mail requests from around the world were distributed to every member of our congregation. As each prayer need was read aloud someone holding that particular request would stand and agree to continue praying throughout the week. Soon, every man, woman and child in the congregation was standing and praying for another.

No longer were we simply asking God to be active in national and world events. We were praying for real people around the world and their specific needs. Somehow our prayers became more significant. The worship service ended with Holy Communion. Groups of people moved to the altar to receive the bread and cup symbolizing the body and blood of Jesus Christ. But this time, each person brought their email prayer requests to the altar and received communion for two.

For us, the time-honored liturgy of Holy Communion took on a new implication, *"Pour out your Holy Spirit on us gathered here, and on these gifts of bread and wine. Make them be for us the body and blood of Christ that we may be for the world the body of Christ, redeemed by his blood. By your Spirit make us one with Christ, one with each other and one in ministry to all the world."*

What started as a problem soon became an exciting opportunity for growth and ministry. Those who asked for prayer are already noticing changes and discovering answers. Our church is excited about being an active partner in a new prayer ministry.   And me? I've changed too. When prayer needs flash across the computer screen, I'm not burdened anymore. I finally realize there is plenty of help just waiting to be asked. Isn't this what being the church is all about?

William Temple wrote: *"When I pray, coincidences happen and when I do not, they don't."*

Shall We Gather At The River?

"Larry, we want to be baptized and join the church," said Rick. Coy, his son and a friend, Buck, nodded in agreement with obvious intensity.

"That's great!" I responded with equal enthusiasm. *"I'll make the arrangements and we can do everything during next week's worship service."*

"No! You don't understand," Rick replied earnestly. *"We love the outdoors and spent most of our lives hunting and fishing in the woods nearby. There is a creek about a mile from our house and we want to be baptized in that creek."*

"Okay," I said but with less enthusiasm. *"You do know that it's October?"*

People from Jerusalem and from every section of Judea and from all over the Jordan Valley went out to the wilderness to hear John the Baptist preach. And when they confessed their sins, he baptized them in the Jordan River.   (Matthew 3:5-6)

There is something astonishing and awe-inspiring about a baptism. I can't really explain it. I just know it to be true. Ordinary cares and concerns are temporarily forgotten as we share in the celebration of a momentous human decision blessed by the power and grace of almighty God.

No one illustrated this better than Jesus: *After his baptism, as Jesus came up out of the water, the heavens were opened and he saw the Spirit of God descending like a dove and settling on him. And a voice from heaven said, "This is my beloved son and I am fully pleased with him."*

(Matthew 3:16-17)

Three men were making life-changing decisions and our church community was determined to support them in any way possible even if it meant going to a creek in the middle of the woods on a cold October Sunday afternoon.

Yet, on the big day, the sun burned bright as if God himself were smiling on us as fifty some folks following Sunday worship hopped into a caravan of pick-up trucks and four-wheel drive vehicles to plow through the mud and debris to the creek bank. Once there we formed a circle to sing, appropriately enough: *"Shall we gather at the river, where bright angel feet have trod, with its crystal tide forever flowing by the throne of God."* We all joined hands to pray and then we were ready.

As I stepped into the chilly water my first thoughts were unfortunately not scriptural… *"Whoa, it's cold!"*

Rick was first to step into the creek and as he crossed his arms I placed a handkerchief over his nose and gently lowered him into the water solemnly saying, *"Rick, I baptize you in the name of the Father and of the Son and of the Holy Spirit."* …oh oh! Big trouble. I couldn't lift him back up. My feet were slipping in the mud. *"Help!"* I cried, imagining the next morning's news headline: "Baptism leads to Drowning!"

Buck, the next person to be baptized quickly jumped in to help bring Rick back to the surface. Taking no more chances, Rick then assisted with Buck and finally together we gently lowered Rick's son, Coy into the water. As we returned to the creek bank, the singing resumed: *"Yes, we'll gather at the river, the beautiful, the beautiful river; gather with the saints at the river that flows by the throne of God."*

Our little gathering at the river became a sacred moment in the lives of three special men and a church that supported and loved them. Years later, we still talk about that day as one of the highlights of our ministry. I can't explain it. I only know it to be true. *And with Christ you were raised to a new life because you trusted the mighty power of God, who raised Christ from the dead.* (Colossians 2:12)

Maybe Baptism is God's way of illustrating for us what it means to have total faith in the grace and power of almighty God. I don't know about you but it definitely works for me!

Will It Take Six Strong Men to Bring You Back?

- *"I'm too busy to go to church."*
- *"The sermons are dull and the music is sleepy. Why should I come just to be bored?"*
- *"Church people are such hypocrites. They don't practice what they preach!"*
- *"I'd rather watch "Touched By An Angel" and stay home."*
- *"The only thing my church wants is my money or my willingness to serve on a committee."*
- *"I'm young or I'm divorced or I'm poor. They don't want me."*
- *"Do you believe in God?"* I reply.
- *"Oh, yes... I'm just not ready to go back to church."*

For years, my own favorite excuse for not attending church was, *"I work six days a week in a suit and tie. I just want to sleep-in, relax and read the paper. Why should I dress up again on my only day off?"* Truthfully, I just did not feel any great need to be in church. Obviously my situation changed but why?

Zig Ziglar a well-known motivational speaker and author, literally sold me on the benefits of becoming a Christian and attending church now rather than later. Zig described the church as the body of Christ showing me a piece of Heaven for today, not just tomorrow. What is that piece of heaven? What are those benefits of attending church? I thought you would never ask:

- ✝ **Longer life**: Insurance studies show regular church attendance adds 5.7 years to your life.
- ✝ **Wealth:** The Bible is full of methods for effectively managing your money.
- ✝ **Peace:** There is a special peace of mind knowing God will always be there, no matter what.
- ✝ **Courage:** God will give you courage and strength to make ethical and moral stands.
- ✝ **Love:** Learning to love others the way God loves you is a source of happiness and comfort.
- ✝ **Forgiveness:** Learning to forgive yourself and others can literally heal your body and your soul.

This is just the short list, but what a picnic basket full of luscious promises! You live longer. Manage your financial resources more efficiently. Enjoy peace of mind. Receive supernatural courage to take a stand. Experience the breathtaking love of God and obtain the healing medicine of forgiveness.

Why do we need to go to church? *"Because the church is still the best way to strengthen your relationship with God and with others and receive those special benefits."*

I went back to church with a new attitude. Yes, at times, I was busy, the music was awful, the preacher was boring and people are still hypocrites... but I also discovered an indescribable love and peace. I found a source for encouragement and a place of acceptance. The church isn't perfect, but what human institution is? The Bible says it best:

Without wavering, let us hold tightly to the hope we say we have, for God can be trusted to keep his promise. Think of ways to encourage one another to outbursts of love and good deeds. And let us not neglect our meeting together, as some people do, but encourage and warn each other, especially now that the day of his coming back again is drawing near.

(Hebrews 10:23-25)

Here is a dramatic way to think about your current relationship with God and the church.

A newspaper ad designed by a company called, Church Ad Project shows a black and white photograph of people carrying a coffin. The caption reads: **"Will it take six strong men to bring you back into the church?"** My first reaction was shock but the ad made me pause and think. What about you?

Let's face it. You do need the church and the church definitely needs you. If you've not been to church in awhile... come back. We've missed you. If you are already active with a church, share this story with a friend and invite him/her to join you. It sure beats the "six strong men" alternative. Ecch!!

Pride and the Preacher

"Are you the preacher?" the voice asked over the phone.

"Yes, I am." I replied. "Why do you ask?"

"A few weeks ago, I was a visitor in your church and heard your sermon. Could I ask a few questions?"

"Sure." I said with a smile, expecting a compliment.

"You told a story of a woman receiving communion? What does that have to do with the Bible?"

I started to explain how stories are an excellent way to teach scripture when he cut me off...

"Actually, I thought your sermon was pathetic!" He then went on to tell me why. When I tried to explain further, he cut me off saying, "I don't understand how you can justify what you do as preaching?"

At this point, my mouth was turning dry and my whole body was beginning to shake. How dare this young man tell me I was pathetic? (That's not what he said.) Who does he think he is? With gritted teeth, I politely told him there are other churches in the area and he should consider attending one.

Later that day I read this story told by Jesus: *"Two men went to the Temple to pray. One was a Preacher and the other was a dishonest businessman. The proud Preacher stood by himself and prayed: 'I thank you, God, that I am not a sinner like everyone else, especially like that businessman over there! For I never cheat, I don't sin, I don't commit adultery, I fast twice a week, and I give you a tenth of my income.' "But the businessman stood at a distance and dared not even lift his eyes to heaven as he prayed. Instead, he beat his chest in sorrow, saying, 'O God, be merciful to me, for I am a sinner.' I tell you, this sinner, not the Preacher, returned home justified before God. For the proud will be humbled, but the humble will be honored."* (Luke 18:9-14 occupations modernized)

If there was ever a famous parable about humility, this is it. The preacher is doing everything right. We should admire someone who consistently does what he is claiming. So why is Jesus giving him a hard time? The businessman was in church to confess a sin. Why is Jesus honoring him? The temptation is to picture the preacher as secretly evil and the businessman as a nice guy who made a little mistake.

Don't do that! Jesus is making an important point. Most of us become Christians by recognizing our sins and seeking forgiveness before God. We change our lifestyle and grow in faith. As we change, we also see more clearly the sins of our friends and coworkers. We want to offer guidance. "Why can't they straighten out their lives and become more like me? Thank you God, I don't make their mistakes."

Did you catch it? Comparing our lives to others may make us look a little better but not for long because the only comparison that ultimately matters is with God. With God, we always come up short. A freshly painted white house stands out in most neighborhoods… until it snows. Then, even the white paint looks pretty dull compared with the pure, freshly fallen snow. We like to comfort ourselves that we are not thieves or drug dealers but we forget the more subtle sins of pride and neglecting others.

Then God's truth hit me right between the eyes… I was the arrogant preacher in the story. Someone called me, looking for answers. His criticism very likely disguised a cry for help. Instead of listening and attempting to understand his underlying concerns, I became defensive and shut him out. I was the one who needed God's forgiveness. I was the preacher who needed to be humbled.

Two men began to pray. One was a businessman with a problem. The other, a preacher, considered one of the best in the community. The preacher compared himself with the businessman and thought he had arrived. The businessman compared himself with God and knew he was in deep trouble. Both were sinners but only one knew it… *"For the proud will be humbled, but the humble will be honored."*

Breaking
The
Peanut Butter
Habit . . .

Following God's Recipe
For A Wonderful Life.

Chapter 3
Examining Some
Old Recipes!
Turning Points
In The Bible

Sowing Seeds Ministry and John

It was a hectic week with little time left to prepare a Christmas message so I hurriedly looked up the first chapter of John intending to simply talk about Jesus being the true reason for the season. But something extraordinary happened. I discovered a gem of scriptural truth that explains much of what I struggle to accomplish as a minister and a writer. So it seems appropriate to share my newfound treasure with you as we begin this new chapter based on "Turning Points in the Bible." After all, you have a right to know.

✟ **What do I believe? What is Sowing Seeds Ministry attempting to teach?**

"In the beginning the Word already existed. He was with God, and he was God. He was in the beginning with God. He created everything there is. Nothing exists that he didn't make. Life itself was in him, and this life gives light to everyone. The light shines through the darkness, and the darkness can never extinguish it." (John 1:1-5 NLT)

We think of words as merely something you read. There certainly is some influence and power within those words but do we really understand "The Word?" For John "The Word" takes on a whole new meaning and becomes the living Christ who shines in the darkness and the darkness can never extinguish it. In Genesis God creates the world by merely speaking: "God said... and it was so." Such is the power of God's Word. So, my job as a pastor and a writer is to simply expose you to the authoritative, living Word and have complete faith that God will do the rest. God's Word is powerful.

1. Jesus is the Word: Foundation of our Faith

I must teach at least one Bible study every year. In addition, I speak or write with the belief that exposing you to the Word will change your life and improve your relationship with God: Areas such as deepening your prayer life, sacrificially giving of yourself and looking for opportunities to share your faith with others. Everything begins when we become serious about God's Word.

God sent John the Baptist to tell everyone about the light so that everyone might believe because of his testimony. John himself was not the light; he was only a witness to the light. The one who is the true light, who gives light to everyone, was going to come into the world. (6-9)

Now what? It may be the most important question you can ask as a follower of God. You've studied God's word... now what? John the Baptist was sent to be a witness to the light but so are you. You are sent by God to be a witness to the true Light of the world... Jesus Christ. Be honest with yourself. Why should you come to church on Sunday if your faith doesn't affect your daily lifestyle and habits from Monday through Saturday? Why should others seek a deeper relationship with God if they don't see God's light reflected in you? You are called to be a light!

2. God called us to witness to the light!

Who me? How? It depends upon your God-given talents and what you have been uniquely shaped to do. This is why studying God's word becomes a critical first step. People who study God's words are inevitably inspired with an interesting idea. One church gives school supplies to children each fall because someone in a Bible study had an idea. Another church started an after-school ministry because someone felt called by God to be a unique witness to the light.

We may all be called to be a witness to the light but it is not easy. When you get serious about being a witness you inevitably face obstacles.

But although the world was made through him, the world didn't recognize him when he came. Even in his own land and among his own people, he was not accepted. (John 1:10-11)

Good people often become discouraged because they don't anticipate this passage of scripture. God touches you in a significant way. You are eager to learn more and become a witness then... you get rejected, encounter an obstacle, face persecution or worse.

Facing obstacles in business could mean taking a stand for higher ethical standards. A schoolteacher may look for opportunities to become a Christian influence even when such activities are discouraged. Being a witness to the light of Christ could mean facing ostracism from fellow employees or even risking your career.

3. Facing Rejection: Christ faced it for you!

There is an old truism in the sales profession: if you hide in your office and never pick up the phone or look for opportunities to talk to a customer you will never encounter problems but you will also have no sales, no income and eventually no job. Rejection is a normal characteristic of business. Rejection is a normal component of life. Facing rejection is also a customary part of witnessing your faith. Successful businesses learn to surmount rejection by providing quality training and continuous encouragement. God provides quality training and continuous encouragement through the church.

Now comes the best part! Here is what makes it all worthwhile!

But to all who believed him and accepted him, he gave the right to become children of God. They are reborn! This is not a physical birth resulting from human passion or plan—this rebirth comes from God. So the Word became human and lived here on earth among us. He was full of unfailing love and faithfulness. And we have seen his glory, the glory of the only Son of the Father. (12-14)

As an employee, you work under a contract. If you goof off or make too many mistakes you could be fired. If the company experiences a business downturn you could be laid off. There are no guarantees in a job contract. Maybe you imagined God as a cosmic employer who could at any time terminate your contract and abandon you...

It may be a reasonable assumption based on worldly experience: reasonable but very wrong!

Many years ago, I worked at a famous hamburger restaurant. There were certain rules that all employees had to follow or lose their jobs. But one employee seldom followed the rules and nothing ever happened. Why? Because he was the owners' son. Are you smiling? Of course you are. You've probably worked with him.

One night while the rest of us were busy working our shifts, this jerk sits at the bosses' desk just behind us and gorges on a pizza. None of us can eat pizza in a hamburger joint. None of us can sit at the bosses' desk. We have to follow the rules and work hard because if we don't... do you get the picture?

Yet, you are never a mere employee of God. You are reborn as the Big Bosses' son or daughter. You are a child of the living Lord. Take a moment and relish this thought while savoring that delicious pepperoni pizza. God's children are never fired or laid off. You may goof up and need a good kick in the pants but you will always be a precious child of God. Isn't grace amazing?

4. No Employees Needed: Welcome to the family.

As a family member you share in God's glory. So, study God's living Word and get serious about your spiritual growth. Dare to become a witness to the light of Christ and trust in the Holy promise God's glory will fill you with perseverance in the face of persecution. **Welcome to the family!**

As a minister and a writer, I passionately labor to help you experience this awesome glory of God: The glory that could motivate you to endure a disappointing week, a stress-filled year or even a difficult life with a smile on your face and a prayer in your heart. **I call it, sowing seeds of faith...**

1. Jesus is the Word: Foundation of our Faith
2. God called us to witness to the light!
3. Facing Rejection: Christ faced it for you!
4. Employees Unnecessary: Welcome to the family.

Thank you God... I really needed that.

In the Beginning...Creation or Children's Story?

The national and international news is unusually gloomy this week. As I write:

♦ Wall Street is in the midst of a record economic free fall that threatens our national economy.

♦ Once Mighty, Russia is fighting to simply feed her people and survive.

♦ The war with worldwide terrorism seems to be rapidly escalating.

What is happening and what can we do about it? My answer may sound trite but when events get out of hand most experts stress returning to the basics. There is nothing more basic than taking another look at your faith by getting involved in a serious Bible study. Most of us own Bibles, but do we really try to read them? Think about how God still shapes our lives. For example:

✞ Our belief in God dictates our moral and ethical standards.

✞ Our faith gives us hope when hardship or tragedy strikes.

✞ Our faith allows us to see the world from a better perspective.

✞ Our belief in God gives us the desire to help others and be more sensitive to their needs.

Each September, we begin several Bible studies designed to deepen our faith. Through active Bible study we rediscover how God is still active in a twenty-first century world. Holy Scripture continues to offer solid solutions even in a fast-paced world of high-tech communications, Jerry Springer-style dysfunctional behavior and unstable economic conditions.

Where do we start? The beginning! When was the last time you read this passage? In a children's Sunday school class? *"In the beginning God created the heavens and the earth..."* Can an educated American still believe in the Biblical account of creation? Many people say, "It's a good story but hardly intellectually stimulating?" That's what people say but most haven't read the passage since childhood. So, why do we ignore it? Could we be afraid of what may be discovered?

Stop reading this, take a minute to open your Bible and then read chapter one of Genesis again, slowly. Read it as beautiful poetry expressing God's power and love. Go ahead... I've got all the time in the world. If you read this passage as poetry there is no need to answer questions of modern science or history. The poet really wasn't interested in answering those questions but instead chose to look for creative ways to express love for God's creation.

But Larry... why the seven days? Good question. Each day is meant as a statement of faith to show God created order and form. Out of nothing, God created the universe and then carefully created and lovingly breathed life into us to manage God's creation.

Next: The seven days are meant to illustrate the importance of celebrating the Sabbath: God worked for six days and then on the seventh day God rested... so should we.

Genesis is not the only scripture that describes God as creator of the universe and still in control:

✞ *In the beginning the Word already existed. He was with God and he was God.* (John 1:1)

✞ *When I look at the night sky and see the work of your fingers - the moon and the stars you have set in place...* (Psalm 8:3)

✞ *Acknowledge that the Lord is God! He made us and we are his.* (Psalm 100:3)

✞To Job: *"Where were you when I laid the foundations of the earth?"* (Job 38:4)

Are you looking for comfort to calm your fears of uncertain world and local events? Do you seek forgiveness and peace to release you from guilt and anguish? Are you looking to deepen your faith? Read the creation story again and behold the wonder of God and God's creation. It's certainly more reliable than Wall Street.

Adam & Eve: Excuses, Excuses, Excuses

What follows is an excerpt of a conversation between a Father and his child. By the way, this really happened.

Child: *Dad, I was in an automobile accident this morning.*
Father: *Are you okay? Was anyone else hurt? How serious was it?*
Child: *I'm okay, dad. No one else was hurt and it's not too serious.*
Father: *What happened?*
Child: *I was backing out of my friends' driveway and hit a pick-up truck. But Dad it wasn't my fault because the driveway had a huge 'S' curve in it. It was hard to maneuver and the truck was parked near the middle of the road...*"
Father: *Wait a minute! Wait a minute! Son, did you say the truck was parked?*
Child: *Well... yes, but it wasn't my fault. It was parked at such an odd angle...*
Father: *I love you, son but if the truck you hit was not moving then the accident was your fault. So don't give any more excuses.*

Does this sound familiar? Maybe you too have been forced to listen while someone uttered lame excuses instead of confessing their mistakes. Worse, have you been the one making excuses? Admit it. We've all been there. That is why Adam and Eve's forbidden fruit escapade is so potent.

(Adapted Genesis 3:8-13)

Another conversation between a Father and his children: *"They heard the sound of the Lord God walking in the garden at the time of the evening breeze and hid themselves from the presence of the Lord God among the trees of the garden."*

Father: *Where are you?*
Child: *I heard you in the garden and I was afraid and hid myself because I was naked.*
Father: *Who told you that you were naked? Have you eaten from the tree of which I commanded you not to eat?*
Child: *It wasn't my fault! The fruit was handed to me!*
Father to the other child: *What have you done?*
Other child: *It was the serpent who tricked me!*

We make excuses when God wants us to confess and repent. We claim to be victims instead of admitting that we are sinners. God warns us time and time again.

⊙**Amos:** *Come back to the Lord and live!* (5:6)

⊙**Jeremiah:** *"And I will forgive their wickedness and will never again remember their sins."* (31:34)

⊙**John the Baptist:** *I baptize with water those who turn from their sins and turn to God.* (Matthew 3:11)

God never asked for perfection… only a willingness to repent when (not if, when) we lose our way.

Maybe you can hear the sound of the Lord God walking in the garden. Are you hiding among the trees? When God finds you, what will you say? "It wasn't my fault! It was the serpent!"

Or… like another wayward son, you could say: *"Father, I have sinned against both heaven and you, and I am no longer worthy of being called your son."* (Luke 15:21)

And like the Father to the Prodigal Son, you could hear these words of comfort: *"We must celebrate with a feast, for this son of mine was dead and has now returned to life. He was lost, but now he is found."* (15:23-24)

It sure beats trying to convince someone that an unoccupied parked truck hit your moving car. Give me a break!

The Columbine Tragedy and Modern Day Cain's

News of the Columbine High School tragedy is no longer on the front page but the debate rages on. We still ask… Why? What provided the spark that drove Eric Harris and Dylan Klebold to plan such a hate-filled scheme and shoot so many people in cold blood? Can we do anything to prevent future outbursts of violent behavior?

A *Newsweek* article written shortly after the tragedy stated: *In survey after survey, many kids – even those on the honor roll – say they feel increasingly alone and alienated, unable to connect with their parents, teachers and sometimes even classmates. They're desperate for guidance and when they don't get what they need at home or in school, they cling to cliques or immerse themselves in a universe out of the parents' reach, a world defined by computer games, TV and movies where brutality is so common it has become mundane.*

Part of growing up has been reflected in our desire to be different, but youthful originality has taken a deadly twist. Sarah Roney, an eighteen year old girl from Madison, Wisconsin wrote: *"I think it's time for our – America's – Mom and Dad to ground us – to say, 'If you don't shape up by the time I count to three...' and then really count to three. Because we are running wild and pretty soon we're going to be too far from home to ever get back. There was once a great saying that has rung true throughout the history of mankind... 'By their fruits you shall know them.'"*

As a parent and pastor, I wonder: What can I do? For years the church was considered *"out of touch"* with real world issues but are we? It has always been the church that took a stand for moral values and ethical standards. God's church provides hope when crisis strikes. We use the Bible to teach responsibility for our individual and societal shortcomings. Our faith, nurtured in the church gives us the desire to reach out to others and make a real difference in the world.

Could it be time to take a fresh new look at the church and Godly faith? Over the years, I've discovered an ever-increasing interest in Bible study, prayer and spiritual development. People are hungry to rediscover their faith in God. But there are hurdles to overcome. One is a persistent myth that the Bible fails to address or fully understand today's complex problems. Absolutely, not true!

For example: There are literally hundreds of places providing sound guidance for raising children. In the first book of the Bible, Cain the oldest son of Adam and Eve had a severe problem with anger and was insanely jealous of his younger brother Abel. At one point, Cain became enraged when God rejected his offering and accepted Abel's. Why? Scripture doesn't say, but we do know that God was concerned enough about Cain's anger to give him a stern warning. *"If you do well, will you not be accepted? And if you do not do well, sin is lurking at the door; its desire is for you, but you must master it."* (4:7)

Cain did not master his sinful anger and lured his brother out to the woods and killed him. Later, when the Lord asked, *"Where is your brother Abel?"* Cain haughtily replied, *"I do not know; am I my brother's keeper?"* (4:9) Are we our brother's keeper? Yes, of course we are and it's time we acted like it!

Cain, just like Eric Harris and Dylan Klebold faced temporary setbacks. All three youth responded with enraged violence. All three desperately needed help and didn't receive it. So what can we learn? First, we take a hard look at ourselves. Then, we begin to take a more active interest in our youth.

✝ **Set an example:** Adults and youth alike must earnestly desire to set an honest spiritual example for our family and community. Be willing to admit your own shortcomings and seek to improve.

✝ **Become a mentor** or a guide for one or several youth in your community. Look for ways to encourage and offer opportunities for growth. Include them in your prayers.

✝ **Get Serious About Your Faith:** Participate in a Bible study at your local church and invite others to join you.

✝ **Be alert:** When you notice signs of trouble in a young person… don't wait. Do something now!

God skillfully combines a warning with a breathtaking promise. Yes, Cain was punished for the murder of his brother and his unwillingness to repent. We too face God's judgment for our sins. But there is a word of hope. Cain was also protected: *"And the Lord put a mark on Cain, so that no one who came upon him would kill him."* (4:15) Even at our very worst, we all receive a breathtaking and continuing promise that God offers divine grace, love and protection. It is the promise that ultimately makes everything worthwhile and gives us all… hope!

Child Sacrifice? You're Kidding!

If you read the Bible, from cover to cover, one of the first characters you will come across is Abram later changed to Abraham. At the tender age of 75, he's told to pack up his tent pegs and move. God adds; *"oh by the way, you are also going to be a father."* A father? A father at 75?! Is God kidding? But Abraham hears this promise at least four different times. Once while God is talking, Abraham can't control himself any longer and falls on the floor and laughs, so does his wife Sarah… can you blame them? A child at their age?

But, sure enough, Sarah gives birth to a son and they name him, Isaac which means, (Are you ready for this?) '*…laughter.*' In other words, God bided his time and eventually had the last laugh. Doesn't he always? So, Isaac was more than a child. He was the fulfilled promise of God. Which is why what happens next makes no sense.

One day the Lord says to Abraham, *"Take your son, your only son – yes, Isaac, whom you love so much – and go to the land of Moriah. Sacrifice him there as a burnt offering on one of the mountains, which I will point out to you."* Wait a minute! Sacrifice your child? (Abraham's story comes from Genesis 22 New Living Translation)

A professor once said this story took a stand against child sacrifice, which was pretty common in those days. Well… if you are thinking about sacrificing your child, I guess it's good to have this case on the docket. I know we parents have our moments but I don't imagine many of us would seriously stoop to that. Would you? So, Larry, what is the real point?

Maybe God was using this story to prepare the world for a different kind of sacrifice. One offering that would be sufficient for us all. Compare the story of Abraham's only son, Isaac with the story of God's only Son, Jesus and you begin to see a clear picture of what God intended from the beginning. Let me show you:

Jesus: *"Jesus took a loaf of and asked God blessing on it. Then he broke it in pieces and gave it to the disciples saying, "Take it and eat it, for this is my body." And he took the cup of wine and gave thanks to God for it. He gave it to them and said; "Each of you drink from it for this is my blood, which seals the covenant between God and his people…"* (Jesus story comes from Matthew 26, New Living Translation) Body, blood, covenant… Jesus, we don't understand?

Abraham: *The next morning Abraham got up early and saddled his donkey… On the third day of the journey, Abraham saw the place in the distance.* Is Abraham really going to do this? Will he sacrifice his only son, the child of God's promise?

Jesus: Pilate tried to set Jesus free but the Jews kept shouting …*"Crucify him!"* Are you really going to let them do this, God? Isn't there another way? Can't you stop it?

Abraham: *Abraham placed the wood for the burnt offering on Isaac's shoulders, while he himself carried the knife and the fire. As they went on together, Isaac said, "Father, we have the wood and the fire, but where is the lamb for the sacrifice?" "God will provide a lamb…" Abraham answered.*

Jesus: *Then they lead him away to be crucified.* Is Jesus the lamb?

Abraham: *When they arrived at the place where God had told Abraham to go, he built an altar and placed the wood on it. Then he tied up Isaac and laid him on the altar over the wood.* You can't let Abraham do this God… Isn't there another way?

Jesus: *At noon, darkness fell across the whole land until three o'clock. At about three o'clock, Jesus called out with a loud voice, "Eli, Eli, lema sabachthani?" which means, "My God, my God, why have you forsaken me?"* But does it have to be this way?

Abraham: *Then Abraham took the knife and lifted it up to kill his son as a sacrifice to the Lord. At that moment the angel of the Lord shouted to him from heaven. "Abraham! Abraham! Lay down the knife. Do not hurt the boy in any way... Then Abraham looked up and saw a ram..."*

Jesus: *Then Jesus shouted out again, and he gave up his spirit. At that moment the curtain in the temple was torn in two from top to bottom. The earth shook, rocks split apart, and tombs opened ...The roman officer and the other soldiers at the crucifixion were terrified by the earthquake and all that had happened. They said, "Truly, this was the Son of God!"*

Can you imagine the agony and pain Abraham must have felt preparing to sacrifice his only child, the fulfilled promise of God? Can you now understand God's anguish watching His only Son suffer and die on a cross?

The story of Abraham and Isaac dramatically points the way toward another child sacrifice. The only one, God would allow. We were spared because God spared Abraham and chose to make the sacrifice himself as an undeserved gift... for you and me! Are you feeling a little speechless at this point? So am I.

Now comes the real question: ***"The gift has been given. How will we respond?"***

Jacob: Confession & Reconciliation

Have you heard the story of two unmarried sisters who lived together but because of an argument stopped speaking to each other? Since neither one could afford to move they continued to live in the same rooms, use the same appliances and eat at the same table all without one word spoken between them. A chalk line divided the sleeping area in half so that each could hear the breathing of the other but because both were unwilling to reconcile, they coexisted for years in numbing silence.

We all have disagreements with friends and family. Some arguments are obviously more serious than others. Yet, refusing to reconcile can have grave consequences on your life, your health and even your relationship with God. A willingness to confess combined with an attitude towards forgiveness can be a major turning point. No one understood the power of reconciliation better than Jacob.

Jacob followed his twin brother, Esau at birth grabbing on to his heel. Hence the name Jacob means "Grabber." Throughout his life, Jacob selfishly grabbed, deceived and conned to get his way. He grabbed his brother's birthright with a hot bowl of stew. Jacob conned his father into giving him a blessing meant for Esau. He was later caught… and ran for his life. Now, after twenty years of grabbing and running, Jacob was coming home.

For years, Jacob escaped the consequences of deceit and lies. No more. He would soon face the truth before Esau and his four hundred armed men who happened to be riding out to greet him. What would they do to him? … to his family? Fearful, Jacob sends everyone across the river to act as shields while he stays safely behind. (Coward!)

But during the long night, Jacob experiences a significant turning point that changes his life forever…At first glance it may be one of the strangest stories in the entire Bible.

"…a man came and wrestled with him until dawn." (Genesis 32:24) Who is this mystery man? Why a wrestling match? Is this just a bad dream? What does it all mean?

"When the man saw that he couldn't win the match, he struck Jacob's hip and knocked it out of joint at the socket. Then the man said, 'Let me go, for it is dawn.' But Jacob panted, 'I will not let you go unless you bless me.' 'What is your name?' the man asked. He replied, 'Jacob.'" (25-27)

Something very significant occurred. First, the hip or thigh in the Middle East symbolizes where vows are made and life is given. So Jacob is literally struck down because of his life of broken vows and shattered promises.

Second, Jacob would not ordinarily divulge his name to a stranger because it was believed to reveal your character and surrender power. So by admitting his name was Jacob, "grabber and deceiver," he was for the first time confessing his true character. "My name is Jacob and I'm a grabber, a liar and a deceiver."

Of course, the mystery man is God. So, if Jacob is locked in a wrestling match with God then he really wrestling with the consequences of his life of deception.

Confession was the major turning point that would transform Jacob's life. What happens next is one of those significant Biblical moments. *"Your name will no longer be Jacob,"* the man told him. *"It is now Israel, because you have struggled with both God and men and have won."* (28) In one significant evening, Jacob the "grabber" became Israel, who "struggled with God and men and won." But what does it all mean for Jacob and eventually for us?

► Where is a Jacob of "grabbing and deceit" within all of us.

► Someday, we must all face our own wrestling match with God.

► Confession is the necessary first step toward divine change and reconciliation.

Did Jacob really change? Absolutely! The former coward who hid behind his family now limps ahead to face his brother and four hundred armed men... alone. But Jacob wasn't the only one who changed. *"As he approached his brother, he bowed low seven times before him. Then Esau ran to meet him and embraced him affectionately and kissed him. Both of them were in tears."*(33:3-4) The one who had every right to seek revenge, instead, chose to embrace his brother.

Is it any wonder that Jacob/Israel would say to Esau: *"to see your friendly smile is like seeing the smile of God!"*(33:10) Such is the power of grace. Jacob's wrestling match with God led to confession and Esau's willingness to forgive led to the miracle of reconciliation.

Are you locked in a disagreement with a relative or friend? Have you stopped speaking and drawn your chalk lines of separation? Maybe it's time for you to have a wrestling match with God. It has been said that confession followed by reconciliation is powerful medicine for the soul. Do you have the courage to try? Like Jacob, it could be the turning point that changes your life.

Turning Points: Moses, Failure and 'Ever After'

Enthusiasm can be misleading especially for ministers. It is so tempting to promote the victory of Christianity without warning of the cost: to broadcast the glory exclusive of the pain. *"Become a Christian and live happily ever after,"* we too quickly say but fail to explain what *ever after* means.

Readers Digest told of two seminary students who decided to go door-to-door sharing their faith. At one house they walked through a gauntlet of screaming children and barking dogs. A tired mother opened the door. *"We would like to tell you how to obtain eternal life,"* they said. She hesitated then looked around for a moment, at the children, the dogs, the mess and then carefully replied, *"Thank you, but no thanks. I don't believe that I could stand it!"*

I don't know of a single person who became a Christian and actually lived happily ever after. There were times of defeat and failure for them just like you and I. There are still so many days and weeks where I feel like an utter failure no matter how hard I try. I sometimes let down my family, my church and yes... I let down God. Have you felt that way? Sure you have!

In the Bible you will find the experience of failure is often where God teaches unforgettable lessons. The hero's of scripture are really ordinary human beings who become heroic because God teaches and uses them despite their flaws. Would you like an example? How about Moses?

Moses? Wasn't he God's man who rescued his people from Pharaoh? Didn't he part the Red Sea and receive the Ten Commandments? **Wasn't Moses Charlton Heston?** (If you don't understand, ask an old person... sigh.) As a baby, he was rescued by Pharaoh's daughter and raised as an Egyptian noble with the best education available. For the first forty years of his life... Moses literally had it made. So, what happened?

"...Moses went out to visit his people, the Israelites and he saw how hard they were forced to work. During his visit, he saw an Egyptian beating one of the Hebrew slaves. After looking around to make sure no one was watching, Moses killed the Egyptian and buried him in the sand."

(Exodus 2:11-12)

Thinking he had won respect from his people, Moses was shocked to find he was scorned and in a matter of days he was forced to flee for his life, an utter and complete failure. For the next forty years, Moses would hide out in the desert as a lowly shepherd. Where did Moses go so wrong?

1. He committed murder. You don't cheat on your taxes and then give a portion to God.
2. Moses did it his way not God's way. Moses looked around but he never looked up.
3. Spiritual leadership only comes from God so you can never just reach out and grab it.
4. Burying your mistakes in the sand never erases them; it only postpones the discovery.

So Moses spent forty years in the desert contemplating his blunders and wondering what might have been if only... Wait! This would all be depressing if we didn't know how it ended. But we know at the tender age of eighty, God called Moses from a burning bush to lead the Hebrews out of Egypt. This time Moses was ready to listen and rely upon God and the rest is... history.

Yes, the life of a Christian promises exciting times on the mountaintop as well as painful lessons learned in the desert. Maybe you've been there recently and you're still feeling the hot sand between your toes. Yet, God has not forgotten you and may be preparing a burning bush for you. Whether you are eight or eighty, God is never absent. Such is the real promise of "ever after."

Andre Crouch wrote it best in a song… *I've had many tears and sorrows. I've had questions for tomorrow. There've been times I didn't know right from wrong! But in every situation, God gave blessed consolation that my trials come to only make me strong. Through it all; through it all; I've learned to trust in Jesus. I've learned to trust in God. Through it all; through it all; I've learned to depend upon God's word.*

Ruth: A Love Story and More

Bad news travels quickly in a small town. There was a tragic accident in a remote area of Prudhoe Bay near the village of Deadhorse, Alaska. A father named Eli and his two sons were among those killed. After the funeral, Eli's wife, Naomi took stock of her situation and decided to go back home to Virginia. There was only one problem. Both sons married native Alaskans and both women still lived with Naomi. Where would they go? They certainly couldn't live in Virginia? Could they?

Naomi told both women of her plans and suggested they immediately return home. One woman took her advice and left the next day but Ruth refused. When Naomi insisted, Ruth refused again saying: *"Don't ask me to leave you and turn back. I will go wherever you go and live wherever you live. Your people will be my people, and your God will be my God."* Together, the two grieving women wept.

Returning to rural Virginia was going to be much more difficult than Naomi or Ruth imagined. Life would be different… especially for Ruth. Before they even arrived, the local rumor mill was churning and the main topic was Ruth. One busybody said, *"I was told Ruth's tribe doesn't believe in God but follows a another religion that worships a whole bunch of different gods with names like Odin and Thor. Who ever heard of such a thing? Wasn't Thor in a comic book?"*

When Naomi and Ruth arrived at the old family house just outside of town, there was a crowd of friends and curious onlookers ready to greet them. *"Is that really you, Naomi? We are so sorry?"*

"God has made my life very bitter," Naomi replied. *"I hope that coming*

112

home will help us heal."

Ruth immediately went to the local restaurant looking for a job. The restaurant owner was Boaz, a distant relative of Naomi. Boaz reassured Ruth, *"Listen, you stay right here and work with us as long as necessary. If you need food or anything else, let me know and I will try to get it for you."*

Ruth thanked him warmly. *"Why are you being so kind to me? I'm not from around here."*

"Yes I know," Boaz replied. *"But I also know about the love and kindness you have shown Naomi since the death of your husband. I have heard how you left your father and mother to live among complete strangers. May God bless you for being so kind."*

That evening, Ruth told Naomi about Boaz and how kind he was to her. When several of the young men in town tried to 'harass' Ruth as she waited on tables, Boaz was quick to rush to her aid. One evening, as Ruth left to drive home, she found a shopping bag full of food and supplies in the front seat. She knew it could only be from Boaz.

"Boaz is a relative and dear friend," said Naomi. Then with a sly wink, she added, *"but he is showing special kindness to you."*

Boaz endured an especially traumatic divorce and long ago gave up any hope of finding another person he could share the rest of his life with. Over the years, he had been content to let restaurant and church become the main focus of his time and energy.

But there was something about Ruth's steely dedication combined with a quiet dignity that attracted Boaz. One Sunday, people at church were making snide remarks about her religious beliefs. Boaz, who was normally quiet, said in an angry voice that all could hear, *"Look, Ruth is respecting us enough to visit our church and learn. Maybe we should show some interest in her culture and background and learn something from her!"*

Naomi and Ruth were sitting at the dinner table talking over the events of the last few months: The tragic accident, moving from Alaska to Naomi's former home in rural Virginia, the emotional and financial adjustments of trying to survive the loss of loved ones.

"My daughter," said Naomi. *"It's time that you gave some serious thought about your relationship with Boaz. He seems to care about you very much. Do you love him?"*

"Yes, very much," Ruth replied. *"Boaz has been so generous to give me*

a job at his restaurant, but it's become more than just appreciation. I really enjoy being with him, talking with him… laughing with him. Oh Naomi, it feels so good to laugh again! But neither one of us seem to be able to find the time or even know what to say that will take our relationship to a different level."

Naomi gave a conspiratorial smile and said, *"Tonight, Boaz will be conducting an annual inventory after his restaurant closes. I want you to volunteer to stay and help him. For the rest of the evening you two will be alone, working. Meanwhile, pray that God will guide you from there."*

Everything happened just as Naomi predicted. Boaz was visibly pleased to have Ruth stay and help him with a necessary but tedious task. Throughout the night, Boaz and Ruth worked side by side talking about each other, their hopes and dreams, even their diverse religious beliefs. *"Would you tell me about your faith?"* Boaz asked.

"Asatru has a lot in common with Christian ideals," Ruth replied. *"We believe the goal of living is to lead a worthwhile and useful life. We emphasize nine noble virtues: Courage, Truth, Honor, Fidelity, Discipline, Hospitality, Industriousness, Self-Reliance and Perseverance. Jesus seems to teach those same values. I have come to admire his teachings!"*

Boaz replied, *"But Jesus is more than that, Ruth. I feel a personal relationship with Christ. I'm no preacher so I can't really describe it. I just know that Jesus is there somehow, within me. I would have never survived the divorce and the other painful incidents in my life without knowing that Jesus and my church were providing comfort and love! Does that make any sense?"*

"Of course it does," said Ruth. *"I am beginning to fall in love with Jesus just as I am with you."*

Boaz was quiet for a moment before he smiled and said, *"I have been in love with you for awhile."* As they continued working side by side, counting, Ruth's hand softly brushed across Boaz's arm. They looked up into each other's eyes, shyly at first but as their gaze grew bolder their faces slowly moved closer together until at last they shared the first tender kiss of love.

Imagine that… Boaz and Ruth have their first romantic moment in a restaurant storeroom. You can guess what happens next or better yet, read the story for yourself in the Bible. The book is titled, "Ruth."

Can two people from different cultures find love and happiness? Yes, of course they can, but it will be a struggle and requires lots of love and patience. *"Love never gives up, never loses faith, is always hopeful, and endures through every circumstance."* (1 Cor. 13:7)

Can Christians respect and love people from other faiths without compromising their beliefs? Yes, but we must learn a new kind of love. Jesus said: *"So now I am giving you a new commandment: Love each other. Just as I have loved you, you should love each other."* (John 13:34) The challenge is for us to love as Jesus loved with compassion and without judgment.

Look around and find someone you haven't noticed recently and offer him/her the love of God in a fresh new way. Meanwhile, I'm going to find a restaurant where my wife and I can enjoy a romantic evening by taking an all-night inventory.

Elijah: Victory to Despair to Faith...Turning Point

Victory: It was the best year ever. Our automobile dealership shattered every sales record. Profits were exceptional. We even set a record for fewest customer complaints. It seemed that we could do no wrong. After the final results were tallied, we congratulated each other and handed out bonus checks. By the next day the celebrating was over and it was back to work as usual.

That's it? No vacation? No party? Unfortunately, there was work to be done. We faced a new year with tougher goals to achieve. It would mean working harder than ever with new employees to train and more problems to solve. We simply had no choice. So, instead of enjoying a period of elation, I struggled with mild depression. Why? Why would success be followed by despair?

Despair: We've seen it effect entertainers, athletes, preachers, parents, teachers and friends. A surge of extraordinary success is followed by a period of despondency and anguish. Christmas is supposed to be a season of joy, gift giving and celebrating the birth of Christ. Yet, December is also a time of increased melancholy and loneliness. Why? It doesn't make sense... or does it.

Are extraordinary successes always followed by bouts of despair? Of course not, yet it happens frequently enough to ask questions and seek guidance. In the Bible, I discovered supportive answers through a prophet of God named Elijah.

Victory: Elijah challenged 850 prophets of Baal to a dramatic show-down before the entire nation of Israel... *"Now bring two bulls. The prophets of Baal may choose whichever one they wish and cut it into pieces and lay it on the wood of their altar but without setting fire to it... Then call on the name of your god and I will call on the name of the Lord.* ***The god who answers by setting fire to the wood is the true God!"*** (1 Kings 18:23-24) Wow! A dramatic showdown!

For several hours, the prophets of Baal put on quite a show of chanting and dancing but nothing happened. Elijah began to taunt them... *"You'll have to shout louder... perhaps your god is in deep thought!* (27) At one point the dancing became so frenzied they began to cut themselves with knives but all for nothing. The sacrifice lay peacefully on the altar undisturbed by fire.

Then it was Elijah's turn. *"...he dug a trench around the altar large enough to hold about three gallons... Then he said, 'Fill four large jars with water and pour the water over the offering...'"* (33) He had them fill the jars again and pour them over the offering again and then a third time until the water overflowed the altar and filled the trench.

Now, what kind of show would Elijah put on?

There would be no show... instead; the people of Israel would witness a miracle! Elijah strode purposefully to the altar and simply prayed. That's it? No show? *"Immediately the fire of the Lord flashed down from heaven and burned up the young bull, the wood, the stones, and the dust. It even licked up all the water in the ditch."* (38) A spectacular display of God's power! What a triumph!

Despair: The Mount Carmel victory should have caused a great cele-bration... but instead; Elijah was soon fleeing for his life. Depressed and afraid, *"...he went on alone into the desert, traveling all day. He sat down under a solitary broom tree and prayed that he might die."* (19:4)

What happened? Scripture refers to a furious Queen Jezebel seeking to kill Elijah but after facing 850 prophets why would he fear one angry queen? How could such a victorious prophet of God lose his confidence and faith in himself and God so completely that he prays openly for death?

At one point, I assumed the Mount Carmel showdown was a major turn-ing point for Elijah but I was wrong... so wrong! Next, I'll show the real turning point that allowed Elijah to go from victory to despair to a strength-ened faith. In the same way, my own struggle with despair became a major turning point that would enrich my faith and literally change my life.

Elijah: Victory to Despair to Faith... Turning Point Part 2

1984 was our best business year ever but I was feeling despair. Why? Elijah stood alone against 850 prophets of Baal and witnessed the awe-inspiring power of God at Mount Carmel but never received the opportunity to savor it. Instead, an enraged Queen Jezebel wanted him dead, so Elijah escaped to the desert, alone and begged God to take his life. Why?

At times, even after a significant accomplishment we can feel unappreciated, vulnerable misunderstood, abandoned and even threatened.

But it was during this time of despair in the desert that Elijah's extraordinary journey of faith would reach a dramatic turning point. *"He went on alone into the desert, traveling all day... Then he lay down and slept... as he was sleeping an angel touched him and told him, 'Get up and eat!' He looked around and saw some bread... Then the angel of the Lord came again and said, 'Get up and eat some more, for there is a long journey ahead of you.'"* (1 Kings 19:2-9)

Elijah assumed God's miracle on Mount Carmel would be the turning point of his ministry. Wrong! Now, he must make a journey to discover the truth. Meanwhile, God quietly feeds Elijah and prepares him for the trip ahead? I assumed that a good business year would be the turning point of my ministry fulfilling my goals to be an astute businessman as well as a solid Christian witness. Wrong! Like Elijah, I needed to make a spiritual journey to seek the truth.

For forty days and nights, Elijah traveled to Mount Sinai, the mountain of God, where Moses received the Ten Commandments. *"'Go out and stand before me on the mountain,' the Lord told him. And as Elijah stood there, the Lord passed by and a mighty windstorm hit the mountain... but the Lord was not in the wind. After the wind there was an earthquake but the Lord was not in the earthquake. And after the earthquake there was a fire but the Lord was not in the fire. **And after the fire there was the sound of a gentle whisper.**"* *(11-13)* Now Elijah was ready to listen.

Do you see the turning point yet? Occasionally, God will surprise us with an awesome miracle like the mighty windstorm or the earthquake but they are seldom understood or even appreciated. It is not our victories that gratify God as much as our day-by-day obedience and attentiveness to God's quiet and gentle whisper.

It is in the quiet and gentle whisper Elijah receives instructions and a promise that he is not alone... *"Yet I will preserve seven thousand others..."* (18) This was the assurance Elijah needed.

Early the next year, I was asked to give a short weekly message for children during the worship service. Normally, I declined such requests because of a hectic work schedule but this time I heard a quiet and gentle whisper encouraging me to say yes. Saying yes turned out to be my major turning point. I discovered a fresh talent and an exciting new way to communicate my faith.

My despair at work was quickly replaced by a fresh vitality. Business didn't change... I changed. 1985 was another record-breaking year but it would not be followed by despair again. For the first time, I felt at peace with my career and my faith. In 1986 I would hear God's quiet whisper again and leave my business career behind to become a full-time church pastor.

So, what did I learn from Elijah?

1. God is always patiently offering spiritual nourishment in victory or despair.
2. We must all occasionally be willing to take a long journey and trust God's guidance.
3. Big victories are not as important as our day-by-day obedience and our willingness to listen to God's voice.
4. God's gentle whisper promises guidance and reassurance that we are not alone.

It's comforting to know that God is not counting your victories, your defeats or your occasional periods of despair. What really matters is the consistency of your journey: humble when on top and determined when on the bottom but always recognizing that God is still in control. You are never alone and God will actively nourish and guide you every step of the way. Thank you, God!

An Audacious Miracle!

The city was surrounded by the enemy and slowly but surely starving to death. Donkey heads were being sold on the streets for food. Even little children were being fought over by parents to be eaten as food. Humanity had sunk to its lowest possible level. It could not get any worse.

A local preacher confronted the city leadership with a message. *"By this time tomorrow, there will be so much food that bushels of flour will be sold on the streets for pennies."* One leader stood to question such a bold prophecy and the preacher pointed his bony old finger in his direction and replied: *"You'll see it with your own eyes, but you will never taste any of it!"*

What a prediction: *A city going from famine to feast in 24 hours? From donkey head soup to a chicken in every pot?* Does it sound like election year politics with too many empty promises? Who is this preacher trying to kid? There would have to be a military victory followed by an economic miracle and all occurring in one day! **Who could possibly accomplish all of this?**

Meanwhile, in another part of the city, near the outside wall were four men with leprosy, a gruesome disease believed to be highly contagious. Anyone with leprosy was considered an outcast from society. These poor men could not even remain in the city to starve with the rest of the people. They were shunned, feared and abandoned. It doesn't get any worse than a starving leper!

But as they are gathered around campfire trying to stay warm, one leper had an idea. *"Why should stay here and just die? Let's go to the enemy camps outside the gate and surrender? If they spare us, we might get some food and live. If they kill us...hey we're dying anyway!"* They all agreed, so in the middle of the night, four starving lepers shuffled and hobbled their way down the hill to the enemy camp to surrender and hopefully bum a free meal.

Here comes the miracle! The sound of their shuffling feet was somehow magnified to resemble the attack of a mighty army. The sleeping soldiers heard the noise, panicked and ran for their lives leaving their weapons, clothes and all of their food behind. What made these hardened soldiers run? The sound of four sick, starving lepers stumbling down the mountain to surrender. (Are you laughing yet? You really should be.)

As the lepers reached the camp they were greeted with silence and the inviting aroma of fresh pepperoni pizza. ***"It's party time!"*** one shouted. They ate and drank, carried away piles of cash, new clothes and all the food they could eat. As dawn broke over the horizon, one of the lepers, feeling a twinge of remorse, said to the others: *"We're not doing right. This is a day of Good News and we are keeping it to ourselves. We must report this to the city."*

At first the city didn't believe the lepers shouting outside the gate, but they sent a scouting party and found everything to be true. The enemy had run away leaving the whole lot behind. The gates were opened and everyone rushed out to eat and take away whatever could be found. Food was so plentiful that a bushel of flour could now be sold for pennies as predicted. The leader who originally questioned the preacher was assigned the duty of counting everything that was brought back. In the confusion, he was trampled to death, all as the preacher predicted.

Wild? Yes, but it's true. (Well, not the pizza) Read 2 Kings 6:24 to 7:20. But Larry, what can we learn from this strange story?

- **Tragedy is a part of life:** The city is suffering horrifically just as you and I occasionally suffer.
- **God is in the midst of our tragedy:** God never abandons you.
- **Ordinary Humans are often used by God to accomplish miracles:** Four Lepers? Can you believe it?
- **Our bold faith and willingness to take risks honor God:** This means you.

Hearing this story gave me the courage to give up my business career and plunge boldly into the ministry. My prayer is that hearing this story inspires you to do something bold for God.

After all, if God can use four lepers to accomplish an audacious miracle, just think what can be done with you and me!

Turning Points: Job & One String

Ouch! I simply wanted to illustrate Job from the Bible suddenly losing his family and all his possessions. I said, *"At any time, your calm and reasonable life can be disrupted and we stumble and fall..."* so to make my point, I deliberately stumbled down the steps fully intending to catch myself. Somehow, I really lost my balance in the act of falling and really hit the floor... hard. In my enthusiasm to make a point, I nearly ruined the service and one of my knees in the process. I'm really getting old!

Despite my idiotic flair for the dramatic, stumbling is an unfortunate element of life. At any time...

- The doctor asks to see you in her office to discuss the results of a recent biopsy.
- Your employer schedules a personal appointment. There are rumors of lay offs.
- Your husband confesses he is unfaithful and wants out of the marriage.

- On the way to work, a sleepy driver runs a stop sign directly in front of you.
- Your daughter is arrested for shoplifting and reveals a three-year-old drug addiction.

What do you say? What do you do? How could this happen? What went wrong? The world around you becomes a blur as you find yourself spinning out of control. The pavement that seemed so firm and sure moments ago has unexpectedly shifted and you find yourself falling hard. I don't like admitting it but if it hasn't happened to you yet, it will. So, Larry… are you just trying to ruin my day? No! I'm trying to prepare you for the next catastrophe.

The best Biblical example of stumbling is the story of Job, a prosperous farmer living in the land of Uz.

Job is described by God as *"the finest man in all the earth – a man of complete integrity."* (Job 1:8) But before you can say "stumble," Job through no fault of his own loses his possessions, his family and even his health until he is left sitting on an ash heap scrapping his itching, boil covered skin with a broken piece of pottery. Sitting with Job are Eliphaz, Bildad and Zophar.

Job cries out to God proclaiming his innocence while his so-called friends begin to offer possible explanations:

- *Maybe, you did something wrong?*
- *Could it be your children's fault?*
- *Somebody must have done something wrong!*
- *You are simply being disciplined.*
- *Don't be angry with God!*
- *Shut up; you have no right to complain.*

Whoa! With friends like these guys, who needs… friends?

But don't get too smug. Job's friends actually represent our own well-meaning response when people around us suddenly find themselves stumbling. Instead of compassion, you offer cheap explanations. Instead of help, I offer unwanted criticism. Instead of empathy we offer slanderous gossip. Meanwhile Job, confused and even angry at times continues crying out to almighty God…

The immensely talented violinist, Nicolo Paganini, was giving a concert accompanied by a full orchestra before a standing room only crowd. Suddenly one string snapped and hung uselessly on his violin. But instead

121

of stopping the concert, Nicolo frowned in concentration, made musical adjustments and continued to play. Then to everyone's surprise another string broke and a third leaving only one string on Paganini's violin. What would Nicolo Paganini do next?

Dr. Victor Frankl, a Jew, became a prisoner during the Nazi holocaust. At one point, the doctor was marched into a Gestapo courtroom for the usual false trial. His captors had taken away his home and family, his freedom, all of his possessions and forced him to endure months of torture and backbreaking slave labor. There he stood under the glaring lights being interrogated and falsely accused in the hands of brutal, sadistic men. Dr. Frankl had nothing left… or did he?

Just when you think all is lost: *"Then the Lord answered Job from the whirlwind."* (38:1) Will Job receive the answer from God he so desperately seeks? What about this mysterious conversation between God and Satan? Can the story of Nicolo Paganini help us survive life's stumbles when all that remains is one string? Will Dr. Victor Frankl help us discover hope when all seems hopeless? Before you read on, look at the book of Job.

Turning Points: Sudden Storms, Job & One String - Part 2

Ouch! I mentioned unexpected storms that cause you to stumble, so I faked a little stumble during our worship service and ended up falling… hard. Dumb! Very dumb! Speaking of unexpected storms: Weathermen told us to prepare for an inch or two of snow today so no one panicked. But instead, the snow came down all night dropping over seventeen inches. That is a lot of snow for us so the whole county has come to a complete standstill. Oh well… at least we didn't lose our electricity *"Hey! Who turned out the lights!"*

Sudden storms are why understanding Job is so important. Why would *"a man of complete integrity"* (Job 1:8) suffer so grievously? Job's three friends provide no help at all as they continue to look for something he must have done wrong. Some friends! Yet when others fall, don't we often shake our heads and offer trite explanations, unwanted criticism and slanderous gossip?

"If only I had someone who would listen to me and try to see my side!" says Job. *"Look, I will sign my name to my defense. Let the almighty show me that I am wrong… I would face the accusation proudly."* (31:35-36) *In other words… where is God when we fall hard? Good question!*

122

"Then the Lord answered Job from the whirlwind. Brace yourself because I have some questions for you... Where were you when I laid the foundation of the earth? Who defined the boundaries of the sea? Have you ever commanded the morning to appear? Where does the light come from? Can you hold back the movements of the stars?" (Parts of Job 38)

I have to admit this sounds impressive but I'm left with more questions than answers. After all, Job was asking, where were you when I was suffering? Why am I suffering when I've followed you loyally? Yet, God only says, where were you when I created the earth? I have to ask: God, what kind of answer is that?

It may be the best answer of all because Job comprehends just who God really is. He responds, *"I know that you can do anything... and I was talking about things I did not understand, things too wonderful for me... I take back everything I said..."* (42:2-3) What did Job understand?

Now may be the time to look back on a mysterious conversation at the beginning of Job between God and Satan. In the beginning, God holds up Job as a shining example but Satan replies: *"Yes, Job fears God, but not without good reason! You have always protected him and his home and his property from harm... But take away everything he has and he will surely curse you to your face!"* (1:9-11)

You see, all the forces of good and evil are carefully watching Job! How would he respond to catastrophe? We see him cry for mercy, beg for answers and scream from the pain but when God finally appears... What will Job do then? He's expected to curse and complain.

Instead, Job chooses to trust and because of his courage all of heaven celebrates.

The great violinist, Nicolo Paganini is left with one string and a concert hall full of expectant listeners. What would he do? Everyone is watching and waiting. Paganini held the violin high for everyone to see and shouted, *"Paganini and one string!"* He nodded to the conductor to begin and with a twinkle in his eye, began to play as the audience shook their heads in amazement.

Dr. Victor Frankl stood before the glaring lights of the Nazi courtroom stripped of everything or was he? He suddenly realized there was one thing they could never take away from him – just one. He had the power to choose his attitude. Would he choose bitterness or forgiveness? Would he submit to the sadistic brutality or would he dare to shout out, *"Dr. Frankl and one string!"*

✝ When the doctor calls… can you trust in God's presence to see you through?

✝ When your spouse abandons you… can you believe in a God who is ever faithful?

✝ When another car suddenly pulls in front of yours… can you believe God is still in control?

✝ When everything seems to break… can you cling to the one string God always provides?

Studying Job fortifies your faith and strengthens the decisive one string on your violin called, "attitude:" The attitude string is part trust and part perseverance, which together can withstand the worst tragedies life can throw at you. Sudden storms will always appear out of nowhere dumping seventeen inches of snow on a community prepared for two. Circumstances can lead to broken strings. The question is… how will you respond when you are down to that final string? What attitude will you choose?

Turning Point: Daniel, Food & Movies?

Often it's the little things that tell the world exactly who we are and what we truly believe.

Take movies for instance. I have always loved watching movies: action, comedy or drama. You name the movie and I probably saw it. My first job in high school was "Usher" at a movie theater. My first promotion, are you ready… was "Head Usher" which paid a whopping ten extra cents per hour. Big deal! I'm not so crazy about movies anymore but I still occasionally rent a video.

Several years ago, I noticed a sign on a door in the back of the video store that prohibited anyone under twenty-one from going inside. *"What in the world is behind that door?"* I thought to myself. *"Well, I'm twenty-one. Let's take a peek!"* Big mistake! The pictures on the video boxes told the whole story. I had no idea pornography was sold in our tiny town. I almost ran out of the store!

What should I have done? What would you do?

a) Turn in my video card and self-righteously tell the owner a thing or two?

b) Continue renting videos? After all, I wasn't looking at the pornography.

c) Organize a petition drive and a boycott to close down the store?

124

d) Celebrate the owner's right of free speech and write a complimentary letter?

Often it's the little things that tell the world exactly who we are and what we truly believe.

Many years ago, the Israelites were conquered and enslaved by the Babylonians. Several youth were selected among the Israelites to live in the kings' palace with the royal officials. They would be taught the language and the literature of the Babylonians and given only the best food and wine. They would be trained for three years and promoted to serve as the King's advisors. It was a grand honor. One of the young men chosen was Daniel.

"But Daniel made up his mind not to defile himself by eating the food and wine given to them by the king. He asked the chief official for permission to eat other things instead." (Daniel 1:8) The official was alarmed. *"If you become pale and thin compared to the other youths your age, I am afraid the king will have me beheaded for neglecting my duties."* (1:10) Daniel suggested a test of feeding him a diet of vegetables and water for ten days. After ten days, Daniel looked healthier.

My mother would say... *"Larry, this is why you should eat your vegetables?"* O.K. Mom, but this is really about having the faith and the courage to take a stand. When the crowd goes one way... will you go another? Daniel faced a turning point early in life that would mark him forever as a servant of God. It would have been so much easier to go along with the kings' program. After all, it was just a little food and wine. Arguing could be dangerous. Wouldn't it be smarter to simply go along? We can always follow God later, can't we? Sometimes, the answer is... take a stand, now!

Often it's the little things that tell the world exactly who we are and what we truly believe.

A couple visited the same video store and decided to do something. In front of the store they distributed leaflets. *"We are concerned about the influence of pornography on the increasing problems of child abuse, spousal abuse and teen pregnancy. We encourage you to temporarily rent videos from another source until this store discontinues the rental of X-Rated material."*

Motivated by their example of courage, I later joined the couple, turned

125

in my video card and eventually convinced the local newspaper to write about the protest. Other churches and ministers took up the cause and urged the community to join in. The storeowner was furious and steadfastly refused to stop… so nothing really changed or did it? Inspired by a couples courage… I changed and others changed. We learned the importance of taking a stand for God, now!

Often it's the little things that tell the world exactly who we are and what we truly believe.

Turning Points: Jonah…It's More Than Just A Fish Story!

The stranger gave me one of those 'dead serious' stares and before I could shake his hand, asked: *"Do you believe the Bible is the Holy Inspired Word of God?"* I was caught off guard and honestly didn't know how to respond. Sensing my hesitation, he gripped my hand even tighter and asked, *"Do you believe Jonah was swallowed by the fish? Well, do you?"* I sensed only one answer would satisfy him. Anything else and I would immediately be "judged" unworthy.

The stranger responded to my hesitation just as I expected. He removed his hand, sniffed and walked away, no longer interested in me. I flunked his litmus test!

I always believed Jonah was a children's story taught in Sunday school. When did it become a pass/fail exam on how to 'correctly' interpret the Bible? Is this the real significance of Jonah? Truthfully, there is a lot more to Jonah then I ever imagined.

The book of Jonah contains only four short chapters but within those chapters is a significant message that Jews and Christians alike should heed and appreciate. "But Larry… can modern people really believe that a big fish swallowed Jonah whole?" Actually, it's not impossible but if you get caught up in this argument you'll miss the real reason why Jonah is in the Bible.

"The Lord gave this message to Jonah son of Amittai; "Get up and go to the great city of Nineveh! Announce my judgment against it because I have seen how wicked its people are. But Jonah got up and went in the opposite direction…" (Jonah 1:1-3) Who is Jonah, really? What is a Nineveh?

Jonah was a respected prophet/preacher like much like "Billy Graham" is today. God called Jonah to leave Israel and travel to Nineveh, a major city within Assyria, the country that conquered and enslaved many countries nearby.

What if God said to you: *"Witness to Saddam Hussein or Adolph Hitler! Visit the murderer, Charles Manson in prison and offer him God's Word! Go to a trusted friend who betrayed you and warn her of God's judgment!"* Wouldn't you be angry and a little fearful? Are you beginning to understand why Jonah boarded a ship headed in the opposite direction?

"But as the ship was sailing along, suddenly the Lord flung a powerful wind over the sea, causing a violent storm that threatened to send them to the bottom." Violent storms in the Mediterranean Sea are certainly not unusual but this storm terrified even seasoned sailors. They were doomed unless something supernatural intervened to save them. *"'Throw me into the sea,' Jonah said, 'and it will become calm again. For I know that this terrible storm is all my fault.'"* (1:12)

Give the sailors credit. They resisted Jonah's advice at first but conditions were becoming worse so they reluctantly threw him into the raging sea... the storm stopped at once. What an awesome miracle for the sailors to witness but the best is yet to come. *"Now the Lord had arranged for a great fish to swallow Jonah. And Jonah was inside the fish for three days and three nights."* (1:17) Jesus himself would refer to this verse as symbolic of His own death and resurrection.

Jonah was disobedient and should have met his fate beneath the seas... but instead received a miracle of God's grace. *"I sank beneath the waves and death was very near. The waters closed around me and seaweed wrapped itself around my head... but you, O Lord my God, have snatched me from the yawning jaws of death."* (2:5-6) Three days later, Jonah was back on the beach and once again heard God's voice instructing him to go to Nineveh. This time he went.

Larry, you keep referring to 'turning points:' those significant events that dramatically spark a noteworthy change. ***"Is this Jonah's life-changing turning point?"*** It should be. Being rescued by a giant fish should transform anyone but sadly, although Jonah outwardly obeys God and goes to Nineveh he has not changed his original attitude at all. The real "turning point" and lesson for all of us comes later.

For three days, Jonah walked from one end of this great city to the other. What was his message? *"Forty days from now Nineveh will be destroyed!"* (3:4) Here is the amazing part. The entire city listened and repented of their sins. Excuse me but did you say everyone? Yes! Every man, woman and child began to fast and pray for God's forgiveness. Wow! That's incredible! Actually a better word might be… absolutely impossible!

Maybe not! We know the Assyrians studied astrology. Some scholars suggest, there was a solar eclipse just as Jonah entered Nineveh with a message from God. A fearful city having seen a sign like a solar eclipse would be ready to listen and obey. The king then issues a decree stating everyone is required to pray and ask forgiveness. In our democratic society we forget that in a society like Nineveh, if the king said to repent, you repented or else!

This may be the biggest mass religious conversion in history. What a major event! Is Jonah happy now? No! He's miserable! Why? Because he wanted Nineveh destroyed. He said to God, *"I knew you were a gracious and compassionate God, slow to get angry and filled with unfailing love… just kill me now, Lord! I'd rather be dead than alive because nothing I predicted is going to happen."* (4:2-3) Why is Jonah so upset?

Don't be too hard on him. We all have our prejudices, our mortal enemies and our personal grievances. Imagine someone who committed such vile atrocities, who is so evil he is absolutely beyond normal redemption. Then he attends your church claiming the miracle of God's grace. "He's faking!" you say. "She's insincere!" you exclaim indignantly. "How can God do this to you?" At this point you are sure, God made a big mistake!

"Is it right for you to be angry about this?" the Lord replied. (4:4)

Jonah, still furious builds a shelter just outside the city walls and waits. He's still hoping Nineveh will be destroyed. As the hot sun begins to pierce the flimsy protection of Jonah's shelter, God provides a leafy plant to grow and provide cool protective shade. Jonah is pleased. But, the next morning, a worm begins chewing on the stem and the plant dies. The afternoon is a scorcher and Jonah grows faint and begins to whine. Again he cries out, "Death is better than this!"

Here comes the lesson…. Don't miss it… God says to Jonah: "You feel sorry about the plant, though you did nothing to put it there. And a plant is only at best, short lived. But Nineveh has more than 120,000 people living in spiritual darkness, not to mention all the animals. Shouldn't I feel sorry for such a great city?" (4:10-11) Lesson taught! End of story! Did you catch it?

A furious Jonah said it best: "God is gracious and compassionate, slow to anger and filled with unfailing love." Jonah sought righteous judgment against his hated enemy. Instead God extended the hand of forgiveness. An intimidating stranger tried using the book of Jonah as a Biblical litmus test but he totally missed God's point as he judged me unworthy. We seek tools for judgment but God extends grace.

In our own way, we are all disobedient before God. We make mistakes and fall short of God's expectations. We judge and condemn others when we ourselves deserve judgment and condemnation but through it all God offers total forgiveness and the healing balm of grace. We don't know for sure but because Jonah wrote this story, I believe he finally understood God's lesson, which then became his life-changing turning point.

Turning Points: A Church, The Messiah... Wait! Why?

Every Sunday for nearly three years Walter had a routine. Just before 10:00 AM he would open the doors to Epworth and prepare the church for worship. If the weather was cold, he would build a fire in the old wood stove. If it was hot he would open all the windows and distribute the hand fans with a picture of Jesus on one side and an ad for a local funeral home on the other.

Next, Walter would open the Bible located on top of the wooden pulpit and read the selected scripture for that week. Then it would be time for prayer. Often there were folks in the community included on Walter's list. The latest national and world news would be mentioned. But always, Walter ended every prayer with a plea for God to remember and bless his beloved church.

Every Sunday, Walter had a routine but what makes this story so unique is that with very few exceptions, Walter began and ended the Sunday morning worship service... alone. Alone? Why? Many years ago, Epworth church was built on land donated by a neighboring farmer but if for any reason they stopped meeting regularly, if Walter stopped opening the church doors every Sunday the property would revert to the original owners... Epworth church would cease to exist.

So what is the big deal? If Walter is the only one bothering to attend, let him go somewhere else or stay at home. Why not face the inevitable and allo✝w Epworth to quietly disappear? What harm would it do? For Walter, it was a big deal. God had a divine purpose for his life and for the church he loved. But for now, Walter must be patient, be faithful… and wait? Wait for what?

"Wait" is not one of my favorite verbs. I define wait as "waste"… as in waste of time. I become frustrated waiting in line at a grocery store. I bought a new computer because it claimed to be faster with less waiting time. So, according to my definition of wait, Walter was wasting his time at Epworth and refusing to face reality for three long years while waiting for something to happen.

Walter waited. Not me! I would move on. So would most of you. Yet, you and I, in our impatience and lack of faith would have missed the miracle of Epworth!

In another time: For nearly eight hundred years, prophets foretold the coming of the Messiah.

✚ *"But you, O Bethlehem Ephrathah are only a small village in Judah. Yet a ruler of Israel will come from you…"* (Micah 5:2)

✚ *"All right then, the Lord himself will choose the sign. Look! The virgin will conceive a child! She will give birth to a son and will call him Immanuel – God is with us."* (Isaiah 7:14)

✚ *"But he was wounded and crushed for our sins. He was beaten that we might have peace. He was whipped and we were healed!"* (Isaiah 53:5)

But for eight hundred long years the people of God waited. Can you imagine that? Generations were born, grew up, lived and died never knowing or seeing the promised Messiah of God. What were they waiting for? In order to fully value the significance of Christmas we must understand why learning the importance of "waiting" can be one of God's turning points in our lives.

In Luke, a man named Simeon who is described as righteous and devout spent most of his time in the temple… waiting: *"He was filled with the Holy Spirit and he eagerly expected the Messiah to come…"* (2:25) Day after day and year after year, Simeon was faithful in his task. Why?

In the same part of Luke, there was also a prophet named Anna. She became a widow at an early age and spent most of her adult life waiting: *"She was now eighty-four years old. She never left the Temple but stayed there day and night, worshipping God with fasting and prayer."* (2:37)

What were Anna and Simeon waiting for? The answer will help you appreciate what happened at Epworth church and help you understand the true meaning of Christmas.

Would it help to understand what is meant by the word, wait? My tendency is to think of waiting as idle time doing nothing such as waiting for a movie to start. Actually, waiting for God is more like receiving word that an honored guest will soon be visiting. You busily clean and decorate your house, prepare special foods, take a shower and search through the closet for just the right outfit. In other words…. waiting on God is essentially an eventful time of preparation and anticipation.

> ✝ *"I waited patiently for the Lord to help me and he turned to me and heard my cry."* (Psalm 40:1) Waiting is learning to trust in God's leadership and competence.
> ✝ *"But those who wait on the Lord will find new strength. They will fly high on wings like eagles. They will run and not grow weary."* (Isaiah 40:31) Waiting renews your strength.
> ✝ *"This time he (Christ) will bring salvation to all those who are eagerly waiting for him."* (Hebrews 9:28) Waiting is a sign of faith and faith in Christ is the source of our salvation.

Simeon waited, filled with the Holy Spirit, expecting an honored guest, the Messiah, to appear at any time. Anna waited by staying busy in the Temple day and night, worshipping God with fasting and prayer. Walter waited by faithfully preparing his beloved Epworth church for worship each and every Sunday morning. God responded to Simeon, Anna and Walter with a miracle.

One afternoon a young couple named Joseph and Mary came to the temple to offer their eight-day-old baby for dedication to God. *"Simeon was there. He took the child in his arms and praised God, saying, 'Lord, now I can die in peace! As you promised me, I have seen the Savior you have given to all people. He is a light to reveal God to the nations…'"* (Luke 2:28-32) Anna came along, *"just as Simeon was talking with Mary and Joseph and she began praising God. She talked about Jesus to everyone who had been waiting for the promised King…"* (2:38)

Simeon and Anna were among the first to witness the Christ child and proclaim Him as the Messiah. Every year they are remembered and celebrated as a part of Christmas. It's a special honor given to two folks who patiently and lovingly learned to wait.

One Sunday morning a young family, new to the area visited Epworth and after meeting Walter joined him in worship. They found something unique about this little church nestled among the trees and the old man who faithfully opened her doors. On the following Sunday they came back and within a few weeks the children were bringing friends. At years end a minister was hired.

Today, Epworth is a small family church situated between several farms and hidden among the trees. Every summer there is Vacation Bible School for the neighborhood and each Christmas there is a pageant performed by the children. Many of the original family have died and some of the children have moved away but the miracle of Epworth has never been forgotten.

On the first Sunday of August people come from across the U.S. to visit the church of their youth and relive the miracle of the old man who refused to let his beloved church die. The worship service is followed by a picnic on the church grounds. While the children are playing and the adults are eating you may notice a family wandering over to the nearby cemetery. If you listen carefully you'll hear a parent telling her child, *"Let me tell you a story about Walter..."*

As you celebrate this Christmas remember the example of Simeon, Anna and Walter and express your faith in God through the power of... waiting!

A Different Way of Looking at Jesus: Angry

"How would you describe Jesus in one or two words?" I asked the youth in our Bible study. They used words such as: love, goodness, humble, pious, kind, caring, devout, meek and gentle. *"So, what would Jesus look like based on what you saw in the movies or read in the Bible?"* They mentioned long hair, pale skin and a constant smile... like a flower child of the 1960's holding two fingers in a 'V' saying... *"I'm for peace, man."* Still, another student's description reminded me of Mister Rogers as he pats a child on the head and says... *"It's a wonderful day in the neighborhood. Will you be my neighbor?"*

But... do you know anyone wanting to arrest Mr. Rogers, torture him for hours on end and then hang him up on a cross until he dies? (Maybe after watching a few hours of reruns?) Nah! I don't think so. Apparently, Jesus was no flower child or Mr. Rogers. Yes, Jesus can certainly be described as loving, full of goodness, humble, pious, kind, caring, devout, meek and gentle but there is so much more...

Why were the Jews so enraged at Jesus? Good question. I found interesting answers in the twenty third chapter of Matthew: *Then Jesus said to the crowds and to his disciples, "The scribes and the Pharisees sit on*

Moses' seat; therefore, do whatever they teach you and follow it; but do not do as they do, for they do not practice what they teach.

(Matthew 23:1-3)

Who are the scribes and Pharisees and why is Jesus chastising them?

Scribes and Pharisees describe a group of experts on Jewish law formed long before Jesus birth. Surrounded by Greek culture and Roman occupation, the Jewish people were slowly losing their identity as people devoted to following God's law. Pharisees took a heroic stand to once again follow God's law whatever the consequences. In many ways, they were heroes for their faith. In other words, scribes and Pharisees were the most dedicated church folks in town. People like you and me.

Imagine a world famous spiritual leader such as Billy Graham or the Pope visiting your church. The entire community gathers to hear the message. On the front row sits the pastor and church leaders. The speaker steps up to the pulpit and calmly faces the congregation. He thrusts his arm toward the front row and shouts: *"You pastors and church leaders sit in nice buildings with thickly padded pews and stained glass windows. You may be good teachers but you do not practice what you teach."*

Are you beginning to understand why the scribes and Pharisees were so offended? Wait! There is more. Throughout chapter twenty three of Matthew, Jesus goes on to proclaim:

- ✟ Verse 13: *How terrible it will be for you teachers of religious law and you Pharisees.*
- ✟ Verse 15: Yes, *How terrible it will be for you teachers of religious law and you Pharisees.*
- ✟ Verse 16: *Blind guides! How terrible it will be for you!*
- ✟ Verse 23: *How terrible it will be for you teachers of religious law and you Pharisees.*
- ✟ Verse 25: *How terrible it will be for you teachers of religious law and you Pharisees.*
- ✟ Verse 27: *How terrible it will be for you teachers of religious law and you Pharisees.*
- ✟ Verse 29: *How terrible it will be for you teachers of religious law and you Pharisees.*

Then Jesus shouts the harshest condemnation of all... Verse 33: ***"Snakes! Sons of vipers! How will you escape the judgment of hell?"*** Wow! Strong language! When someone you know becomes angry frequently you don't pay much attention to each outburst but when a person like Jesus who is known for being loving, calm and compassionate blows his top... you wake up and take notice.

Why is Jesus so angry? Also, why is he so angry at pastors, Sunday school teachers, choir members, Administrative Board chairpersons, deacons, elders and other leaders of local churches?

Most of all, why is Jesus so angry at me?

The answers may surprise you or even infuriate you. Then you will begin to understand why Jesus had to die so that we may live. Meanwhile, read Matthew 23 for a different way of looking at Jesus: angry.

A Different Way of Looking at Jesus: Angry - Part 2

"Blind guides! How terrible it will be for you... Snakes! Sons of vipers! How will you escape the judgment of hell?" Strong language from a Jesus most of us would describe using only loving and compassionate language. Even more surprising, his outburst was aimed at Pharisees who were considered among the most religious folks in the community. They could be your Sunday school teacher, a member of your choir, an elder or even your pastor. Ouch! Why was Jesus so angry?

In chapter 23 of Matthew: Jesus said, *"How terrible it will be for you..."* Then he explained why:

❖ *"Everything they do is for show. On their arms they wear extra wide prayer boxes..."* Traditionally, Jews wear prayer boxes on their arms or foreheads but Pharisees had to wear big boxes. Many Christians wear crosses but yours has to be a "big" cross, complete with flashing lights. Big deal!

❖ *"You won't let others enter the Kingdom of Heaven..."* You almost had to be born a Jew to become a Jew. There was solid evidence that Romans and Greeks were interested in the one God of the Jews but there was little or no encouragement from the Pharisees. We too frequently condemn someone for what is humanly lacking rather than offer praise for what God is changing.

❖ *"You cross land and sea to make one convert and then you turn them into twice the son of hell as you yourselves are..."* The Pharisees were teaching Jews to obey the law and be good Pharisees rather than holy people of God. Which is more important? What are we teaching Christians today?

❖ *"You say that it means nothing to swear 'by God's Temple'... but then you say that it is binding to swear 'by the gold in the Temple.'"* Pharisees were experts at swearing oaths then changing the rules. Today, it's called aggressive advertising to announce a ridiculously low price and then bury the truth in fine print. We marry for life but also seek prenuptial agreements… just in case. Sad!

❖ *"You are careful to tithe even the tiniest part of your income but you ignore the important things of the law – justice, mercy and faith."* It would be like finding a dollar on the street and while driving to church to give a tenth you pass right by an auto accident and a house fire. Cold! Really cold!

❖ *"You are so careful to clean the outside of the cup and the dish but inside you are filthy…"* I have a bad habit of leaving half-filled coffee cups throughout the church. If you happen to find one several weeks later, it may be potential penicillin but what's inside that cup is not a pretty sight. Sunday is often the day we put on our best outfits but what about the inside? It isn't pretty. Ugh!

❖ *You are like whitewashed tombs – beautiful on the outside but filled on the inside with dead people's bones and all sorts of impurity."* Jesus is repeating the same point so it must be important. The tombs may be beautiful on the outside but just inside is still dead bones. Ecch!

Let's see if I understand what Jesus is saying:
1. *Everything we do is for show… We must really think we are hot stuff…*
2. *We are far too quick to condemn and way too slow to praise…*
3. *We place a higher priority on serving the church than serving God…*
4. *Our word is no longer sacred… even our contracts have escape clauses…*
5. *We major in the minors and completely miss the foundations of our faith…*
6. *We may be clean on the outside but inside we are filthy…*
7. *We may look good on the outside but inside we are dead…*

No one enjoys receiving a tongue lashing. Especially when those being lashed consider themselves respectable, law-abiding, upright citizens. ***"How dare Jesus talk to us like we are common thugs! Who does He think he is… God!"*** Are you beginning to understand where this is leading? The Pharisees began to gather in their meetings to talk about how to deal with Jesus. They soon had an answer… Jesus was arrested on trumped up charges, whipped, beaten and crucified until he died.

Are you beginning to understand why the Pharisees reacted to Jesus' harsh condemnation with rage? Do you also understand that this response is wrong and not what Jesus wanted from them or expects from us? This is the crucial part of the story. If the Pharisees were wrong... what is right? What reaction did Jesus want? What response does Jesus expect from today's church leaders... from you... from me?

A Different Way of Looking at Jesus: Angry: Part 3

A few years ago, I watched an interview with Dick Morris. Dick was President Clinton's political advisor who resigned in disgrace after pictures showing him with a prostitute surfaced in the news. He wrote a book portraying his savvy political advice as the secret weapon which saved Clinton's presidency. Frankly, I was not impressed but something he said during the interview caught my attention.

"There are two personalities at war within us," Morris said. "One is the hard working professional who handles everything with ease. Another personality is addicted and cannot control his or her desires whether it be sex, drugs, alcohol or other pleasures." In other words, *"I confess to being caught red-handed but please buy my book or watch my interview because I was sick and couldn't help myself."*

Excuses! Excuses may make good talk show material or books but they do not impress God.

The Pharisees were experts at making excuses, which is why Jesus was so angry. Among the most religious folks in the community, Pharisees could be your Sunday school teachers, members of your choir, your pastor or... even you. Jesus said, *"How terrible it will be for you..."* Then in the 23rd chapter of Matthew, he began listing all of our faults:

1. *Everything we do is for show... We must really think we are hot stuff. . .*
2. *We are far too quick to condemn and way too slow to praise...*
3. *We place a higher priority on serving the church than serving God...*
4. *Our word is no longer sacred... even our contracts have escape clauses...*
5. *We major in the minors and completely miss the foundations of our faith...*
6. *We may be clean on the outside but inside we are filthy...*
7. *We may look good on the outside but inside we are dead...*

We know how the Pharisees responded to their tongue-lashing. Jesus was arrested, whipped, beaten and murdered. Wrong answer but how should we respond? "I have two personalities at war within me?" Give me a break! This is the crucial part of the story. If the Pharisees were wrong… what is right? At this point, Jesus is intense, passionate and yes, angry: as angry as you will ever see him as he cries out to the Pharisees and us:

"O, Jerusalem, Jerusalem, the city that kills the prophets and stones God's messengers! How often I have wanted to gather your children together as a hen protects her chicks beneath her wings, but you wouldn't let me. And now look, your house is left to you, empty and desolate. For I tell you this, you will never see me again until you say, 'Bless the one who comes in the name of the Lord!'" (Mat. 23:37-39)*You kill the prophets.* No Excuses! Righteous indignation will do you no good. God is looking for courage, which involves absolute honesty and integrity. **Face your wrongdoing! Confess your sins!**

✝*…as a hen protects her chicks beneath her wings.* We expect and deserve God's wrath. What we receive is a loving parent eager to shield a cherished child. **Confession restores God's love.**

✝*But you wouldn't let me.* An unwillingness to confess is actually worse than the sin itself because you deny God the opportunity to be a loving parent. **Refuse to confess and you reject God.**

✝*…your house is left to you, empty and desolate.* As wrongdoing accumulates, fair-weather friends disappear, leaving you to face the consequences alone. **Refusing to confess leads to isolation.**

✝*Bless the one who comes in the name of the Lord!* There comes a time when all of us need to ask, "Who should be in charge of my life?" **Confession places ultimate authority with God.**

Jesus is giving us all the answers. Face your wrongdoing. Have the courage to confess your sins. Accept God's authority. At this point, I picture Jesus with tears in his eyes as he describes a loving mother hen shielding her chicks beneath her strong wings. What a beautiful portrayal of God's longing to comfort, protect and restore you and me. The alternative is refuse to confess, reject God's love offering and face a future of emptiness.

Jesus was angry because people who should know better were avoiding the truth. We may look good on the outside but inside, we are filthy. The Pharisees responded with rage. Dick Morris wrote a book filled with excuses. It won't help him nor will excuses help you. The question is: How will you respond? It may be the most important decision you ever make.

Breaking The Peanut Butter Habit . . .

Following God's Recipe
For A Wonderful Life.

Chapter 4

Snapshots in Time . . .

What If? A Look at the Future

I was handed a mini-disk that resembled a music CD but half the size. On it written in large letters were two words: *What If... "This is my new calling card,"* he said with a smile. *"Take it home and play it on your computer."* As soon as I inserted the disk, the screen burst to life with colorful photographs while futuristic music played in the background. A voice began asking: *"What if...*

What if you had the foresight to recognize major trends? What if... you had a new business idea? What if... you could build a business from your home? What if... you missed it?" For the next fifteen minutes I was given a glimpse into the future, provided by a company that had the foresight to plan ahead and offer products that might meet the needs of tomorrow's world.

Proverbs puts it another way: *"My child, don't lose sight of good planning and insight. Hang on to them. For they fill you with life and bring you honor and respect. They keep you safe on your way and keep your feet from stumbling."* (3:21-23) Good automobile drivers constantly look ahead anticipating potential hazards. Champion chess players plan at least five or six moves in advance. Successful corporations regularly schedule strategic planning sessions. Good planning is important.

So, I conducted my own strategic planning session and came up with ten major trends that could be life changing. After reading this you may be tempted to add a few of your own.

1. The World Wide Internet will continue to affect our daily lives in dramatic new ways.
2. Home-based businesses will have an ever-increasing effect on the marketplace.
3. Ovens will cease to become standard equipment in the typical kitchen, as typical households will seldom eat cooked meals.
4. We will face increased terrorism and violence due to economic disparities and ethnic hatred.
5. Baby Boomers will create new health related industries as they fight to slow down the aging process.
6. Paper currency and filed tax returns will become extinct as computers handle all financial data.
7. Hispanics will become the largest ethnic minority in the US causing a language debate.

8. Gene Therapy and biotechnology will replace traditional medicine as treatment of choice.
9. Traditional churches and denominations will continue their slow decline.
10. A search for spirituality however will rise as people seek answers to life's deepest questions.

Now what? New trends mean new problems but they also present unique opportunities for you and God's church to offer ministry to those affected by the changes. Maybe, we could respond to each of the ten trends by seeking God's will and asking our own, "What if..."

✟ What if... your church could use the power of the Internet as a spiritual force for God?

✟ What if... you could provide support for someone struggling to start a home business?

✟ What if... your church provided a regular place where people could eat and socialize?

✟ What if... you could support outreach ministries to victims or even terrorists themselves?

✟ What if... your church could sponsor health clinics and offer aging support groups?

✟ What if... you offered financial guidance and support to those caught in the credit squeeze?

✟ What if... you studied Spanish to understand a culture and become a better witness?

✟ What if... your church offered basic classes taught by pharmacists, nurses or doctors?

✟ What if... you took a more active role in your church and helped to stop the decline?

✟ What if... you personally become involved with someone seeking spiritual answers?

One explanation often given for why churches, businesses and institutions fail is because they choose to live in the past rather than respond to the opportunities presented by the present and the future. As the new millennium unfolds, what choices will you and your church make?

For fifteen minutes a little mini-disc gave me a glimpse into the future. The announcer concluded his presentation with a question we would all be wise to ponder prayerfully. *"What if... you had the opportunity to do something about the future and missed it?"*

Computers, Cruise Missiles and Shepherds

It's been a horrible day. At least, God offers grace for life's mistakes, but computers are not so forgiving. It all started when I switched files from one place in the computer to another... dumb mistake. Within seconds, I lost my entire e-mail ministry mailing list, my schedule and even most of my financial records. As I feverishly tried to fix the computer my problems simply increased. I was having a royal pity party and my normally cheery disposition was growing dark and nasty.

By 2:00 PM, I was too frustrated to do anything. Looking for a break, I turned on the television only to be snapped out of my little dilemma into a worldwide tragedy. At that moment eighty cruise missiles were flying toward terrorist bases in Afghanistan and the Sudan. It was called "striking back" at Osama bin Laden, the alleged mastermind of the American Embassy bombings in Kenya and Tanzania. But questions remained. Were the attacks justified? Would they do any good?

Whether it is one of life's daily frustrations or world tragedy there is no passage of scripture better able to give comfort and hope than the "Song of the Shepherd." Psalm 23 is better known than any other part of the Bible. Most of us can recite it by heart. The words are beautiful, but to really appreciate them you have understand what it is like to be a sheep guided by a loving shepherd.

The Lord is my shepherd; I shall not want. He maketh me to lie down in green pastures — Sheep frighten easily and can run over each other in their panic. A shepherd will fix this by catching the sheep and gently, but firmly forcing them to lie down. A good shepherd does that.

...he leadeth me beside still waters. — Even thirsty sheep are afraid of rushing water. So a group of sheep will often stand in front of a running stream and stare at the water but refuse to drink. The shepherd will move a few stones around to slow down the water and create a pool. In the middle of the rushing river, the good shepherd provides needed water.

He restoreth my soul: he leadeth me in the paths of righteousness for his name's sake. Yea, though I walk through the valley of the shadow of death, I will fear no evil: for thou art with me; — We were never promised an easy life, but during the worst of our troubles we should not fear for God promises that we will never, ever... be alone! The good shepherd always guards the flock.

...thy rod and thy staff they comfort me. — The rod is actually a thick
142

club to protect the sheep against predators. The staff is a long stick with a curved end that is used to pull the sheep back into the fold. A good shepherd protects us from others, while also protecting us from ourselves.

Thou preparest a table before me in the presence of mine enemies: thou anointest my head with oil; my cup runneth over. — In a mountainous region, a table describes a flat section of land. Before entering a new table, a shepherd inspects the ground for holes, which are potential hiding places for poisonous brown snakes. In each hole he will pour some thick oil and then anoint the sheep's head with the same oil offering protection against snakebite. A good shepherd does that.

Surely goodness and mercy shall follow me all the days of my life; and I will dwell in the house of the Lord for ever. This is the final promise of the Good Shepherd who watches over us. No matter what difficulties you may be going through… goodness and mercy will follow you and in the end you will dwell in the House of the Lord… forever!

Are you having a terrible day? Have the troubles of the world soured your disposition and even your faith? Get out your Bible and turn again to Psalm 23. Read the words slowly and enjoy the heavenly protection of the good shepherd. I feel better already. Do you?

O.J., Bill & David

Do you remember Ron Goldman? He was the innocent bystander who was cruelly murdered while trying to protect Nicole Simpson. A book about him written by the Goldman family described the subsequent O.J. Simpson trial they were forced to watch, in a way that I will never forget.

"The arrogance that permeated the courtroom was suffocating. You could smell it, taste it… We decided that Defense Attorney Robert Shapiro needed a third eye. As the camera panned, he and Carl Douglas constantly monitored it, so that they could alert the defendant to stop joking and grinning and tapping out a tempo with his fingers. Lights! Camera! Action! Time to wipe the eye. Time to bite the lower lip."

In other words… there were two pictures of O.J. Simpson during the trial. One was the emotional, contrite individual we saw on television. The other Simpson was described by the Goldman family as arrogant, selfish and completely capable of brutal savagery. Which picture do you believe?

There are also two sides of President Bill Clinton. One is a man who oozes sincerity and compassion when he says, "I feel your pain!" Another side of Bill shows him saying whatever is necessary to stay elected. Do you

143

remember this? "I may have smoked pot, but I never inhaled!" (or this one) "I did not have sex with that woman!" Does anyone recall Jennifer Flowers or Kathleen Willey?

Do you believe the side of Clinton who said this? "I don't think there is a fancy way to say that I have sinned. It is important to me that everybody who has been hurt know that the sorrow I feel is genuine – first and most important my family, also my friends, my staff, my cabinet, Monica Lewinsky and her family, and the American people. I have asked all for their forgiveness."

Is he sincere or just another O.J. Simpson panning for the cameras and arrogantly laughing behind our backs? After all of the lies, why should the American people believe him yet again?

Finally, there is David: Do you remember his tryst with Bathsheba? Instead of fighting with his troops, David becomes intimately involved with the wife of one of his finest soldiers. She becomes pregnant. He covers up the affair by having her husband killed. Does all of this sound familiar?

Well David almost gets away with it, but for the prophet, Nathan. He skillfully traps David with the story of a poor farmer who has his one and only lamb stolen by a wealthy landowner. David's reaction is fury…"any man who would do such a thing deserves to die!"

Nathan dramatically points his bony finger toward the throne and says to David, "You are that man! …For you have murdered Uriah and stolen his wife." Here is the important part. David needed no lurid Starr Report costing 40 million dollars to recognize his sin. David immediately confessed to Nathan and said, "I have sinned against the Lord." (From 2 Samuel 12) David paid an awful price for his sins, but God forgave him because he confessed and expressed a genuine desire to change.

What can we learn from O.J., Bill and David?

- ✝ We are to appreciate and utilize what God has given us… not lust after someone or something we were never meant to possess or enjoy.
- ✝ When we do sin… it is vital that we be willing to confess and accept the consequences.
- ✝ Genuine repentance means striving to really change… not just the appearance of change simply to avoid punishment.

No matter what punishment ultimately overtakes O.J. Simpson and Bill

Clinton, they have lost a priceless treasure: their integrity and our nation's trust. May we learn from their grievous sins and strive all the harder to be the Godly people we've been called to be.

A 'Pie In Your Face' Award: 1998

A recent ad in the paper claimed that for a modest fee, someone would visit anyone you choose, knock on the door and when the unsuspecting victim answers, cream him/her with a pie. You're minding your own business with a certain air of dignity. Life as you know it is calm and relatively serene. Suddenly the stillness is shattered with a splat! And a stranger in uniform says: "Hi! I'm from Acme Cream Them with Love, Inc. You have been honored with a pie and a poem:" Trust me. I am not making this up!

You try to be so clever and cute, With your cruel remarks and wild lies.
Your mean, malicious behavior deserves rebuke,
Instead, we offer you a pie, right between the eyes!

What a great idea! Think of the possibilities!
- Don't stew over insensitive jerks who walk all over you... let them have a fresh piece of your... pie.
- Did a boyfriend just dump you or a wife walk out on you? Let them know how much you care!
- Has your boss been a pain lately? Apply some first aid relief!
- Maybe a friend has been teasing you too much? Enjoy the last laugh!
- Do you know a preacher who's been a little stiff around the collar? (Forget I said that!)

Nothing shatters your dignity and pride better than a pie. Even Bill Gates of Microsoft fame was not immune. With one creamy splatter in the face and the click of a camera, the wealthiest man on earth was reduced from a technological guru to a very ordinary and vulnerable human covered with meringue.

Which got me thinking... who else could benefit from a little "humble" pie? After all, this could be a time for us to reflect on where we would be without God in our lives. Confession and repentance is good for the soul. So here is my first (maybe last?) annual pie in your face award for those notable individuals or institutions that refuse to repent of their arrogance and pride and display a grave need for a "whip-cream-filled" dose of

145

humility.

The Vatican — Remorse was expressed for the cowardice of some Christians during the Holocaust while defending the actions of the wartime pope, Pius XII. Meir Lau, Israel's chief rabbi and a Holocaust survivor said: "It's too little, too late. I have no doubt that the church did not do everything it could have done to save people... His (Pius XII) silence cost millions of lives.

Sergeant-Major McKinney who after being accused by six different female staffers of sexual harassment and assault was only reduced one level in rank: a virtual slap on the wrist.

Linda Tripp — The mystery woman at the center of "Bimbogate," claimed friendship with Monica Lewinsky but secretly taped hours of intimate conversations about her alleged affair. Some friend!

Bill Clinton — who has successfully involved the whole world in a 'he said, she said," soap opera of lies, sexual misconduct and presidential mischief. Grow up, Bill!

Hear the warnings from Proverbs about our foolish pride and God's desire for humility:

- Pride leads to disgrace, but with humility comes wisdom.
  Good people are guided by their honesty; treacherous people are destroyed by their dishonesty.   (11:2-3)
- Haughtiness goes before destruction; humility precedes honor. (18:12)
- Pride ends in humiliation, while humility brings honor. (29:23)

Admittedly, we all could use a "creamed pie" occasionally to smash our prideful attitude. The lesson is to never allow pride to interfere with improving our spiritual walk. As Christian Holy Week looms, remember how much God loves you and wants to enjoy an honest, intimate relationship with you, warts and all. Don't wait for a "pie in the eye" to be your wake-up call!

Y2K: A Formula For Disaster?

Quiz Question: What in the world is Y2K?
  a) A new formula for Bug Spray.
  b) 'You're **2 K**ind!'
  c) Computer-geek symbol for "Big Oops!"
  d) The fall of humankind and the end of the world.
Answer: Probably c) or possibly d) but it depends on who you're read-

ing. Here is an example:

As the new millennium begins, millions of computers throughout the world will begin to crash. The lights will go out where the computers that run the electric power grid fail to make the transition to the next century. Many government agencies and business will be unable to function as their essential computer programs either shut down or produce false data. The failure to correct this massive problem before the year 2000 deadline will threaten jobs, our food and our finances.

Grant R. Jeffrey – The Millennium Meltdown

What happened? Apparently, during the early days of computers when memory was scarce the programmers took a shortcut and eliminated two digits from the date. For example: 12/12/1965 became 12/12/65. No problem… until now or at least, January 1, 2000. When the 19 becomes 20 no one really knows how computers will respond. They could shut down or simply go back to 00, which means 1900. Either reaction spells catastrophe according to some experts.

Computer programmers around the world are frantically racing against time to make the millions of corrections necessary to avoid disaster. Unfortunately, they will not succeed! So the billion-dollar question is: "What will happen?" A *Newsweek* article gives five interesting alternatives:

1) **Y2AOK**: Relax: The government has it under control. Y worry?
USA = no Y2K: The real problems are overseas. You'll be fine if you don't fly abroad or invest in Asia.
2) **Cautious Buzz**: Nothing big will go down. But it can't hurt to print out bank statements and buy a gas mask. Welcome to the future.
3) **Zealot Buzz**: Millennium bug as apocalypse. The worthy ascend; the rest of us… well, it looks bad.
4) **Y2K = H2O .357**: Stockpile water and ammo: it's gonna hit the fan. Cities collapse; nukes rain. I've got my home cannery, my silver dollars and booby traps.

Think of all the areas where the Y2K problem could cripple our lifestyle:

▷ Banks – All your records could be lost as computers shut down or go back in time.
▷ Travel – Air traffic control is guided by gigantic computer systems. What will happen to our aiplanes?
▷ Communications – Computer switchboards control all of our telephone lines.
▷ Military – All of our missiles and modern weapons are dependent upon computers.

▷ Energy – Power plants and even local gas pumps are computer controlled.
▷ Social Security – All checks are printed and mailed by computer.
▷ Stock Market – Computers regularly handle all records and transactions.

In other words, come January 1, 2000 you could wake up with a dead telephone line, no electricity, no heat in your house and no access to the money you need to survive. Does all of this sound farfetched and alarmist? Maybe. That's the problem… no one really knows.

So the question is: If Y2K cannot be fixed then how do we avoid panic and prepare for the coming crisis?

Proverbs 6:10 says, "Take a lesson from the ants, you lazybones. Learn from their ways and be wise!" Being wise in this case means working hard and being prepared. Are you ready for the coming Millennium? If you are like me, probably not, but there is a story about someone in the Bible who can help us prepare: Joseph

Y2K: Joseph and Being Prepared

Some of you may remember the great stock market crash of '29 like it was yesterday. It was a pivotal event in your life. I can still recall my whereabouts on the day President Kennedy was assassinated and when the Challenger Spacecraft exploded. In the future, will people be saying: "Where were you on Y2K day?"

If the computer programmers can't win the race to fix all the bugs the billion-dollar question becomes: How do we avoid panic and prepare for the coming crisis? Also, why does a country preacher (Who me?) think he's qualified to answer this issue?

Of course, I am not qualified, but God is. In Genesis, approximately 4000 years ago: "Pharaoh dreamed that he was standing on the bank of the Nile River. In his dream seven fat, healthy-looking cows suddenly came up out of the river and began grazing along its bank. Then seven other cows came up from the river but these were very ugly and gaunt. These cows went over and stood beside the fat cows. Then the thin, ugly cows ate the fat ones!"   (Genesis 41:1-4)

The Pharaoh looked everywhere for someone to interpret the dream before they found a young man named Joseph, who had been sold into slavery by his own brothers, falsely accused of sexual harassment, locked up and forgotten in prison. But God had been preparing him for just this crisis. Joseph's interpretation of Pharaoh's dream could be part of our solution to Y2K.

Joseph said: "It is beyond my power to do this, but God will tell you what it means and will set you at ease... The seven fat cows represent seven years of prosperity. The seven thin, ugly cows represent seven years of famine... Let Pharaoh appoint officials over the land and let them collect one-fifth of all the crops during the seven good years... and store it away..." (Genesis 41:16-36)

A Y2K style crisis was coming that would have disastrous impact on Egypt. Seven years of prosperity followed by seven years of famine. Can God's words to Joseph help us prepare?

1. *It is beyond our power, but God will tell us...* **Faith**: Being prepared starts with faith.
2. *There will be years of famine...* **Listen**: Are we listening to God's warnings?
3. *Appoint officials over the land...* **Leadership**: Are you willing to support capable leaders?
4. *Store it away...* **Sacrifice**: Are you willing to sacrifice today for a better tomorrow?

Seven years of prosperity were followed by seven years of famine just as God promised but thanks to the leadership of Joseph, Egypt was well prepared. In addition to feeding their own, they were even able to offer aid to other starving countries. A potential catastrophe turned into an opportunity to help those less fortunate. That is how God works.

Here are some practical steps you can take today to prepare for Y2K:
▷ Get current copies of all your records: Bank statements, stocks, etc.
▷ Put enough cash aside to last you two to four weeks or longer.
▷ Do you have an alternative source of energy or heat for your home?
▷ Do you have an adequate supply of food and water?
▷ Do you have copies of your medical records?
▷ Do you have emergency tools such as flashlights, batteries, etc.
▷ Stockpile enough to be able to share with those less fortunate.

Will Y2K be a catastrophe for you and your family or an opportunity to show God's amazing love to someone in need? The answer lies in your willingness to learn from God's counsel through Joseph. "Have faith. Listen to God's warnings. Support capable leadership and be willing to sacrifice today to prepare for a better tomorrow." Like Egypt, you too could be used by God to bring someone much needed aid in the midst of tragedy. What an awesome thought!

An Act of Kindness: A Different Sort of War Story

Amidst the confusion and controversy of the conflict in Kosovo you may wonder: Can America get involved in a war without doing more harm than good? Of course we can, but there is no easy answer to the problems in Yugoslavia nor is there ever an easy war. Memorial Day is a poignant reminder that conflicts and war are unavoidable. Yet each conflict has a way of also presenting experiences of God's love and old-fashioned human kindness.

For example: If you visit a certain museum in Eindhoven, Holland you may notice aerial photographs taken on the day American paratroopers liberated the city from the Germans in 1944. The fascinating story of how those photographs came to the museum is an amazing series of coincidences that shows how kindness can stretch across continents and even cultures.

"Skee" Ramsey, a member of a church I served in Keysville, Virginia told me about her daughter Katherine who was given the opportunity to tour Europe with a concert band. In Holland, she stayed with a couple in Bergeyk. A friendship developed and the two families kept in touch regularly. When Katherine went back to Europe to continue her college studies, it was this same Dutch family that went out of their way to pick her up at the airport and drive her safely to the University in Belgium.

Several years later, the same family visited the United States and stayed with their American friends. At one point, "Skee" began to thank them for taking such loving care of their daughter. The husband replied, "I have always felt that if I ever had the chance to do anything for an American, I would do it."

He went on to describe one special day in 1944 when he and his father went up to the roof of their house in Eindhoven to watch the 101st Airborne of the United States Army drop from the sky in parachutes and special gliders. The boy turned to his dad and asked: "Are the Germans leaving?" The father replied, "No son, the Americans are coming."

A relative of "Skee's" who served as an Intelligence Officer during the war and helped to plan the campaign that liberated the Netherlands, heard the story of the grateful Dutch family and began looking through his old souvenirs. He found several aerial reconnaissance photographs of Eindhoven that were made that day even detailing some of the gliders used by the paratroopers. The photographs were given to the couple who then donated them to a local museum.

Can you imagine having the opportunity to witness the stunning rescue of your countrymen and your family? Because of this awe-inspiring moment a Dutch couple would forever look for opportunities to show kindness to a nation that sent the very best of its population oversees to rescue others from tyranny! No wonder celebrating Memorial Day is so significant!

Memorial Day is a day to remember the times our country met the challenge to fight and refused to bury its collective head in the sand. Good men and women died for our country so Memorial Day is a way to remember. Like most citizens, our country's presence in Kosovo concerns me. How deeply do we get involved? The story of a grateful Dutch couple in Holland serves as a reminder that sometimes the kindest thing we can do is fight.

Paul's short letter to Philemon says a lot about kindness: "I always thank God when I pray for you, Philemon, because I keep hearing of your trust in the Lord Jesus and your love for all of God's people. You are generous because of your faith. And I am praying that you will really put your generosity to work, for in so doing you will come to an understanding of all the good things we can do for Christ." (1:4-6)

The definitive act of kindness is to trust God enough and love God's people enough to be willing to sacrifice everything... even your life. Few can claim that sort of courage without the supernatural love of God.

Will Your Child Be Safe?

Dark clouds hover over our schools this year. News of the Columbine High School tragedy is no longer on the front page but the debate sparked by the senseless attack rages on. We still ask... Why? Other attacks occurred this year in Colorado, Georgia and Arkansas. Are they isolated incidents or is it the tip of an iceberg of violence among our nation's youth? Can we do anything to prevent future outbursts? "Will our children be safe in school this year?"

If you think that it can't happen in your area... think again. In our area of central Virginia during the last week:

▷ Several students were arrested for carrying concealed weapons.
▷ A bomb threat forced a school evacuation for several hours.
▷ Web pages were discovered at a junior high school teaching other students how to build a bomb.

A recent *Newsweek* article: "In survey after survey, many kids – even those on the honor roll – say they feel increasingly alone and alienated, unable to connect with their parents, teachers and sometimes even classmates. They're desperate for guidance and when they don't get what they need at home or in school, they cling to cliques or immerse themselves in a universe out of the parents' reach, a world defined by computer games, TV and movies where brutality is so common it has become mundane." Increasingly children feel alienated and are desperate for guidance.

Larry Dunn, Charlotte County Superintendent, warns of the danger of overreacting: "We will be careful not to treat our students as criminals. Schools are still the safest places in student's environments. Our students have a much better record of violence and crime than do our communities. Our students are exemplary because we expect such. We need to continue to have high expectations for students, for academics and more importantly for behavior."

So... how can we help our children have a safer and more productive school environment?

1. **Get Involved**: Offer to volunteer at a local school. Become a tutor. Attend meetings and get to know the teachers and parents. Watch how students interact with each other.
2. **Become a Mentor**: Look for ways to guide one or several youth in your community. Be encouraging and approachable. Include them frequently in your prayers.
3. **Talk and Listen**: How well do you know your child? Who are his friends? What are her interests? Spend a few extra minutes each day deepening your relationship with him/her.
4. **Heed the Warning Signals**: Has his appetite changed? Have her grades fallen? Have they lost interest in favorite activities? Are they becoming more aggressive or sullen?
5. **Take A Faith Inventory**: Is your family religiously active? Do the children have peers at church offering support and love? Are you praying for or with a child?

The Bible teaches: "...you must love the LORD your God with all your heart, all your soul, and all your strength. And you must commit yourselves wholeheartedly to these commands I am giving you today. Repeat them again and again to your children." (Deuteronomy 6:4-7)

For years, the church was considered "out of touch" with real world issues but is it really? After all, the church often takes a righteous stand for moral values and ethical standards. God's church provides hope when crisis strikes. The Bible teaches responsibility for our individual and societal shortcomings. Our faith, nurtured in the church gives us the desire to reach out to others and make a difference in the world. No organization teaches life's moral fundamentals better.

Recently, eight high school seniors in our area were honored with scholarships: partly for academic excellence and partly for being the very first in their family to ever attend college. In their acceptance speeches, all of them mentioned obstacles and sacrifices to overcome. But every senior had a clear goal and cited faith in God as a significant influence in his or her life.

How can we help our children? Get involved and become a mentor. Spend more time with your children and be on the alert for the warning signals of trouble. More importantly… take a careful faith inventory and become active in a local church. Your encouraging influence in the life of a child could spell the difference between two "S" words: a scholarship… or a shooting.

Kosovo: How Should We Respond?

A missionary in Albania wrote: *"Pray for the genocide to stop. Please do not be misled: This is real genocide! There is no other term for it. The stories we are hearing from the refugees in Kosovo are horrific. I cannot conceive of such atrocities - and they have experienced them…" The Serbs are trying to erase, by using "identity elimination" tactics, all records that the Albanian Kosovars ever lived by taking away passports, drivers licenses, removing plates off of vehicles, destroying public records, such as land deeds, financial records, birth & marriage certificates, etc.' This is a total form of ethnic cleansing."*

Regardless of your political viewpoint, it's obvious that a major catastrophe is occurring in a province of Yugoslavia known as Kosovo. As I write, NATO warplanes have intensified their attacks on the Serbian forces of Slobodan Milosevic in an attempt to stop what seems to be a calculated attempt to relocate or destroy the Kosovars. In other words: genocide.

Why is this happening? The breakup of Yugoslavia following the cold war reopened centuries old wounds between the Kosovars and Serbs. Kosovo holds historical and religious significance for both sides going back more than six hundred years. In the late 1300's a decisive battle resulted in defeat of the Serbs and led to Turkish rule, which only ended in the early 1900's. For six hundred years racial and religious hatred between these two peoples has steadily intensified.

Before the recent hostilities, ninety percent of Kosovo's population was Muslim Kosovar with only ten percent described as Christian Serb. Milosevic, the leader of Yugoslavia, however, is Serbian and on a mission to reclaim the territory lost to the Muslims hundreds of years ago. The key to securing peace in Kosovo is to recognize and resolve this deep cultural and religious animosity.

How big is the crisis? The Serbs have forcibly evicted nearly one million Kosovars. Testimonies and evidence brought out by the refugees along with satellite surveillance strongly imply mass executions along with other atrocities. NATO air strikes are primarily aimed at stopping the ethnic cleansing and forcing the Serbs into a peaceful settlement with the Kosovars.

What can we do? When the Biblical Nehemiah heard of a crisis among his people he wrote: "When I heard this, I sat down and wept. In fact, for days I mourned, fasted, and prayed to the God of heaven. O LORD, please hear my prayer! Listen to the prayers of those of us who delight in honoring you." (Neh. 1:4 &11) Nehemiah realized a fundamental spiritual law: Pray! That's it? Pray? Prayer was never meant to be just a mental exercise. Prayer is an act of faith in itself that emphatically declares our trust in a God who listens and responds either through us or someone else. First... we must pray. A worldwide prayer vigil has been organized asking all of us to pray for Kosovo for at least two minutes beginning at 3:00 pm EST every day.

☦Pray... individually, in small groups and as a church. Hold a prayer service.

☦Pray... for God to bring peace and for the leaders to act with Godly wisdom.

☦Pray... for the refugees and the victims of ethnic cleansing.

☦Pray... for the men and women of the armed forces and those held prisoner.

☦Pray... for guidance on how you can help those heading up the relief efforts.

Prayers will guide additional action. You could contribute to relief organizations that are already getting involved. You may feel the need to do something more extensive. A doctor flew over and volunteered her services at a refugee camp. A church organization sent blankets and health kits full of basic medical supplies. Another group sent thousands of batteries.

What ever you do, please carefully read the closing statement of this Albanian missionary: *"This letter is an appeal – don't forget us! Please make mention of us and the Balkan nations in your prayers. Keep interceding for our political leadership for various parties, factions and nations. Persist until you see a spiritual change, until a great salvation of our people comes."*

The Tragedy at Wedgwood Baptist Church

"Jesus called his disciples and the crowds to come over and listen. 'If any of you wants to be my follower,' he told them, 'you must put aside your selfish ambition, shoulder your cross and follow me. If you try to keep your life for yourself, you will lose it. But if you give up your life for my sake and for the sake of the Good News, you will find true life.'"

(Mark 8:34-35)

"And as they stoned him, Stephen prayed, 'Lord Jesus, receive my spirit.' And he fell to his knees, shouting, 'Lord, don't charge them with this sin!' And with that, he died." (Acts 7:59-60)

Most have heard or read these passages many times but never in our wildest dreams would we think they would apply to modern Americans. It's one thing to read about someone named Stephen being brutally stoned to death 2000 years ago for defending his beliefs. It's quite another to helplessly watch as television screens display the funerals of innocent children cruelly murdered by an angry gunman, ironically during a youth service held at Wedgwood Baptist Church to encourage nonviolence.

✝**Kristi Beckel** was a fourteen-year-old volleyball player described as an "awesome server." Every night she would wish her parents well and then shout from her bedroom wall, "Good night, I love you!"

✝**Shawn Brown** was twenty-three and studying at the seminary for his master's degree and hoped to become a youth minister. He was described as fun loving and eager to learn, studying the guitar and sign language.

✝**Susan "Kim" Jones** was also twenty-three and lived on campus at the seminary, loved missionary work and was described as having a ready smile that lit up a room.

✝**Sydney Browning** was the children's choir director and was a teacher at Success High School who specialized in working with dropouts. She was shot while sitting on a couch in the foyer with a friend. She was thirty-six years old.

✝**Justin Ray** was seventeen, a devoted Boy Scout who wanted to pursue a career in film and sound production. He was videotaping the service when the gunfire started.

✝**Joseph "Joey" Ennis** was fourteen, loved playing basketball and spending "family nights" playing board games at home. Just four months ago he wrote this mission statement for a class assignment: My mission in life is to be kind and trustworthy with humor, always keeping promises, especially as a friend, a son and a pet owner."

✝**Cassandra Griffin** at fourteen was laid to rest in a bold blue casket with clouds painted on the lid. It was fitting for a young woman described by many as an angel. On either side of the casket floated lime-green balloons in the shape of a frog, representing the motto of the church youth: Fully Rely On God.

Rev. Al Meredith, the pastor of Wedgwood Baptist church asked at Cassandra's funeral, "How many of you have been to the funeral of a martyr before? This is my fifth one in three days."

The Bible teaches that Stephen was not martyred in vain. Thousands of people became Christians immediately following the stoning because of Stephen's faithful life and his courage facing death. Across the centuries, many Christians faced death simply because they believed in God. History teaches… the death of a martyr is never wasted. Their examples inspired millions.

Our best response is to first, pray and offer God's comfort and support to the families of those who were slain and injured. Second, we honor the memories of seven martyrs and renew our commitment to "shoulder our cross and follow Christ." Third, we look for ways to make a positive difference in the lives of lost and forgotten children in our community.

Will this ease the pain and suffering at Wedgwood Baptist Church? Of course not! God never promised a life free of tragedy. We are promised comfort during our trials and a holy confidence that the ending will always justify the pain. In the end, we must believe it is a faith worth dieing for!

'Pie in Your Face' or 'Pat on the Back' Awards: 1999

It all started when I wrote about a company that for a modest fee would visit anyone you choose and cream him/her with a pie. What a great idea! Think of the possibilities!

- Do insensitive jerks walk all over you? Let them have a fresh piece of your... pie!
- Has your boss been a pain lately? Apply some first aid and enjoy the last laugh!
- Do you know a preacher who's been a little stiff in the collar? (Forget I said that!)

Now, who else could benefit from a little "humble" pie? After all, confession and repentance is good for the soul. Right? So here is my second (maybe last?) annual pie in your face award for those notable individuals who refused to repent of their arrogance and pride and displayed a grave need for a "whip-cream-filled" dose of humility. But, this year to appease my sense of fairness and my innate desire to be positive, I am also giving a pat on the back to those notable individuals who accomplished great feats yet displayed humility.

World Events & National Politics

☹ For continued violence and outright cruelty against humanity: *Saddam Hussein and Slobodan Milosevic* richly deserve their pie in the face. (Stuffed with a missile?)

☺ For continuing to promote the causes of peace and freedom worldwide: *Pope John Paul II and King Hussein* of Jordan richly deserve a pat on the back and our gratitude.

☹ For diverting our attention from critical issues and forcing us to dwell on your pursuit of cheap thrills and bald-faced lies: *Bill Clinton* deserves a cream pie between the eyes.

☹ For wasting a much-needed opportunity to focus on our moral values and instead pursuing a political 'get Bill' agenda: *Congressional Republicans* equally earned a pie.

☺ For offering a voice of reason in the midst of mud slinging and continuing to creatively serve and give to our country: *Jimmy Carter* deserves a pat on the back.

Sports & Entertainment

☹ For allowing us to see the Olympic games at their worst: *The*

International Olympic Committee needs to feel the splat of fresh cream pie.

☺ For being positive role models and simply making baseball exciting again: *Mark McGuire and Sammy Sousa* deserve a pat on the back and our gracious thanks.

☹ For lowering television standards to sewer level: *"The Howard Stern Show."*

☺ For raising television standards and offering a gracious view of God: *"Touched By An Angel"* deserves an extra pat on the back.

Church Issues

☹ Was it to make a point or a publicity stunt? Either way, *Rev. John Fado* deserves his pie for overseeing a "holy union" between two homosexuals and circumventing a carefully and prayerfully debated by his national church.

☺ A pat on the back for *Andrew Pearson*, a youth delegate who stood before thousands of church delegates and persuaded them to take a stand against alcohol at college.

☺ A special pat on the back for *Rev. Billy Graham* who over the years has consistently spoken to us and modeled for us a wonderful message of salvation and hope.

You and I

☹ For all the times when we had a golden opportunity to take a stand as Christians and lacked the courage. We too deserve the same creamed pie between the eyes.

☺ For those times when you had a golden opportunity to take a stand as a Christian and found the courage you needed. Accept your pat on the back with grateful humility.

Maybe this is where Proverbs speaks with such authority:

- Pride leads to disgrace, but with humility comes wisdom. Good people are guided by their honesty; treacherous people are destroyed by their dishonesty. (Proverbs 11:2-3)
- Pride ends in humiliation, while humility brings honor. (29:23)

Admittedly, we all could use a "creamed pie" occasionally to smash our pride. So, remember how God loves you and wants to enjoy an honest, intimate relationship with you, warts and all. Act now! Don't wait for a "pie in the eye" to be your wake-up call!

A National Crisis or Politics Run Amok? Bush vs Gore

Are you disgusted with the 24 hours a day "Who won?" news coverage yet? Me too, but for some reason, I'm still glued to the TV, day and night straining to hear the latest development in a continuing political soap opera. "Who will be our next president?" Sadly, I'm ready to answer, "Who cares?"

As I write, George W. Bush has been certified the winner in Florida by a whopping margin of 537 votes. Immediately Al Gore announced he would contest the results. Now, according to one network, forty-eight separate lawsuits have been filed. One voting precinct wasn't finished with their recount. Another stopped the recount, knowing they couldn't make the deadline. Thousands of absentee ballots were declared ineligible. We learned more than we ever wanted to know about dimples, chads and butterfly ballots. How many times must we be forced to watch as groups of people hold ballots toward the ceiling in a futile attempt to divine 'true voter intent'? Give me a break!

Fortunately we had a lot of opportunities to laugh along the way. Have you tried the Palm Beach Pokey? "You put the Gore votes in. You put the Bush votes out. You put the Gore votes in. And you do another count. You do the Palm Beach Pokey and you turn the count around. That's what it's all about!" Maybe you've seen the newest book in the famous series, "Voting for Dummies: A Reference for Florida Voters." One article is titled, "Hole Punching Techniques made Simple." Finally there is the new Democratic Party official seal featuring a picture of a crying baby.

When I stop laughing, I worry. What about our future? The stock market is plunging. Sales of big-ticket items have slowed to a trickle. If someone doesn't eventually concede defeat what will happen next? Will the victor have any mandate to govern with? Will the controversy and court cases tear at the fabric of our democratic way of life? Could the Bush vs. Gore conflict become more than rhetoric and briefs?

Well, I've watched and read enough political advice. It's time to seek guidance from God!

Many years ago, Jerusalem was overrun and in ruins. Her people were taken captive and hauled off to Babylon. All seemed lost, yet In the midst of their misery, the prophet Isaiah made a bold promise: "But now, O Israel, the Lord who created you says: "Do not be afraid, for I have ransomed you. I have called you by name; you are mine. When you go through deep waters and great trouble, I will be with you. When you go through rivers of difficulty, you will not drown! When you walk through the fire of oppression, you will not be burned up; the flames will not consume you. For I am the Lord, your God, the Holy One of Israel, your savior." (Isaiah 43:1-3)

Do not be afraid… is reassurance that God is in the midst of us. I have called you by name… is the promise that God knows our predicament. When you go through rivers of difficulty, you will not drown… is the comfort of knowing you will be safe. For I am the Lord, your God, the Holy One of Israel, your savior… is a statement of faith. God is firmly in control and still loves you and me.

What have I learned from all of this?

1. In the end, either Bush or Gore will concede and the victor though humbled and slightly weakened will still be President of the United States.

2. There will be no terrorism, guerrilla warfare or tanks in the street. There are few places in the world offering this promise. We will learn from our mistakes. For the next few years: how we vote and how our votes are counted will be studied, argued, changed and hopefully improved.

3. We belong to something bigger than any political candidate or party. As Americans we put our faith in democracy and the law. As followers of God we know Who is always in charge.

The prophet Isaiah also promised: "For a child is born to us, a son is given to us. And the government will rest on his shoulders." (Isaiah 9:6) In a few short weeks, we will celebrate the fulfillment of Isaiah's promise: Christmas. As years pass, there will be other presidents, more critical issues to argue over and yes, even a few new political crises. But just as fall surely moves toward winter there will always be the promise of Christmas offering a gentle reminder… "For I am the Lord, your God… your savior

A Letter of Faith…   from Esther Kim

Tired and discouraged, Esther Kim recently finished a grueling round of chemotherapy and drove to a nearby church, looking for a quiet place to pray. She ended up at our church but couldn't find the chapel. She was miraculously discovered wandering the halls by one of our prayer groups and within minutes all of them were crying and praying together as Esther shared her struggles with cancer and told the incredible story of Pastor Dong-Shik Kim, her husband held prisoner in North Korea.

For months we have been in contact with governments and organizations around the world urging Pastor Kim's release. Above all, we have prayed. On the one-year anniversary of the kidnapping, representatives from the Korean church and others throughout the community joined us in a special service to pray both for Pastor Kim's release and the peaceful unification of Korea. As a part of the service, Esther Kim wrote and read a letter... of love and continuing faith in God.

"On January 16, 2000, North Koreans kidnapped Pastor Dong-Shik Kim, my husband. I appreciate those who have joined the prayer movement for him. I wish for you to pray not only for my husband but also for the people who are suffering in North Korea."

"My husband was inspired by the biography of Pastor Ju Kichul. He attended the Ungchun Church in which Pastor Ju ministered. Ungchun church was also the place he prayed about marrying me."

"My husband lived for the smallest. In 1986, he was involved in a serious traffic accident, which left him unable to walk without the use of a cane. After that, he began to emphasize that he and I should take better care of our five adopted children than of our own three children. He believed that if every Korean church adopted at least one orphan, they would no longer need foreign adopters and Korean churches themselves would benefit. He himself led such a life."

Pastor Kim worked for handicapped people. He opened a talent conference and a ski camp in Korea for the handicapped. He interpreted "To Live is Enraptured" by Dahara Uneko and "Dream of the Wheelchair" by Jang Heduck into Korean. With the help of several South Korean churches he built noodle factories in North Korea. He sent containers of clothes and socks to protect people from harsh winters. He supported several orphanages and kindergartens in North Korea and sent provisions."

"While working in China, Pastor Kim began taking care of escapees from North Korea and looked for ways to bring them into South Korea via a third country. On November 30, 1999, he miraculously succeeded in leading five families (13 people) into South Korea through Mongolia where they were detained for seven days. He reentered China on January 15, 2000. The next day, shortly after worshipping at church, he was kidnapped by North Korean spies."

"Each year my husband chose for our family a hymn such as: 'The Lord Who Helps Me Behind My Back' in 1997, 'On a Hill Far Away' in 1998,

'God is Our Refuge' in 1999, and 'We are Bound for Canaan Land' in 2000. He wrote Scripture verses on our calendar. His favorite was 2 Kings 6:16,17: 'Don't be afraid. Those who are with us are more than those who are with them.'"

"After surgery for rectal cancer on September 30, 1999, when his body became weak, people urged him to look for a successor. He said, "There is no one who would die for this work. We should make up our mind to die for the LORD if we really want to do the work of the LORD." He continued to take care of the weak without taking care of his own body."

"I don't know where my husband is or how he has been. North Korea is a country in which people have no freedom and do not know God. Would you, who enjoy freedom and know the Gospel, pray for the evangelism of North Korea and the unification of all of Korea? It is what my son, Heaven, and I and my husband Dong-Shik Kim want. As for us, there is nothing we can do but pray. In Christ, Esther Kim."

World events and politics are often hard to comprehend but we can all appreciate a devoted wife and family who want their loved one home and the country they love reunited. Will you join us in prayer?

'Pie in Your Face' or 'Pat on the Back' Awards: 2001

It all started when I wrote about a company that for a modest fee would visit anyone you choose and cream him/her with a pie. What a great idea! Think of the possibilities!

- Do insensitive jerks walk all over you? Let them have a fresh piece of your... pie!
- Has your boss been a pain lately? Apply some first aid and enjoy the last laugh!
- Do you know a preacher who's been a little stiff in the collar? (Forget I said that!)

Does this sound like fun to you? I thought so and wrote a story about some folks who definitely needed a pie in the eye. What happened next surprised even me.

I received an email complimenting the pie-in-the-face article. But then the writer asked: "I love being hit with pies. Don't you? Would you like to see some pictures?" (No! I wouldn't!) More letters came with the same message. For months, I was bombarded with weird photos of folks creamed from every angle and loving every minute of it. Does that sound strange to you?

"What is wrong with you folks? Get a life and leave me alone! Don't you know the difference between satire and cheap thrills? You're sick, sick, sick! Please… Stop sending those pictures! So, this year I throw my first pie at "Creamed Pie Whackos!" I know, I know. It's what they want. I can't win!"

Now, who else could benefit from a little "humble" pie? After all, confession and repentance is good for the soul. Right? So here is my third (maybe last?) annual pie in the face award for those notable individuals who refuse to repent of their arrogance and display a grave need for a "whip-cream-filled" dose of humility.

I am also giving a pat on the back of recognition to individuals who accomplish great feats yet display a Christ-like humility.

Enough of introductions… let's get started. Who gets the next pie?

Pie Splat! Enough is enough! Would someone please tell the media that *Bill Clinton* is no longer president? Shades of Monica-gate… Now we read about unethical pardons, missing furniture, last minute deals, and hidden money transactions: It's enough to make you gag! Please Bill, disappear.

Pat on the Back! Our always-professional, former *Vice President Gore* has behaved quite honorably after all the confusion and questions surrounding the recent election. He is quickly finding his role as teacher and statesman. Newspaper articles report him as content and adjusting to his new lifestyle. Who knows? If he ran again, I might even vote for him. Congratulations!

Pie Splat! *Robert Noel and Marjorie Knoller* were known to spoil their two Presa Camario mastiff dogs with special food and walks along the beach. Unfortunately there was not as much attention or remorse expressed over the cruel death of Diane Whipple mauled to death by those same dogs.

Pat on the Back! *Father Fortunato Di Noto* spent more than four years tracking down Child Pornography sites on the internet and proved to be a key factor in breaking an international ring of pedophiles. Asked why, he simply remarked: "Silence is what allows pedophiles to win."

Pie Splat! For the times you had a golden opportunity to witness your faith and lacked courage.

Pat on the Back! For when you had the same opportunity and found your nerve.

Maybe this is where Proverbs speaks with such authority:

●Pride leads to disgrace, but with humility comes wisdom. Good

people are guided by their honesty; treacherous people are destroyed
by their dishonesty. (Proverbs 11:2-3)
- Pride ends in humiliation, while humility brings honor.
(Proverbs 29:23)

Admittedly, we all could use a "creamed pie" occasionally to smash our
pride. Remember how much God loves you and wants to enjoy an honest,
intimate relationship with you, warts and all. Act now! Don't wait for a
"pie in the eye" to be your wake-up call!

Timothy McVeigh, Oklahoma and Waco

It's been eight years since an obscure cult led by David Koresh chose
suicide rather than surrender to the FBI, resulting in the horrible fire which
took the lives of so many in Waco Texas. One newspaper article began with
the following haunting words: "They were innocents. Trapped inside the
prairie compound's walls, they had no voices, no recourse, no protector.
Seventeen young children, some of them babies, had the hour of their
deaths dictated by David Koresh, the religious zealot who was father to
many of them and who controlled every aspect of their existence."

Two years later, another passionate zealot, Timothy McVeigh, sought
revenge over the Waco tragedy. He filled a Ryder truck with explosives and
parked it in front of a government office building in Oklahoma City. The
resulting explosion killed 168 people, many of them children attending a
day care center. Who can ever forget the image of a dazed fireman walking away from the carnage gently cradling a dying infant? Along with millions of others I could only watch in horror.

Today there is a memorial in Oklahoma City to forever remember the
tragedy and those who perished. What about Timothy McVeigh? Soon, he
will be executed: The first person executed by the federal government in
many years. Should this be where it ends? Are there lessons for us all?

I noticed that David Koresh and Timothy McVeigh had something in
common. The both passionately believed their particular cause transcended any consequences that may occur. "If innocent men, women and children suffer and die... so be it! What's important is our passion for the
cause!"

We see the same passion in business, where company loyalty and profits mean more than ethics and morality. We see the passion in athletics,

164

when a team sacrifices anything and everything for a winning season. We even see the passion in church, where one group claims to have all the answers and anyone who dares to disagree is going straight to... well, you get the picture.

Ouch! I talk often of becoming more passionate about our faith so is this where our passion inevitably leads? Of course not but there are subtle dangers we all face. We may not ignite a bomb but every time we act smug or condescending or self-righteous we are hurting someone just as effectively.

So what can we learn from the mistakes of David Koresh and Timothy McVeigh? Among the last words on earth Jesus said to his disciples were these: "Yes, I am the vine; you are the branches. Those who remain in me and I in them will produce much fruit. For apart from me you can do nothing." (John 15:5) I found four critical lessons within this one verse:

1. "I am the vine; you are the branches..." The Christian life should always be a balance between two extremes. One extreme is to ignore our need for God and struggle to make it on our own. Another extreme is promoting your particular interpretation of God while giving no respect to others. Does our ministry consistently point to the vine of God's grace and love?

2. "Those who remain in me..." Prayer is how we 'remain in God' and should always be our top priority. Prayer reminds us that God is ultimately in control of our ministry and our lives. Prayer is recognizing God's strength and our weakness.

3. "...will produce much fruit." Does our ministry seek excellence? Do we strive to excel and set a good example in every area of our daily life? Do our actions reflect our beliefs? Do I listen as well as I talk? Are you a positive influence in your community?

4. "For apart from me you can do nothing." Are we doing what God wants us to do? Are we reaching those who really need us? Do I have a humble attitude? Do you offer an encouraging word to those who suffer? Can people see God within us as we serve?

How can we avoid the sins of David Koresh and Timothy McVeigh and learn from the tragedy of Waco and Oklahoma City? We work at keeping our faith in balance, maintain an active prayer life, seek to excel in all that we do and never forget that apart from God... we can do nothing.

This is our chance to pray for Timothy McVeigh, for families in Oklahoma City and for ourselves.

September 11, 2001: A Day of Terror

▶Linda hurriedly left the Boston hotel room for her morning flight to Los Angeles. It had been a long weekend for the young flight attendant but soon she would be home. Her fiancé called on the cell phone to confirm their dinner date. *"I'll be there to pick you up. What flight are you on?"* A little impatiently, she reminded him… "Flight 11! Flight 11."

▶David wolfed down a bagel and scanned the baseball scores before grabbing his brief case and heading out. It was dark as he drove to New York. *"This could be my biggest sale ever,"* he thought as he checked off the features for a new line of copy machines he was presenting to the insurance agency… located on floor 104 in building two of the World Trade Center.

▶Connie paused at the front door of her teenage sons bedroom. For a moment she thought of waking him. Last night's argument had been worse than usual. She didn't mean to get so angry. *"It's too early to wake him,"* she thought. *"I'll apologize after school and we can go out for pizza."* Feeling reassured, she wrote him a note and went to work… at the Pentagon.

Linda, David and Connie represent thousands of ordinary Americans. For them, September 11, 2001 started normally enough but soon, everything would change… forever.

At 8:45 AM, American Airlines Flight 11, a Boeing 767 en route from Boston to Los Angeles with ninety-two people aboard slammed into the north tower of the World Trade Center and initiated a day of terror such as the United States has not seen since Pearl Harbor. Approximately eighteen minutes later, United Airlines Flight 175, a Boeing 767 also en route from Boston to Los Angeles with sixty-five people aboard hit the south tower of the world trade center. Thirty minutes later a third plane crashed into the Pentagon in Washington D.C. A fourth passenger jet would crash just outside of Pittsburgh.

All four planes were hijacked by a well-coordinated band of terrorists. Based on cell phone calls from frightened passengers we know many of the crew members were stabbed to death, while at least one terrorist, who must have received pilot training took over flying the plane, disabled safety equipment and turned an ordinary passenger airliner into a weapon of terror and destruction.

166

President Bush addressed the nation: "Today, our fellow citizens, our way of life, our very freedom came under attack in a series of deliberate and deadly terrorist acts. The victims were in airplanes or in their offices: secretaries, business men and women, military and federal workers, moms and dads, friends and neighbors. Thousands of lives were suddenly ended by evil, despicable acts of terror."

Jesus warned his disciples: "...and the time is coming when those who kill you will think they are doing God a service. This is because they have never known the Father or me. Yes, I am telling you these things now, so that when they happen, you will remember I warned you." (John 16:2-4)

As Christians and Americans: How should we respond to this despicable act of terror?

1. Pray: Around the country, millions have joined together to pray for the victims.

2. Maintain our Schedule: We must not be stopped or the terrorists can claim victory.

3. Support our Leadership: We rally behind those we elected to serve and guide us.

4. Sacrifice Freely: Money and volunteerism is desperately needed. We give generously.

5. Seek Justice not Revenge: We put our ultimate trust in our government and God.

6. Reexamine our Priorities: Life is a precious gift from God. How are you using it?

7. Pray: We pray that somehow these events will draw us closer to God.

Donna and Tony Scurlock from our email ministry offered the following prayer: "In light of today's terrorist attacks, let us pray for wisdom for our leaders especially President Bush; let us pray for the families of the dead and injured; let us pray for the safety of fireman, police, and recovery crews; let us pray for the peace, protection and safety of our nation; let us pray for the safety of our airlines and all transportation centers; let us pray that God's peace will rule our hearts, not fear; let us pray that these events will draw our entire nation close to God; let us pray that these events create a greater dependency upon our Lord; let us pray for the repentance and salvation of all; let us pray that God would be glorified above all things."

For Linda, David, Connie and thousands of others we can do no less.

September 11, 2001: A Response

God where were you yesterday? I looked for you everywhere
You were so hard to find... my father came home from Bible study,
dropped his car keys, a bag of groceries, his Bible to the counter and
looked at me:
"This is a crazy world," he said in a voice pained and flat.
I did not understand until he turned on the T.V.
God did you see?
The television flashed black and white footage of two hijacked planes
flying into New York crashing into the World Trade twin towers
God where were you?
New Yorkers ran through the streets tucking their faces in their shirts.
The ash and smoke, death and dying were all around in my America?
There were men and women... did you see them, God?
Jumping from the buildings like birds with clipped wings.
Did you hold their hands when they made the leap into your world?
The Trade buildings came tumbling down like a child's wooden block
tower.
God did you see?

— From "One Nation Under God" by Kirsten Porter

There are days recorded in history, so crucial, so memorable that we even remember the details of where we were when the event occurred: Stock Market Crash, Pearl Harbor, The President Kennedy Assassination, The Challenger Explosion, The Oklahoma City Bombing. Now we add, September 11, 2001 as a day, which will forever be seared in our brain as a day of unspeakable horror.

There was the corporate president who was delayed taking his son to school. Upon hearing the news, he rushed to his world trade center office and even went partly up the stairs before being forced back. All seven hundred employees are missing. He cried and cried before national TV cameras and vowed to keep the corporation running in order to support those seven hundred families.

There are the firemen and rescue workers working tirelessly night and day, digging through tons of wreckage hoping to find any sign of life. Through cell phone calls, we learned of several passengers who assaulted the hijackers in the fourth plane and averted another possible attack aimed at the Capital or the White House. But what a price they paid for their bravery. Kirsten continues her poem.

God I tried to eat yesterday but my cereal tasted like ash and death.

God I tried to sleep yesterday but my heart hurt and I kept waking

to the memories of police officers pulling people from the wreckage like treasures from a buried chest.

Brave firefighters choking on smoke and tears fighting the fires, the death.

Americans saving themselves, each other and then I found you, God.

An email from a church member asked: "Here is a question that I have pondered since the bombing. In the Old Testament there are numerous accounts of battles, many of which involved tremendous loss of life. These were warranted and often (but not always) threaded with statements that God was on the side of the victors. In the New Testament Jesus tells us we should turn the other cheek: Pretty blunt."

"To me this presents a real paradox. My initial feelings were shock, followed by anger, followed by a desire for retaliation. Part of me wants to say we follow the words of Jesus and turn the other cheek, but honestly my strongest feelings are toward solving the problem, which would result in a massive loss of life. I have heard comments that God can forgive; His forgiveness does not remove the consequences of your actions. If the U.S. doesn't take care of our enemies, they will continue to escalate attacks against the free world. If we do take care of them, a lot of innocent people will suffer. My gut feeling is these concerns are chewing away in our minds."

September 11, 2001: A Response – part 2

Did you see the tears of Americans?
I thought I heard you crying with the country.
You were with us yesterday and today
when we move through the debris waking from a terrible dream.

(from "One Nation Under God" by Kirsten Porter)

Speaking of grade school, an elementary school student wrote shortly after the terrorist attack: *"Dear God: We hope there will be no war and no more plane crashes because we don't want anybody to get hurt again! God bless America."* How do we respond? Do we turn the other cheek? Do we strike back with all the fury America can deliver? What would God have

169

us do… as Christians…. as Americans?

Mayor Guiliani is on the screen his face is drawn like a dark curtain;
his shaking hand is squeezed by another leader and he speaks sadly but
proudly.
Insists we go back to life. Live as normal as possible.
Eat at restaurants, drink coffee at cafes… talk, walk the streets holding
hands
but also pray, give blood, pull the last of the living from the rubble.

Jesus says in the Gospel of Matthew, *"But I say, don't resist an evil per-*
son! If you are slapped on the right cheek, turn the other, too." (5:39) As
my email friend wrote last week: "Petty blunt!" Maybe, Jesus is just talking about a personal confrontation. Right? He's not talking about our
country refusing to go after deadly terrorists! Is he? Maybe but what
Jesus may be more concerned about is our attitude.

God you are with us today and I need to feel you remember
God, this happened in my America
but so did the saving, the prayer services, the candlelight vigils,
the long line to donate blood, the officers giving their lives.
You were with us yesterday.

Maybe the real answer is found later on in the same message from
Jesus in Chapter seven:

1. Stop Judging Others… (1-5) Do not judge people of Arab descent
based on the terrorists.

2. Don't give what is holy to unholy people… (6) Be Realistic. We
really are fighting a war.

3. Keep on asking and you will be given what you ask for… (7-11)
Ask God's guidance first.

4. Do for others what you would like them to do for you… (12) Seek
justice not revenge.

5. Enter God's Kingdom only through the narrow gate… (13-14)

There are no easy answers. Fighting this war will take time, persistence, patience and much courage…

God, you are with us today and I need to feel you remember
the saving in my America
because my dad said this is a crazy world and I'm only 22, God
learning to put trust in a world I can't always trust
so for now I'll put my trust in you and my trust in America
because this is still my America my waving flag of the stars and stripes,
my promised freedom.

Four weeks ago you would think me crazy but here is what you should do. Look for coworkers, friends or even strangers and sincerely ask them: "How are you doing, really? Can I pray for you?" First thing in the morning, ask your fellow workers or students to join you in a prayer group. Pray for each other. Pray for guidance. Pray for our leaders. Pray for the terrorists. Most of all… pray for our country. Four weeks ago, you would have thought I was crazy but today… things change. Things really change!

God I see you so clearly today. You are holding my America;
crying for my America; opening your hands.
You set my America free because we are ready to fly on our own
because God was with us yesterday and God lives in America today.

One Nation Under God

God where were you yesterday?
I looked for you everywhere
You were so hard to find
my father came home from Bible study
dropped his car keys, a bag of groceries, his Bible to the counter
and looked at me
"This is a crazy world," he said
in a voice pained and flat
I did not understand
until he turned on the T.V.
God did you see?

the television flashed black and white footage
two hijacked planes flying into New York
crashing into the World Trade twin towers
God where were you?
when New Yorkers ran through the streets
tucking their faces in their shirts
the ash and smoke, death and dying all around
in my America?
a woman on the radio said it was like confetti
white confetti falling from the skies
I thought of Virginia's white snows in winter
the silvery fall from the skies
was that what death was like?

Virginia winter confetti
there were men, women
did you see them God?
jumping from the buildings
like birds with clipped wings
did you hold their hands
when they made the leap
into your world?
the Trade buildings
came tumbling down
like a child's wooden block tower

God did you see
another hijacked plane crash into the Pentagon
and still another crash in Pennsylvania?
were you sitting next to the woman
who called her husband on the cell phone
and said good bye

did you know there were children at school
studying Geometry, History – the neat type-set of grammar texts
did you know some of these children
came home, fatherless or motherless, changed in one day?
God I tried to eat yesterday
but my bowl of cereal tasted like ash and death
God I tried to sleep yesterday
but my heart hurt
and I kept waking
to the memories of police officers
pulling people from the wreckage
like treasures from a buried chest
brave firefighters choking on smoke and tears
fighting the fires, the death
Americans saving themselves, each other
and then I found you God

later " Attack on America" was the headline
I tried to say it out loud
but the words sounded strange on my lips
in my America?

land of the free , the 4th of July,
desert storm, the America I pledged to in grade school
the 50 stars I counted over and over from my desk
the flag I learned to fold in Girl Scouts
parades and campaign buttons,
the field trips to DC museums and monuments
the pride in my voice on the trip to Europe
when the German man asked where I was from
and I smiled back and answered

"I am from the United States"

"one nation under God-Liberty and Justice for all"
 dear God this all happened in my America
did you see the tears of Americans
I thought I heard you crying with the country
You were with us yesterday
and today
when we move through the debris
waking from a terrible dream
yesterday is a toss and tangle of sheets

Mayor Guiliani is on the screen
his face is drawn like a dark curtain
his shaking hand is squeezed by another leader
and he speaks sadly but proudly
insists we go back to life
live as normal as possible
eat at restaurants, drink coffee at cafés
talk, walk the streets holding hands
but also pray, give blood
pull the last of the living from the rubble

God this happened in my America
but so did the saving, the prayer services
the candlelight vigils
the long line to donate blood
the officers giving their lives
You were with us yesterday

God you are with us today

and I need to feel you, remember
the saving in my America
because my dad said this is a crazy world
and I'm only 22, God
learning to put trust in a world I can't always trust
for now I'll put my trust in you
and my trust in America
because this is still my America
my waving flag of the stars and stripes,
my promised freedom

God I see you so clearly today
You are holding my America
crying for my America
opening your hands

You set my America free
because we are ready to fly on our own
because God was with us yesterday
and God lives in America today

- Kirsten Porter

Breaking The Peanut Butter Habit . . .

Following God's Recipe For A Wonderful Life.

Chapter 5

Surfing Through The Obstacles. . . Of Our Faith

Surfin' for the Lord

You don't hear much about it any more but during the 1960s and early 70s there was nothing cooler than surfing for someone my age. (If you're doing the math, I was - 3. Stop laughing.)

Surfers dared to be different. Most teenagers wore blue jeans with buttoned shirts but surfers wore corduroys with holes in the knees, T-shirts with surfer logos and tennis shoes with no socks. We drove mom's car but surfers drove converted vans with boards on top. Thanks to the influence of Beach Boy's music and movies, surfers were cool dudes and I wanted to be one.

Looking back on my foolish quest, I discovered some lessons and appropriate scripture that can help us all be more successful in life and improve our relationship with God. So, let's go surfin'!

Why Use A Battleship when A Surfboard will do?

To surf, you needed a board. Virginia Beach had small waves so surfboards were small and light. What did I do? I bought a board... *'Cheap'*... from a sailor, out of Hawaii that was over nine feet long, made of oak, weighing seven tons and appropriately nicknamed 'the battleship.' People on the beach laughed when they saw me coming. Surfers in the water avoided me like the plague.

Lesson Learned: Good preparation beats frettin' any day. Nike says, "Just do it!" God says, "Pray first and I will guide your doing!" *Don't worry about anything; instead, pray about everything. Tell God what you need, and thank him for all he has done.* (Philippians 4:6)

Are you doing too much paddlin' and too little surfin'?

Do you know how much energy it takes just to paddle to the surfing area? (Especially with a battleship.) I would huff and puff, thrashing my arms, only to have the next wave pick up the surfboard and fling us back to shore. When I finally arrived, I was too pooped to surf.

Lesson: Is your *'work at it'* too large and your *'faith in it'* too small? Frank Sinatra sings, *"I did it my way."* God says, *If you do this, you will experience God's peace, which is far more wonderful than the human mind can understand. His peace will guard your hearts and minds....* (Verse 7)

A sleeping surfer could get stung.

After finally reaching the surfing area, I could take a few minutes to rest. Dumb move! One time, I woke up, rubbed my eyes, looked around and...

saw the biggest jellyfish in the world. It must have been a deadly Portuguese 'Man of War.' (Of course they aren't normally in Virginia Beach, but it's a good story.) So much for teenage coolness as I screamed and fell off the board setting a new speed record swimming to shore. The surfboard could take care of itself.

Lesson: Do you know when to relax and when to be alert? In this scary world, working to have a better relationship with God can set our priorities straight. Then we are more able to rest peacefully and also be more alert when necessary. *And now, dear friends, let me say one more thing as I close this letter. Fix your thoughts on what is true and honorable and right.* (Verse 8)

Good preparation is as important for life as it is for surfing. Strengthening our relationship with God through prayer, Bible study and church involvement can be the key ingredients to an improved outlook in this world and the next. So grab your board and catch a wave. Surf's up!

Still Surfin' for the Lord

Have you ever been surfin'? After reading the last article, was there a wistful look in your eye that implied, *"No, but I've always wanted too!"* Did you break out the old 'Beach Boys' albums only to discover there isn't a single record player in the house? Admit it we're getting a little old!

But this is about more than surfin' and nostalgia. Good preparation is as important for life as it is for surfing. Strengthening our relationship with God through prayer, Bible study and church involvement can be the key ingredients to an improved outlook on this world and the next. So grab your board and let's see what lessons await us. Surf's up!

Waxing your board beats breaking your gourd.

After finally getting into position, I was ready for my first ride. I could picture myself hangin' five... maybe ten. For you nonsurfer dudes that's the ability to stand on the front of the board and curl either five or ten toes over the edge. Awesome stunt, huh! In my lifetime, I managed to hang... maybe one.

The right wave was coming my way. The 'Battleship' (my oversized board) was in position and I started paddling like mad and caught it. I really did! *"Man, this is easy,"* I thought and stood up... No one ever told me that a surfboard needed to be waxed. It was like trying to stand on a 'slip n slide.' Well, I slipped and slid off the board like it was a gigantic banana peel. So much for hanging ten.

Lesson: A willingness to prepare can save a lot of despair. *Think about things that are pure and lovely and admirable. Think about things that are excellent and worthy of praise.* (Philippians 4:8)

How do you steer this thing?

After applying at least three inches of wax, I went out again, caught a wave, stood up and stayed up. But there was just one tiny problem. ***How do you steer this thing?*** Steering was critical because the surfing area was limited and extremely crowded. The 'Battleship' and I were bearing down on some poor schmuck and all I could do was shout... LOOK OUT! It is simply amazing what a moving surfboard can do. He stepped back just as my board landed and was flipped high enough in the air to qualify for a pole vault competition... They asked me to leave the beach that day.

Lesson: A continual willingness to get up after failing is often the crucial ingredient for success. Never, never, never give up! *Keep putting into practice all you learned from me and heard from me and saw me doing...* V9

Shootin' the tube makes a happy surfer dude!

Finally... I began to get the hang of surfing. There are few thrills that compare with catching a wave and riding it all the way to the shore. Surfing is ultimately a combination of preparation, patience, a never-give up attitude and a deep love and respect for the power of the ocean wave.

Could this also be the secret of living a godly life? A combination of preparation, patience, a never-give-up attitude and a deep love and respect for the power of God? Once you get the hang of it... there is no thrill that can compare with totally surrendering your life to God. Nothing!

Lesson: The right journey is always worth the sacrifice. *...and the God of peace will be with you.* V9

May the wind of the Holy Spirit be at your back and the waves of opportunity tall as you surf and serve for God! So... what are you waiting for? Surf's Up!

Breaking the Endless Cycle of Guilt and Shame

On our first visit, after a few moments, she began to weep. *"I'm so sorry."* For the next hour, I heard a sad story of mistakes, misunderstandings and family disagreements. None of them seemed all that serious, but her speech was tortured with words of guilt and hurt. *"Will God ever for-*

give me?" she asked. For another hour we talked of God's healing comfort and grace and studied the appropriate Biblical passages. Finally we said a prayer together with her asking God for forgiveness. All in all, it was exactly what a pastor should do on a visit. I felt satisfied.

On our second visit, after a few moments, she began to weep. *"I'm so sorry!"* For the next hour, I heard the same sad story of mistakes, misunderstandings and family disagreements. Just like before, her speech was tortured with words of guilt and hurt. *"Will God ever forgive me?"* she asked. For another hour we talked again of God's healing comfort and grace and studied the appropriate Biblical passages. Finally we said a prayer together with her asking God for forgiveness. All in all, it was exactly what a pastor should do on a visit. This time, I felt puzzled.

On our third visit, after a few moments, she again started to weep and I began to worry. The sad story of mistakes, misunderstandings and family disagreements came as if every word had been carefully memorized. Like a broken record, her speech was tortured with the same words of guilt and hurt. *"Will God ever forgive me?"* she asked. Again, I reminded her of God's healing comfort and grace as we studied appropriate Biblical passages. We said a prayer together with her still passionately asking God for forgiveness. All in all, it was exactly what a pastor should do on a visit. So why was I so confused?

What was this poor woman's problem? Why did she continue to torture herself with guilt and bitterness? God had forgiven her so why couldn't she forgive herself?

Jesus spoke often of God's forgiveness, but he also spoke of the need for reconciliation. He said: *"So if you are standing before the altar…, offering a sacrifice to God and you suddenly remember that someone has something against you, leave your sacrifice there beside the altar. Go and be reconciled to that person. Then come and offer your sacrifice to God."*

(Matthew 5:23-26)

Reconciliation means to settle an argument or to make adjustments in a difficult relationship. You cannot reconcile without getting actively involved and making the compromises necessary to resolve a particular situation. One reason this woman suffered was because she wanted God to wave a magic wand of forgiveness without any active participation from her.

Armed with newfound knowledge, I prepared to visit her a fourth time.

179

Again, she began to weep and tell her sad story of mistakes and misunderstandings. This time, I interrupted her and began to talk about God's gift of healing reconciliation. At first, she looked as if I had lost my mind, but didn't stop me. After a moment we prayed and I left having no idea what would happen next.

Months later, during a family gathering, she was given the opportunity to tell her story. It wasn't easy, but after hours of talking and crying, years of misunderstandings and deep hurts were brought into the open and God's wonderful grace began to heal a broken and deeply divided family. Reconciliation may be one of the most difficult responsibilities we could ever face but the potential rewards make it all worthwhile.

On a later visit, after a few moments, she began to weep. *"I'm so sorry,"* but then she began to laugh. *"So much has changed!"* For the next hour, I heard about family get-togethers and exploits of wayward grandchildren. Her speech was more animated and full of life and hope. For another few minutes we talked about community and church concerns. Finally we said a prayer together. All in all, it was exactly what a pastor should do on a visit. I felt enormously thankful.

:- (Demotivators: A Key to Success?

I love motivational products! One of my favorite pictures shows a lighthouse brightly shining in the midst of a fierce storm. The caption reads… *"**Possibilities**: The only way to discover the limits of the possible is to go beyond them into the impossible."* Isn't that great? But sometimes too much of a good thing is well… too much. After all, how many soaring eagles and lighthouses can one person own?

Several years ago, I received a calendar from Despair, Inc. On the cover was a picture of the infamous Leaning Tower of Pisa. The caption read: *"Mediocrity – It takes a lot less time and most people won't notice the difference until it's too late."* Can you believe that? Another page on the calendar showed a snow skier in mid-flight heading for a big fall. Underneath were the words: *"Ineptitude – If you can't learn to do something well, learn to enjoy doing it poorly."*

E.L. Kersten, designed this publication titled: "Monthly Inspirations for Underachievers, Pessimists and the Chronically Unsuccessful." In the introduction he writes: *"For over a decade, motivational products have promoted 'Success,' 'Quality' and the importance of 'Determination.' As wonderful as these notions sound, the sad fact is that not everyone wins, cares or even tries. That's why our Demotivators champion the often-over-looked merits of 'Mediocrity,' 'Pessimism' and even outright 'Failure.'"*

How about this one: A photo of a teenage baseball player sitting alone on the team bench. The shadows of the sinking sun highlight his lowered head and slumping body. Obviously, the game is over for him. The caption: *"Losing – If at first you don't succeed, failure may be your style."* Crash! Do you ever get tired of hearing, "No Pain – No Gain?" Here is Demotivators version: A boxer being hit so hard that his face is contorted in – *"Agony – Not all pain is gain."* Ouch!

Let's face some hard facts. The events of September 11, 2001 are a permanent reminder that life can be incredibly difficult and unfair at times. Hard work does not always lead to success. Some people are more gifted than others. Lightning strikes good people and bad. For every winner there are dozens of losers. The list goes on and on... Becoming more motivated is no guarantee of happiness. So the real question becomes, *"If life is so unfair with no promises of success, where do we go for help?"*

The author of Ecclesiastes wrote in despair that life is... meaningless. But he ultimately found meaning... How? By obeying and following God's will. *"People who do this rarely look with sorrow on the past, for God has given them reasons for joy."* (Ecclesiastes 5:20) Here are God's promises:

✝ *It is useless for you to work so hard from early morning until late at night, anxiously working for food to eat; for God gives rest to his loved ones.* (Psalm 127:2)

✝ *I look up to the mountains— does my help come from there? My help comes from the LORD, who made the heavens and the earth! He will not let you stumble and fall; the one who watches over you will not sleep... The LORD himself watches over you! ... The LORD keeps watch over you as you come and go, both now and forever.* (Psalm 121)

✝ *So I tell you, don't worry about everyday life – whether you have enough food, drink and clothes... Can all your worries add a single moment to your life? Of course not.* (Matthew 6:25,27)

✝ *Don't worry about anything; instead, pray about everything. Tell God what you need and thank him for all he has done. If you do this, you will experience God's peace, which is far more wonderful than the human mind can understand.* (Philippians 4: 6-7)

Put these four scriptures together and what do you get?

1. Hard work and motivation alone will never ultimately satisfy. Trust in God to give you rest.
2. Look to the mountains… your help comes from a God who will watch over and protect you.
3. Worries about everyday necessities interfere with your faith and add nothing to your life.
4. Replace worry with prayer and you will begin to experience God's peace to guard your heart.

Maybe in today's environment, this is the motivation we really need. *"People who do this rarely look with sorrow on the past, for God has given them reasons for joy."* I feel better already. Do you? Now if I could just find a way to put this on a poster. First, I need a lighthouse… (Larry, please spare me.)

For a catalog of Demotivators products, visit their website at www.despair.com.

Sometimes You're the Windshield…
Sometimes You're the Bug!

I was feeling on top of the world. There were no calls of distress and the pile of paperwork was finally beginning to shrink. Then came the shrill ring of the phone.

"Mr. Davies, this is the high school. Your son is not in school today."

"You must be mistaken," I said, trying to sound calm. *"He left the house on time. Are you sure, he's not there?"*

"Yes sir. We have a new policy of notifying parents when students are absent or tardy. Our records show your son as absent," replied the calm professional voice.

"Thank you for letting me know."

Like any reasonable parent with a sixteen-year-old son, I responded immediately. **I panicked!** My little car nearly did a wheelie as I spun out of the driveway and flew down the highway toward the high school. (Of course my speedometer never went past 55!)

"Has he been in an accident on the way to school?" I thought. *"Oh God, please protect my son."*

"Maybe he's skipping school with friends." I wondered. *"Oh God, I'm gonna kill him! I'll take his car keys away and he'll ride the bus! He'll be*

grounded for a month! A year! For Life!"

While spinning into the parking lot, tires a-smokin', I noticed the familiar brown car that could only be my child's. After running into the office and checking with the secretary, I was assured that it was only an administrative error and my son was safely inside the classroom.

"Whew! I can breathe again!"

Have you heard the country song: *"Sometimes you're the windshield. Sometimes you're the bug?"* I'm beginning to understand what that statement means. In the few short seconds of one phone call, the peace and tranquility of my "windshield" morning was shattered. Instead of being in control, I was a helpless "bug" hurtling down the highway with no way of knowing what tragedy would occur next.

This time, I was fortunate because nothing happened but what about next time? I may not be so fortunate. *"What about you?"* It's true, you know. As much as you may try to remain a "windshield," (pay close attention to these next words) you will occasionally be the "bug." You may get squashed!

This is why you and I need God! Jesus told a story about two builders. The foolish one built a house on a foundation of sand. The winds and the storms came and the house collapsed. The wise builder used a foundation of rock. (Pay close attention again) "The rain came down, the streams rose, and the winds blew and beat against the house; yet it did not fall." (Mat. 7:25) Both builders faced the same storms, but only one house survived. **God is our foundation.**

God never promised a storm-free, bug-free life. God provides a solid survival plan.

Are you feeling like a "windshield" or a "bug?" (You can trust me here.) Occasionally, there will be both experiences. Your continued struggle to follow God in the midst of either experience will become the solid foundation of rock against the inevitable storms.

May God give you humility and love when you feel like a "windshield." May God give you a solid foundation of peace and strength when you feel like a "bug."

The Power of One: Inside & Outside

You are called by God to make a difference in your own unique way. Usually, it is by utilizing your talents and abilities to work within your

183

church, family or occupation. Occasionally you could be called to say or do something dramatic that at first stands against the majority but like the rudder of a great ship eventually causes an organization or family to altar course. Dramatic examples of both happened during our statewide denominational meeting in Roanoke, Virginia.

Bishop Pennel made a difference on the inside by using the influence of his office to help our conference accomplish two major goals:

1. Leave Roanoke, Virginia and the world a better place than before. The list speaks for itself: Four Habitat for Humanity houses dedicated, 21 tons of potatoes bagged, $398,000 worth of World Service kits containing medical supplies and other needs, $310,000 collected to benefit children around the world and much more.

2. The primary focus of our four-day meeting was shifted from mostly business to worship, Bible study and helping others. Reports were shortened or eliminated to make room for more worship services, a study of Ephesians and celebrations of how our denomination made a difference in people's lives.

On day three during a long and tiring session, Bishop Pennel made an inappropriate comment to one of our delegates. It was a minor verbal gaffe that was noticed and quickly forgiven and forgotten by most. But within a few hours, the Bishop stood before our entire gathering and confessed his poor choice of words and asked our forgiveness. It wasn't necessary but became a potent lesson on humility. Pennel's leadership had an impact on all of us.

One person, an insider used the authority and influence of his position to make a difference. Could this be the work of God?

Another individual, an outsider who had no institutional authority or influence stood alone before the establishment and pleaded for change… and we changed.

Andrew Pearson, a youth delegate from Winchester wrote a resolution requiring United Methodist colleges to "discontinue use of alcohol in any form or place or by any personnel on campus." The Board of Higher Education responded by politely thanking Mr. Pearson and submitting a substitute resolution calling for continuing the alcohol awareness programs already in progress.

Andrew stood before our conference and told of his desire to attend one of our schools but could not because of the alcohol problem. "Awareness and treatment programs are not enough. Our conference needs to take a stand," he said. For nearly an hour, the issue was passionately debated. The close vote had to be counted several times but Andrew's resolution passed.

One person, an insider used the authority and influence of his position to make a difference. Could this be the work of God? Another person, an outsider had the courage to stand before a statewide gathering and call for change. The insiders tried to stop him but in the end... we listened and changed. Could this too be the work of God?

Paul described the church in Ephesians like this: *Under his (Christ's) direction, the whole body is fitted together perfectly. As each part does its own special work, it helps the other parts grow, so that the whole body is healthy and growing and full of love.* (4:16)

Do you have a valued place within the body of Christ? "Of course you do!" We are all necessary. Are you doing your part to help us stay healthy and growing and full of love? That is up to you. Insider or outsider makes no difference. You are given unique abilities by God to make a difference in our community and our world. So, what are you waiting for? Permission? Go for it!

Ways to Improve Your Integrity

The ancient Chinese built the "Great Wall" which stretches for several thousand miles, to ensure their security from foreign invaders. Yet during the first hundred years after the wall was completed, China was successfully invaded three times, not by going over the wall or tearing it down, but by bribing the guards and simply marching through the gates. China spent years building the "Great Wall" but didn't spend enough time building the character of the gatekeepers.

America is the strongest country in the world today... by far. There is no equal, militarily or economically. The communist threat has disappeared so whom do we have to fear? The answer: ourselves! I received a joke giving the root definition for politics: "poli" which is Latin for many and "tics" which are blood-sucking creatures. Put it together and what do you have? Ouch!

Wall Street has been filled with cases of insider trading and even religious leaders have been involved in sex scandals and misappropriation of church funds. All of these instances serve as examples of serious erosion of our integrity.

David wrote Psalm 15 to help us set strong standards that would define our integrity as people of God. First he asks the question: *Who may worship in your sanctuary, Lord? Who may enter your presence on your holy hill?* In other words, "What kind of individual has an intimate relationship with God? What standards does God expect of us?"

1. *Those who lead blameless lives...* Do we live out what we believe? Do we walk and speak with integrity?
2. *...and do what is right...* This involves our day-to-day habits and choices in life.
3. *...speaking the truth from sincere hearts.* Do we really mean what we say?
4. *Those who refuse to slander others...* You cannot claim to love your neighbor while spreading gossip and rumors behind their backs.
5. *...or harm their neighbors or speak evil of their friends...* We avoid being judgmental and treat people with respect.
6. *Those who despise persistent sinners...* It may be good to witness to the wrong crowd, but it's dangerous to run around with them. Who is influencing whom?
7. *...and honor the faithful followers of the Lord...* We often become like the people we hang with so we should spend our time wisely with those who can help strengthen our faith.
8. *...and keep their promises even when it hurts.* We do what we say, even when it is not in our best interest. The baseball player, Ted Williams, is famous for voluntarily cutting his salary after a bad year. It's been over thirty years and people still talk about it. That's integrity.
9. *Those who do not charge interest on the money they lend...* This is not about banks or business but how you help a friend in need: generously and unselfishly.
10. *...and who refuse to accept a bribe to testify against the innocent.* We have positions of trust. We do not accept favors to corrupt our conduct...ever.

Ten standards designed to guide our Godly integrity. Can you possibly do all of them? Of course not! That is why you and I need God and why we need to be in church. We do our best and trust in God for the rest. Psalm 15 ends with this promise: ***"Such people will stand firm forever."***

A preacher once gave a sermon on honesty. The next day, she took the bus into town and after taking a seat noticed she was given too much change. She tried to convince herself that the extra money was a gift from

God but knew better. Before getting off the bus she handed the driver the extra money and said: *"You made a mistake and gave me too much change?"*

"That was no mistake," said the driver with a smile. *"I was in your church yesterday and heard your sermon on honesty. So this morning, I gave you a little test!"*

People are watching. What will they see in you?

That Didn't Hurt!

Playing around sewing machines was a dumb thing to do, even for a four-year-old. Too much running and not enough looking eventually causes accidents and mine was a big one. The shelf for holding the fabric was just above eye level and I hit it hard and started screaming. Blood was spurting everywhere. Normally sane adults were panic-stricken as I found myself being thrown into a car and rushed to the local hospital emergency room.

"He'll need three stitches just over his left eye," said the doctor. The three adults who brought me all nodded in agreement. Of course, I didn't know any of this. Instead, I saw a big man walking over towards me preparing to cover my head with a sheet. (They did that in those days!) Blind and scared, I did what only comes natural for a four-year-old in a fix. **I screamed and kicked my bloody head off.**

They told me later that one man held my head, another laid across my body while four more held a leg or an arm, all as the poor doctor applied the local anesthetic and three little stitches. What made this experience so memorable was that immediately following the surgery, I sat up and looked around the room, smiled and said, **"That didn't hurt!"**

The adults involved laugh now, but at the time, they wanted to give me a demonstration of real pain by tanning my backside! Why was I so frightened? Was I just a wimp? (Don't answer!)

I was feeling the real pain of the head injury plus a fear of something unknown represented by the mysterious sheet covering my eyes. The combination made for one scared little boy. The reality, however, was not nearly so bad as what I feared so in the end... I could smile (while everyone else groaned) and confidently say... that didn't hurt or that wasn't so bad!

As we grow older we often face situations that cause real pain but the danger comes when we combine the actual pain with the fear of the

unknown. It then becomes a formula for disaster.
- The boss wanders into your office unexpectedly and asks to meet with you in the morning...
- Your doctor calls and wants to discuss your latest test results personally...
- A good friend has become more distant lately with no explanations...

What would be your response? Would you stay up all night worrying then charge in the next morning demanding an explanation? Maybe there would be a few phone calls in the middle of the night to friends while you cry over imagined tragedies? Would you visit a local tavern or liquor store and quietly drink your troubles away?

Life is like that. We get scared of the unknown and start kicking and screaming instead of trusting in God to see us through. Here are some realistic spiritual remedies to help calm your fears:
- Psalm 34:4 — *I prayed to the Lord, and he answered me, freeing me from all my fears.*
- Matthew 6:25-27 – *"So I tell you, don't worry about everyday life— whether you have enough food, drink, and clothes. Doesn't life consist of more than food and clothing? Look at the birds. They don't need to plant or harvest or put food in barns because your heavenly Father feeds them. And you are far more valuable to him than they are. Can all your worries add a single moment to your life? Of course not."*
- 1 John 4:18 — *Such love has no fear because perfect love expels all fear. If we are afraid, it is for fear of judgment, and this shows that his love has not been perfected in us.*

What do you really fear? Can you learn to replace that fear with faith in God's love for you?

In the end, we can rely on the promise that God offers us all the chance face our fears with boldness and say... ***"That didn't hurt!"***

Three Stories of Courage and Faith

"It's been a rough week! You too? Would you like a little inspiration? Here are the stories of three brave souls who have demonstrated extraordinary courage in the face of difficulty."

For some, 'Vietnam' is only an appalling memory. For others born after 1970, the war represents a few pages in a history book and an occasional, *"remember when..."* discussion around the kitchen table. But for our vets, the injuries, physical and emotional are as real today as they were thirty

188

years ago when our nation's finest were fighting and dieing by the thousands overseas.

Recently, our church Missions Team was asked to provide a little help for **David Roberts**, a Vietnam vet working to finish building his dream house. Most of the frame was up, but he needed a little help with the roof. While working on his house, we discovered that Dave, in addition to being a pretty good builder, was also a gifted poet and a championship bowler. Normally, none of this would be considered all that unusual except that David also lost both legs fighting in Vietnam.

We expected to find a helpless, dejected human being dealing with tragedy. Instead we found a human dynamo of energy and enthusiasm that easily outworked and out hustled most of us. It was amazing to watch how he creatively managed to work, even on the roof. Before long, he was just one of the guys, laughing and telling jokes while hammering away: His handicap forgotten.

Courage can also be found in **Eddie Harris,** a talented musician and gifted minister. For several years, Eddie and his wife, Laurie had been a creative influence behind many of our church's musical projects. More importantly, his enthusiasm and love for God was displayed in everything he did. I recently received word that doctors discovered a dangerous parasite in his brain. The only known treatment is a drug commonly called sulfa. Unfortunately, Eddie is allergic to sulfa.

Eddie has lost most of his motor skills and is barely able to eat or talk. From a medical point of view, the doctors offer little hope. He has every right to be bitter, but a loving family refuses to allow it. When I arrived, Laurie was pushing his wheel chair in a race with another patient. In his room, there are plants and cards everywhere. Next to the bed is a beautiful electric piano. You see, Eddie can still play and does frequently. I'm told you often hear the sounds of laughter and singing as the Harris family continues to celebrate God's love in the midst of personal tragedy.

Margaret Yancey is the mother of a close friend. For the last several weeks, she has been in constant pain from something the doctors cannot seem to diagnose. She eats little and as her health and energy continues to deteriorate her family must make critical decisions: Should Margaret be at home with professional care? Should she be in a nursing care facility?

A minister friend visited the hospital to offer Margaret comfort and the prayers of his church. When asked if she would like to pray she said,

"Certainly." As everyone bowed their heads the pastor prepared to speak but was interrupted by the voice of Margaret who began her own beautiful prayer praising God. The pastor could only reply: *"I can't add anything to that!"*

Three stories of tragedy yet we also see three stunning examples of courage and faith.

Maybe this explains why Paul could confidently write: *"Can anything ever separate us from Christ's love? Does it mean he no longer loves us if we have trouble or calamity, or are persecuted, or are hungry or cold or in danger or threatened with death? No, despite all these things, overwhelming victory is ours through Christ, who loved us."*   (Romans 8:35-37)

No one would blame David, Eddie or Margaret for becoming bitter in the midst of his or her suffering. Yet all of them chose courage and their living examples of faith serve as motivation for us all. So, despite every tragedy life can throw at us, the promise of God is… *"overwhelming victory is ours through Christ who loved us."* Isn't that great? I feel better already. Don't you?

Finding and Pursuing Success

"How would you define success?" Must you be rich? Own your company? Become famous? Does it include world travel? Extensive education? Becoming the best in your field? Does success include happiness, good health and a sexy body? A strong marriage and family? God?

Recently I was one of over eight thousand people jammed into the Richmond, Virginia Coliseum at Peter Lowe's Success Seminar. A dear friend sent a ticket and I used it to explore my own path to success and receive a little positive motivation. For eleven hours, I listened to ten of the best speakers in the world share their ideas on success. For example:

★**Elizabeth Dole** talked about how old-fashioned values still succeed in a modern world.

★**Zig Ziglar** spoke of the importance of relationships as a part of success: business relationships, family relationships and especially our relationship with God.

★**John Walsh** founder of "America's Most Wanted" openly shared his personal struggles with coping with the murder of his son to show how we can turn tragedy into triumph.

★**Dr. Jack Groppel** helped us understand how proper eating habits and exercise can actually tune our bodies and minds into more productive tools for success.

★**Brian Tracy** showed how appropriate goal setting could transform our lives.

★**Peter Lowe** spoke of five levels of success and how we are often allow ourselves to be trapped at a lower level. How can we push beyond what we know into what we can be?

★**Christopher Reeve,** famous as an actor and of course, survivor and tireless advocate for victims of spinal cord injury made a comment to Peter Lowe that will forever define success for me. *"Success means so many things. I think it really means letting the relationships in your life grow and transcend into the highest possible levels they possibly can. It also means not putting yourself first in life and remembering that the more you give away, the more you have."*

Mr. Reeve has earned the right to cry out… *"I'm a victim. Take care of me. Let me wallow in my pain."* Yet he chose to do the best he could with what he had by concentrating on two essential ingredients of success:

●*Letting relationships grow and transcend into the highest possible levels.* This level of success often calls for a willingness to shift your priorities and work at developing stronger relationships in business, friendships, family and especially with God.

●*Not putting yourself first in life and remembering that the more you give away, the more you have.* Putting others first is often portrayed as a sign of weakness, but actually it is an indicator of vast strength. Zig Ziglar says: *"You can have everything you want if you will just help enough other people get what they want."* Success means learning to give.

The Apostle Paul wrote about this kind of success: *"I can never stop thanking God for all the generous gifts he has given you, now that you belong to Christ Jesus. He has enriched your church with the gifts of eloquence and every kind of knowledge. This shows that what I told you about Christ is true. Now you have every spiritual gift you need as you eagerly wait for the return of our Lord Jesus Christ. He will keep you strong right up to the end…"* (1 Corinthians 1:4-8)

 ✟ Success means… *learning* to thank God for the generous gifts given to you.
 ✟ Success means… *knowing* you belong to Christ.
 ✟ Success means… *understanding* that you have been enriched with gifts and knowledge.
 ✟ Success means… *using* those gifts as you eagerly wait for Christ's return.

✝ Success means... *relying* on God to keep you strong right up to the end.

Are you looking for that elusive obsession called success? First, discover what success truly means and then be willing to work for it with every talent you possess. Paul near the end of the same letter wrote *"...be strong and steady, always enthusiastic about the Lord's work, for you know that nothing you do for the Lord is ever useless."* (1 Corinthians 15:58)

Words that Hurt or Words that Heal

Words can hurt! Our family moved to a new area as I entered the seventh grade. During the first week of school, I decided to try out for the chorus. Since I already participated in our church choir singing sounded like a great way to make friends and have fun. But as I timidly opened the door to the music room, the singing and the laughter stopped as everyone stared at the new kid... me.

I was summoned to the piano and the teacher handed me a piece of music. She then started playing with the expectation that I would sing. Reading unfamiliar music while also trying to sing was nearly impossible and it was obvious by the knowing looks and snickers of the other children that I was not doing well. The next words out of the teacher's mouth devastated what little self-esteem I still possessed. *"I'm sorry... you are not qualified to sing in our school chorus."*

I remember being upset and crying but I got over the initial hurt quickly enough and went on to other interests. I still made a few friends and enjoyed a normal childhood. I'm happy to confess that I didn't grow up to be a mass murderer, drink orange juice out of a baby bottle or have a torrid affair with an intern. *"So Larry, why are you making such a big deal about it now?*

Words can hurt! Looking back on it, I'm amazed how much effect those words had on my life. To me, the teacher was an authority figure who understood music. *If she said I can't sing then... I can't sing therefore I won't sing.* Over the next few months, I quit the church choir and when singing with others, began to lower my voice so no one would actually hear me.

Words can hurt! While reading this were you reminded of a time when someone said something that hurt you deeply? Very likely! We've all been victimized by words just as we have damaged others with hurtful criticism and inappropriate comments. Yet, occasionally we must offer criticism and if we are to experience growth we must also accept disapproval. So, what are we to do?

The lesson is in understanding and utilizing the power of one word: encouragement.

The author of Hebrews wrote to a struggling church: *"Without wavering, let us hold tightly to the hope we say we have, for God can be trusted to keep his promise. Think of ways to <u>encourage</u> one another to outbursts of love and good deeds."* (10:23-24) To <u>encourage</u> means to inspire another with courage. We hold on to our hope by trusting God and inspiring others with courage.

Becoming an encourager doesn't simply mean speaking in flowery platitudes but analysis should be offered respectfully and prayerfully for the purpose of inspiring another with courage. As an encourager, I learn to be confident of God's love and understand that unsuitable and even hurtful comments should be lovingly but firmly ignored. With God's encouragement we can all do that.

Yes, the music teacher was cruel in the way that she dealt with my musical abilities but I now understand that it is a choice to accept the criticism as valid and have the courage to adjust or reject the comments as inappropriate and have the courage to reject them. The choice is mine.

Encouragement means that words can also heal! Nearly twenty years later, a choir director walked up and said: *"I heard you singing during worship today and really liked the sound of your voice. Would you be interested in joining our choir?"* Thanks to her continuing encouragement, I did join the choir and rediscovered that I could really sing after all… sort of. *Words can heal!*

Words can hurt or words can heal. God lovingly gives us the freedom to choose how we use words and how we receive them. My prayer is that we will all strive to be encouragers and use our words wisely to inspire others to outbursts of love and good deeds. Maybe that is what being the church is all about. We could certainly do worse! *Hey, maybe I should sing a solo? Not!!*

Worry, Trust & Chairs

Worry is like a rocking chair... *"It will give you something to do, but won't get you anywhere."* Worry is like a disease that infects everyone yet no one seeks a cure. Worry is considered a legitimate past time, almost an honor, but worry is still a sin: a dangerous sin that can ruin our physical and spiritual vitality and drain our lives of joy. Yet, knowing that, I still worry... a lot!

▸ I worry about my nearly grown children.
▸ I worry if I'm being a good husband.
▸ I worry about my job and the church I serve.
▸ I worry over my friends and family.

There is a story about a farmer meeting "Death" on the road. "Death said, "I'm going to kill ten thousand people tomorrow." Recoiling at the horror, the farmer decided to spend the rest of the day warning everyone about the coming catastrophe. That night as death passed by again, the frustrated farmer said, "You were going to kill ten thousand people, yet seventy thousand died." Death replied, "I killed only ten thousand. Worry killed the others!"

Can we really stop worrying? Probably not but we can learn to replace *worry* with *trust*.

We can start learning about *"trust"* from the book of Proverbs. Imagine a wise parent giving advice to their teenager and you begin to understand the message of this wonderful book. At one point, the parent says: *"Trust in the Lord with all your heart; do not depend on your own understanding. Seek his will in all you do, and he will direct your paths."* (3:5-6)

There are three commands and a promise:

If you learn to... *Trust in the Lord with all your heart?*

If you practice... *Do not depend on your own understanding?*

If you are careful to... *Seek his will in all you do?*

Then, God's promise is to... *direct your paths.*

Trust is God's antidote for worry. The more we trust... the less we worry but how? Stop depending on yourself and seek God's will. You do that by spending more time on your knees in prayer. A friend suggested: *"Larry, rather than worry all night, wouldn't it be smarter to pray half the night and then sleep comfortably until morning?"* Sound advice.

▸ Replacing worry with trust enables me to pray for my children but allow them to grow up.

- Replacing worry with trust gives me the ability to enjoy and appreciate my wife.
- Replacing worry with trust permits me to work hard and leave the results to God.
- Replacing worry with trust helps me relax and truly value my friends and family.

During a routine visit with an elderly member of the church, a minister noticed an empty chair was always by his bed and asked about it. The old man replied, *"As a child, I had a difficult time learning to pray. A pastor suggested that I place a chair in front of me and picture Jesus Christ sitting with me as a friend. What would I say to Jesus? That chair has helped me ever since."*

A few days later, the daughter called to tell the pastor that the old man was dead. *"I was only out of the room for a minute. When I returned, he was gone. There was no change in him except I noticed that his hand was resting on the chair... the empty chair."*

It's been said that ulcers are caused not by what you eat, but by what is eating you! Are you being eaten alive by worries? Maybe you need to replace your rocking chair of human worries with an empty chair of heavenly trust. All it takes is a commitment to pray. Let's face it: It beats staying up all night.

1-800-2HEAVEN

Children have a way of asking the most interesting questions. Many years ago, I was busy studying when my then eleven-year-old son, Stephen, walked into the office and asked: "Dad, how did you ever become a minister?"

"I received a 'call' from God, son."

He obviously wasn't satisfied: "What does that mean, dad? Did God call you on the telephone?"

Looking up, I said in jest, "Why of course, God did call me on the phone."

Stephen with a trace of a giggle: "What telephone number did you use to call God...1-800-HEAVEN?"

I mentally counted out the letters and answered, "That's close, but the actual number is 1-800-2HEAVEN!" At that Stephen grinned and left the room while I continued reading.

A few minutes later, my mischievous son came back into the room with a twinkle in his eye and smile on his face: "I called 1-800-2HEAVEN. Do you want to know what happened?"

Quickly putting down my book, "I've got to hear this!"

"I called 1-800-2HEAVEN and an answering machine said they were closed now, but please call back between the hours of 8:00 AM and 5:00 PM Monday through Friday."

After we finished laughing, we both concluded, God does answer "Calls," but only from 8 - 5, Monday through Friday.

Does God really "Call" us?

Yes, of course, but don't take my word for it. I did a word search in the Bible and found "call" or "called" or "calling" appears in the Bible 779 times. Here are a few examples:

- Are you looking for answers to tough questions? *"Seek the Lord while He may be found; call on Him while He is near.* (Isaiah 55:6)
- Do you wonder if God hears your cry for help? *"I call on you, O God, for you will answer me; give ear to me and hear my prayer."* (Ps 17:6)
- Do you need to know God forgives you? *"But I call to God, and the Lord saves me."* (Ps 55:16)
- Are you feeling poorly? *"Is any one of you sick? He should call the elders of the church to pray over him..."* (James 5:14)
- Do you feel unworthy of hearing God's call? *"Jesus said: 'It is not the healthy, who need a doctor, but the sick. I have not come to call the righteous, but sinners."* (Mark 2:17)
- Are you wondering what God has planned for you? *"For God did not call us to be impure, but to live a holy life."* (1 Thessalonians 4:7)

God's call is an exciting part of our regular Christian walk. Are you ready to hear it?

By the way, 1-800-2HEAVEN is still not the correct answer. While writing this column, I called and received yet another recording. This time a sweet, soft voice replied, "Heavenly Tahoe Vacations Inc., which happily promised a angelic vacation package to meet every need."

Is this a great country or what?

Alien Visitors

I was raking leaves… (I hate it.) Suddenly a space ship appeared out of nowhere and landed in a field less than fifty yards from our house. Immediately I put down the rake and ran to investigate. (Any excuse to quit raking!) Two creatures stepped out. They looked almost human except for their green, crusty skin. They walked up and introduced themselves as Mort and Mirth from the planet, Morph. *"We are on a fact finding tour. Is this a typical earth town?"* he asked? (I think it was a he.)

"As typical as Mayberry, RFD!" I answered.

"We are studying religions. What Gods do you worship in this town?" Mirth, the other alien asked.

Like the puffed-up preacher I can occasionally be, I exclaimed, "We worship the One Holy God and His Son, Jesus Christ our Lord who lives in us through the Holy Spirit."

Mort paused for a moment and said, *"Where do you worship God?"*

"Why in church buildings like the one across from my house." I answered, beginning to wonder if these aliens from Morph knew anything about us earthlings at all.

Mirth quickly replied, *"We have visited your churches. They are seldom used and often empty. We have concluded very few earthlings actually follow this God you named. After careful observation, we discovered most humans actually worship idols."*

"Idol worship!" I scoffed. "You must be joking. We haven't practiced that since Old Testament days."

"Oh but you do worship idols," exclaimed Mort. *"There are idols in every earthling house."*

"Are there any idols in my house?" I asked nervously.

Mirth looked at Mort. They both looked at my house bowed their head and began to moan. After a moment the moans stopped and Mirth turned to me and said, *"Yes, we count five."*

"**Five!** How could you see five idols in a Methodist ministers home?" I asked. "Where are they?"

"There is one in the kitchen and another in the den. There is also one in each of your three bedrooms."

"Do you mean my televisions? Are you kidding? TV's aren't idols. They're earthling entertainment."

"Oh no," said Mort. *"Earthlings watch the idols hour after hour. You*

197

even have a Holy Book."

He reached inside his bag and pulled out a recent "TV Guide". *"This Holy Book tells you when to pray before the idol and what you will see. I especially like this worship time called* 'The X Files.' *"*

"One of the characters in the show looks just like my cousin Mymph." Added Mirth.

"If you think that's good, you ought to see "Third Rock From the Sun.' " I said. "Wait a minute, you can't seriously believe that TV is our idol just because we spend three hours a day watching it?"

"What else do you earthlings spend three to four hours a day doing beside working?" Mort replied.

I couldn't answer him. Can you? God says, *"Do not worship any other gods besides me. Do not make idols of any kind..."* (Exodus 20:3-4) Television can be a useful informational tool and occasional source of entertainment but too much TV robs you of precious hours that are better spent improving a friendship, spending time with your family or with God. Choose wisely and occasionally turn off the TV. Now if Mort and Mirth would only tell me to stop raking leaves.

It's Been A Really Bad Day, Lord!

Sometimes, you are better off just staying in bed. I recently received the following prayer request:

"Rev. Larry… it has been a BEAR of a day to be sure! I recently received a ticket for an expired inspection sticker. Unfortunately, in the midst of other problems, losing my job, divorce and being forced to move… I totally forgot about it! Yesterday, I received a notice that my license had been suspended! So, I promptly went down to the courthouse to pay the fine and was on my way to DMV. A police officer pulled me over because I was driving with an expired license plate. I told him where I'd been and where I was headed. He said he'd have to check on it. He came back and told me he was sorry but he was going to have to give me another ticket and he was being nice not to take me to JAIL! He asked if I knew anyone to call who would come and pick me up because I could not drive away."

"Larry, I told him that I didn't know anyone because I was new to the area. He said to think about it while he was writing the ticket. (As if a friend would materialize out of nowhere because I got stopped!) So I sat there and thought about it. After writing the ticket, he asked if I had thought of anyone to call, and I explained to him for the fourth time about my divorce, being forced to move and that I didn't have anyone's number in the area. He said, *"Too Bad, I can't take you. So... Good Luck"* and drove away while it was raining! Thankfully, a nice lady offered a ride. What a day! Larry... please pray for me!"

(Note: I checked with a police officer friend who made it very clear this was not normal procedure. He would not have abandoned her under any circumstance excluding emergency.)

Have you ever had days, months or even years, that start bad... and then get worse? Where your problems don't just add up... they multiply? When you think you've finally reached the floor of your difficulties only to discover a basement of woe? Of course you have! Me too. It's hard to avoid.

So, the questions is... How can God help us deal with those inevitable, really bad days?

The Apostle Peter wrote a letter to several churches feeling the harsh sting of persecution. Overwhelmed and devastated this struggling Christian community was pleading for help. In other words... they were dealing with some really bad days. What could Peter write to ease their suffering... to provide hope in the midst of suffering? The answer may surprise you.

"Be truly glad! There is wonderful joy ahead, even though it is necessary for you to endure many trials for a while. These trials are only to test your faith, to show that it is strong and pure. It is being tested as fire purifies gold – and your faith is far more precious to God than mere gold. So if your faith remains strong after being tried by fiery trials, it will bring you much praise and glory and honor on the day when Jesus Christ is revealed to the whole world.   (1 Peter 1:6-7)

Be truly glad while enduring a really bad day? Are you crazy? Maybe... but I found four crucial lessons that offer enduring hope:

1. Really bad days... must be endured but there is a promise of joy ahead.
2. Really bad days... strengthen your faith just as fire purifies gold.
3. Really bad days... in God's eyes produce a tested faith that is more precious than gold.
4. Really bad days... will bring you much praise and glory and honor in heaven.

How many honors we receive: our accomplishments, our financial rewards, our years of service don't seem to matter near as much to God as a tested faith strengthened and purified by our pain and struggle. In other words, how each of us learns to cope with really bad days often shapes our outlook on life and defines our relationship with God. How we overcome really bad days represents our witness to the outside world.

Is it easy? Of course not! Which is why you and I need to continually pursue a deeper relationship with God. The comfort is that in the end, the really bad days will all be forgotten as we bask in the praise and glory and honor of heaven. That's enough to get me out of bed in the morning… how about you?

How Should We Live? By Ree Cathey

For several years, Ree Cathey has been faithfully writing a devotional column in our church's monthly newsletter. Ree's insight and greatest aptitude has been her extraordinary ability to turn everyday experiences into spiritual gems of truth. This particular devotion uses an ancient art form to help us ask and contemplate the age-old question: "How should we live?"

There was a recent article in our local newspaper about a beautiful sand creation made by a group of Buddhist monks visiting Williamsburg, Virginia. Nine men worked slowly and meticulously for several days to create an intricate sand painting called a mandala, which is a work of art, utilizing interlocking designs of gold, red, blue, and black, all in tiny grains of sand. The mandala symbolizes harmony and the beauty of life, and the connectedness of all living things. What is especially intriguing is that soon after the mandala is complete, the monks stir the sand-picture with a paintbrush, thus reducing it all to a wild jumble of colors.

The purpose of the exercise is to demonstrate the impermanence of life - how easily everything we have built or worked for can be taken away. But is everything impermanent? Are there some things in our lives that will last?

When I was a child there was a popular morning show on the local TV station called "Cooking with Betty Feezor". For years she shared homemaking tips with loyal viewers - a North Carolina, 1960s version of today's Martha Stewart. When she became terminally ill with cancer, her message to her viewers was to "Live so that when you are gone, it will have mattered."

"Live so that when you are gone, it will have mattered."

My mother never watched Betty Feezor's show, but her motto inspired her so much that she had it framed and placed above her desk. As a result, my brother and sister and I grew up with that purpose for living, and we have seen it acted out daily in our mother. She has shown us that the things that last are not the things we do with our hands as much as what we do with our heart - the words we say that make a difference in someone's life, the love we share, the encouragement of someone's faith, the gifts we give that can never be repaid. These are the things that will outlive us, and that will matter long after we're gone. — Ree Cathey

Jesus' disciple, Peter wrote: *So make every effort to apply the benefits of these promises to your life. Then your faith will produce a life of moral excellence. A life of moral excellence leads to knowing God better. Knowing God leads to self-control. Self-control leads to patient endurance, and patient endurance leads to godliness. Godliness leads to love for other Christians, and finally you will grow to have genuine love for everyone. The more you grow like this, the more you will become productive and use-ful in your knowledge of our Lord Jesus Christ... Doing this, you will never stumble or fall away. And God will open wide the gates of heaven for you to enter into the eternal Kingdom of our Lord and Savior Jesus Christ.*
(Parts of 2 Peter 1:5-11)

In other words:
- ✞ A life of moral excellence leads to knowing God better...
- ✞ Knowing God leads to self-control...
- ✞ Self-control leads to patient endurance...
- ✞ Patient endurance leads to godliness...
- ✞ Godliness leads to love for others...
- ✞ The more you grow like this... the less you will stumble...
- ✞ Therefore: God will open wide the gates of heaven for you to enter the eternal Kingdom...

"How should we live?" The Apostle Peter and Ree would both agree: *"Live so that when you are gone, it will have mattered."*

Living in the 'Planet of the Apes'

As humor columnist, Dave Berry would say, *"I am not making this up."* My mother-in-law sent a wild article from her hometown newspaper titled, "'It sounds crazy': Monkeys pelt cars with fruit."

"Three monkeys pelted cars on Interstate 95 with bananas and crab apples before running across the highway and fleeing into the woods... A woman flagged down a state trooper and told him a monkey had thrown a banana at her car. "I started laughing," said the trooper but he drove back to the scene of the attack and found a van and a station wagon pulled off the highway. "I know this sounds crazy," one driver said, "but a monkey threw an apple at our car." At that moment a crab apple came out of near-by trees and hit the van. "Lo and behold there were three brown monkeys in an oak tree throwing crab apples," the trooper continued. The primates jumped out of the trees and ran across the highway."

"A 6-year-old boy in the van had watched the movie 'Planet of the Apes' before leaving home a half-hour earlier. As the monkeys ran across the highway, the trooper heard the boy say: 'Look, Mama, we're living in the planet of the apes.'" (Edited from Associated Press Story)

Maybe we are living in the planet of the apes... Life can be strange at times. Like an automobile cruising along the highway, you are minding your own business when suddenly... *SPLAT!* Out of the trees a monkey throws a crab apple, squashing your routine, your day and possibly your life.

- The phone call from the doctor who wants to see you immediately...
- A letter from the Internal Revenue Service that can be condensed to one word... audit...
- An interoffice memo announcing that your company plans to downsize...
- Your child brings home a note from school: *"Please come to the principal's office right away..."*
- The message on the answering machine from your spouse: *"We have to talk..."*

Squash! Abruptly, your peaceful journey is shattered. All resources must now be focused on this latest crisis. Do you resume your trip and pretend nothing happened? Do you immediately stop to investigate? Do you quiet-ly wait and hope the crisis will go away? Should you call for help? Instead of being in control, you become a helpless target worrying over what the monkeys might throw next.

Is this why we must continually strengthen our relationship with God? Jesus once told a story about two builders. The foolish one built a house on a foundation of sand. The inevitable storms arrived, the rain came down, the winds blew and beat against the house and it collapsed. The wise builder used a foundation of rock. "The rain came down, the streams rose, the winds blew and beat against the house; yet it did not fall." (Mat. 7:25) Both builders faced the same storms but only one house survived. The secret to survival has little to do with the storm but instead lies within the foundation.

God is our foundation!

✚ Reverence for the Lord is the foundation of true wisdom…

(Psalm 111:10)

✚ But God's truth stands firm like a foundation stone…

(2 Timothy 2:19)

✚ After you have suffered a little while, he will restore, support and strengthen you and he will place you on a firm foundation…

(1 Peter 5:10)

✚ But you, dear friends, must continue to build your lives on the foundation of your holy faith. And continue to pray as you are directed by the Holy Spirit…   (Jude 1:20)

Do you see the point? Reverence for the Lord… God's truth… After you have suffered… Continue to build… No empty promises to remove crises, rather a commitment to restore, support and strengthen.

Are storms clouds approaching? Feeling the sting of a monkey's crab apple attack? Has your journey been sidetracked by crisis? Maybe this is a good time to build on the foundation of your holy faith. How is your relationship with God? Does it need a little strengthening? When is the last time you attended a Bible study? Prayed with someone? Talked with your pastor? It's never too late, you know.

And another thing… watch out for the flying fruit.

Oh Lord, I Pray… Help Me Lose Some Weight Today!

Prayer and dieting have a lot in common.

I have a confession to make. There has been too many covered-dish suppers and too few fasts in my life lately: too much sitting at the computer and too little running around the church. My belly might as well be stamped "Made by Budweiser," which is not a pretty sight for a preacher who doesn't drink. If you haven't guessed by now, let me be blunt. I've gained a little weight.

But it's not my fault. I'm a victim of uncontrollable circumstances caused by others:

• *My kids:* It would be cruel not to buy them cookies for snacks, deserts and lunches and it would be impolite not to eat a few with them. (No more than six or eight at a time!)

- *My wife:* She comes home from school hungry and needs a refreshing snack so to be a good husband; I eat just a little with her. (A whole bowl of popcorn is a little?)

- *My church:* Can I help it if they have so many covered-dish suppers with delicious food?

- *My house:* Much of my time is spent in the house within easy reach of the treats.

- *My job:* I work so hard there simply is no time to exercise.

- *My lifestyle:* There is no time to cook nutritional meals; so quick-fix junk food is a necessity.

- *My Childhood:* Can I help it if my parents spanked me at a tender age, therefore, causing my uncontrollable urge to consume large quantities of chocolate?

Are the violins softly playing in the background? Does anyone out there feel sorry for me? How does the country song go? *"Here's a quarter. Call someone who cares!"*

What's the point, Larry?

The point is simply, I need to lose weight and there is really only one basic way to succeed. Forget the latest fads and learn the secret of the three D's: **Discipline, Diligence and Devotion to exercise.** All of my creative excuses fall flat because diet and exercise will help me do more work, spend time with the kids, feel better, live longer and have extra energy for fun. The discipline practiced today reaps rewards of health, happiness and a slim waistline tomorrow.

So, what does this have to do with prayer? Everything!

Charles Wheeler once said: *"Prayer should be like the steering wheel of a car."* How could a car possibly function without a steering wheel? Instead, we more often treat prayer as a spare-tire. We only use it when there is something flat in our lives. But wait; Lord… it's not my fault. I'm a victim!

We sound like the title of a recent book. *"O Lord, I Have Sinned, but I Have Some Great Excuses!"* Our prayer life failures sound a lot like my diet and exercise excuses. We're busy with the children, the spouse, the job, the chores and a hectic lifestyle that allows no time for God. *"I watch 'Touched By An Angel' every week. Does that count?"*

God's attitude toward prayer is obvious: *"I love them that love me; and those that seek me early shall find me."* (Proverbs 8:17) *"Listen to my voice in the morning, Lord. Each morning I bring my requests to you and wait expectantly."* (Psalm 5:3)

The point is: God wants to have a relationship with us, which can only happen through habitual prayer. This brings up those same three D's: **Discipline, Diligence and Devotion to God.** Again the creative excuses fall flat because a good prayer life will help us do more work, spend extra time with the kids, feel better, live longer and guarantee us an extraordinary eternal life!

That was a good lesson, wasn't it? Now the million-dollar question: (Is this my final answer?) Can the preacher practice what he preaches? ***"O Lord I pray... Please, help me lose some weight today!"***

Oops & Calculators

"Oops" is one of those extraordinary sounds that can stir up joyous laughter and gut-wrenching fear all in the same historic moment. For example:

During the cold winter night a light rain covers the ground, which soon freezes. Early the next morning you step out with two dogs eager to do their morning business. As Molly and Honey eagerly yank on their leashes your right tennis shoe comes in contact with the slippery ice on the front step... *"Oops!"* Do you get the idea? (*"Oops,"* may not have been the only word I used.)

The picture of you collapsed on the ground with two yelping dogs running all around can be quite funny to anyone... but you. *"Oops,"* is that kind of sound.

Here is another example. You are inside a hospital operating room, heavily sedated but awake. The surgeon is standing over you issuing instructions to the nurse.

- *"Scalpel."*   *"Check."*
- *"Swab."*   *"Check."*
- *"Oops..."*   *"What the..."*

Would you stay calm and serenely ask: *"Doctor, did you just say... Oops?"* (Right!) You would more likely say, *"Where's the phone? Get me a lawyer!"* Or, how about a good old-fashioned loud scream for... *"Help!!??"*

"Oops," is that kind of word.

Have there been any major *"Oops"* in your life? Missed opportunities?

205

Ruined relationships? Something said in anger that hurt a dear friend? Perhaps someone has committed an *"Oops"* against you? A fellow worker stabs you in the back? A trusted friend betrays you?

Maybe your *"Oops"* was against God. You've blown it… big time and now you need help.

The answer could be as close as a calculator. I'm no whiz at arithmetic so a calculator is always nearby. I crunch a series of numbers and the calculator works perfectly but often in haste I hit the wrong key. *"Oops!"* (There's that word again!) No problem… I just push the button marked "C." You can't miss it. Mine is marked in red. Instantly, everything is erased and I can begin again.

God promises to forgive our *"Oops"* in life the same way. There is a "C" button on God's calculator unmistakably marked in red just for you. The "C" stands for Jesus Christ and the red is a vivid reminder of the cost Jesus paid to clear all of your *"Oops."* Confess your mistakes before God, then push the "Red C" button and everything is erased so that you can begin again.

Can seeking forgiveness from God be that straightforward? Ask a woman about to be punished for adultery. Jesus said to her accusers, *"All right, stone her. But let those who have never sinned throw the first stones!"* Jesus then forgave her. (John 8:1-11) Ask the criminal beside Jesus on the cross. *"I assure you, today you will be with me in paradise."* (Luke 23:24) Ask Peter, the disciple who denied Jesus, received forgiveness and became a leader of the church.

This could be your opportunity to hit the "Red C" button on God's calculator and clear some major "Oops" in your life. God's calculator is ready… Don't wait! Go ahead and push that button!

Speaking of "Oops." I need to stop writing. I think my dogs just did an "Oops" on the kitchen floor.

A River Journey, Waiting and A Button Called Faith

Just before leaving, Jesus promised the disciples. *"But you will receive power when the Holy Spirit has come upon you; and you will be my witnesses in Jerusalem, in all Judea and Samaria and to the ends of the earth."* (Acts 1:8) A great promise but before receiving the power of the Holy Spirit, the disciples must wait. One way to understand waiting comes from an evangelist who told the following story…

Picture yourself standing at the wheel of a ship cruising down a river. There is a forest on one side and fields of corn on the other. The river is flowing smoothly and the scenery is beautiful yet something seems strangely wrong. You look in the distance and notice the ship approaching what seems to be a mountain. There doesn't appear to be any way around it. This presents a problem. What will you do? Meanwhile, you are getting closer and become increasingly fearful.

The ship represents your life as it follows the river. The scenery symbolizes events along the way. The mountain represents the obstacles and frustrations that lie ahead. Sometimes difficulties can appear to be so large you wonder if there is any solution. You feel helpless and even hopeless.

As you come closer, you discover not a mountain but a lock. Once inside, the ship comes to a stop. You can no longer go forward or see what is ahead. Large steel walls on three sides block your view. You are now faced with a dilemma. Everything you know and understand about the river, your life and your relationship with God is behind. You do not know what lies ahead.

This is one of those special moments. You can stop the journey and say, "I have traveled with God far enough. I do not want to go any further." But deep down you know that God wants you to keep going. To do that you must push a button near the ship's wheel. On the button is printed one word: Faith. But pushing that button is scary because it cuts off the one thing you still comprehend... your past.

Somehow God gives you the courage to push the "Faith Button" and immediately you regret it. Those great big steel doors begin to close behind you so that you can no longer see in any direction unless you look up and right now there doesn't seem to be anything skyward. It's a scary feeling. The courage that enabled you to push the "Faith Button" begins to weaken. Maybe you made a mistake?

Slowly water begins to flow into the lock and you sense the ship beginning to rise. But it happens slowly, very slowly. Why does waiting take so long? There isn't much to do while you are waiting except clean the ship. (Not a bad idea!) After what seems like forever the ship finally rises high enough so that you can see again but since you are higher everything is much clearer now.

"This is wonderful," you exclaim. As the front gate gradually opens you feel exuberant and alive. Your journey with God seems clear and the river ahead appears smooth. *"Praise the Lord!"* you shout. *"Praise god in his heavenly dwelling; praise him in his mighty heaven!"* (Psalm 150:1)

Yet before very long… you spot an obstacle ahead and you sail into another lock and the whole process starts over. Not again! What will you do? Once again you can say that you have sailed with God far enough. But to continue moving forward you must be willing to push the "Faith Button" that will close doors to your past. Again God gives you the courage to reach out and push that button. Once again you are afraid but you begin cleaning the ship and you wait. "Why does it take so long, Lord?"

The water flows and the ship rises. As the doors open you are again higher than before. You are able to see further ahead and more clearly than ever. You turn around and even your past makes more sense. Your relationship with God is strengthened. "Praise the Lord!" you shout and continue your journey. But your happiness is short-lived as once again you sail into another lock.

At any point during the journey you may be tempted to stop but then you miss the tremendous opportunities God has for you. *"But you will receive power when the Holy Spirit has come upon you; and you will be my witnesses in Jerusalem, in all Judea and Samaria and to the ends of the earth."* Meanwhile, we keep pushing "Faith Buttons," we clean the ship, we look up and yes… we wait.

Breaking The Peanut Butter Habit . . .

Following God's Recipe For A Wonderful Life.

Chapter 6
For Those
Who Like
Their Food . . .
Hot!

Abortion: A Personal Story

Jennifer (name changed) was an active member of our congregation, a successful business woman and single mother to an eight-year-old boy. Yet, Jennifer was in my office crying about a terrible burden that she must talk through.

"It was five years ago, today!" she said. "I had only been divorced a short time with a baby to support and living in my old home town. My parents were nice, but resented having to provide financial aid. Most of my former friends had moved. The one man who showed any interest in me was married. I felt terribly lonely and pretty much abandoned by the whole world."

"My ex-husband came to visit his son and took us both to dinner. We had a few drinks and talked about old times. One thing led to another and you can guess what happened next. It was a huge mistake, but I was determined to go on, learn my lesson and never let it happen again. A few weeks later, I didn't need the test results to know that I was pregnant."

"What would I do now? My parents would never understand. I couldn't afford another child. The blow to my fragile self-esteem just seemed too much to bear. I took what I thought was the easy way out and visited a doctor friend who quietly performed the abortion: five years ago... today!"

What would you say to Jennifer? How would you help her cope?

All too often, what you read about abortion boils down to a shouting match between pro-choice and pro-life extremists. Both sides have compelling emotionally charged reasons to support their claims. In the twenty-five years since Roe Vs Wade, the Supreme Court decision which made abortion legal in the U.S. there has been an average of 1.5 to 2 million abortions per year in this country alone. This is an issue that offers little middle ground. You must choose... but can you take a firm stand while offering compassion and love to those who disagree with you?

Jennifer doesn't need to hear our arguments over whether she is justified in having an abortion. She needs compassion... not judgment. Doctors use the term: Post Abortion Depression to describe her emotional trauma. I call it guilt and God gives excellent answers in dealing with it.

Shortly after the prophet Nathan exposed an affair with Bathsheba, David wrote this confession: *"But you desire honesty from the heart, so you can teach me to be wise in my inmost being."* (Psalm 51:6) In other words, our willingness to be painfully honest with ourselves, with each

210

other and with God is the beginning of our path toward wisdom and healing.

David goes on to describe the benefits of honesty, confession and a willingness to repent: *"Purify me from my sins, and I will be clean; wash me, and I will be whiter than snow. Oh, give me back my joy again; you have broken me—now let me rejoice."* Our willingness to be honest in facing our shortcomings actually gives God the chance to heal us and even bring back our joy.

Over time, Jennifer learned to accept God's forgiveness and began to heal. She began to share her story with others, first to her parents, then at church and finally to groups of young women. She said something in her talk that I will never forget...

"Don't ever delude yourself with the hoax that abortion is a quick, painless solution. The ordeal of telling my parents and the embarrassment I feared would have been temporary. The grief of 'What my child could have been, if only I had let him live...' will last forever. Only God's grace gives me the strength to stand before you now!"

Today, Jennifer is a stronger Christian because she personally knows what it means to feel God's loving, forgiving, compassionate and simply amazing grace. That is a message we all need to hear time and time again.

Sex, Moral Values and Our Youth

Mary is in love. He was sweet, fun to be around and so cute! One Saturday afternoon, while both parents were away they relaxed in Mary's bedroom watching TV. Soon, the television was forgotten as they found themselves locked in a passionate embrace. It seemed only natural to express their love in a physical way.

The parents returned home discovering them both in bed. After the boyfriend left the heated argument began. "What's the big deal?" asked Mary. "I really love him! Everyone else is doing it!" The parents honestly don't know how to argue with her except to say that it is wrong.

What would you say? How do we help our youth grow up with morals and values?

John and a friend discovered it on Dad's computer Internet connection: pornography. The perversions that once were available only in seedy bookstores could now be accessed for free over the World Wide Web. Every day after school, the two boys would rush home and check out hundreds of web sites displaying graphic pictures of everything imaginable pertaining to the act of sex. One click of the printer and full color pictures were instantly available to share with friends.

John's dad turned on the computer one night to check information he had downloaded from the Internet earlier in the week. He noticed a lot of new file names in the directory. Several of them had the word sex within the name. Curious he opened one of the files and gasped at the picture that suddenly appeared on screen.

If you were Dad, what would you say to John? How do we help our youth grow up with morals and values?

If you believe this is a problem only for our generation... think again. Moses gave this warning:

"Hear, O Israel! The Lord is our God, the Lord alone. And you must love the Lord your God with all your heart, all your soul, and all your strength. And you must commit yourselves whole-heartedly to these commands I am giving you today. Repeat them again and again to your children." (Deuteronomy 6:4-7)

In Josh McDowell's book, "Right from Wrong," there was a survey taken of Christian youth... and I emphasize, Christian youth. There were some surprising results.

- •2 of 3 admitted lying to a parent or teacher
- •1 of 2 admitted sexual contact
- •1 of 3 cheated on an exam
- •1 of 5 tried to physically harm someone
- •1 of 10 used illegal drugs

Many of these Christian youth admitted to feelings of confusion and were looking for real answers. Many questioned the authority of the Bible and the relevance of the church in today's world. In other words, our generation is not teaching our children about the importance of understanding the values and morals of following God. But it's not too late to start!

A couple was looking to buy an old fix-me-up house at a great price. But a repair estimate showed that no matter what was fixed on the surface the house would soon collapse because of cracks in the foundation. The foundation of society is our faith in God. If we do not consistently and lovingly pass on that faith to our children ... society is in danger of collapse.

Sex & Our Youth: Conclusion

Dad didn't tell his son, John, about the sexually explicit Internet files he discovered in the computer. He had a better idea.

A few days later, John and his friends came home from school, logged on to the Internet and began surfing for the 'good stuff' they found earlier. This time, a message kept appearing: *"access denied... try another search."* Every word for sex they tried brought *"access denied."*

Dad came home from work and checked his new "Cybersitter" computer protection program. The print out showed hundreds of attempts to access pornographic areas. With the evidence in his hand, Dad entered John's room and said: "We have to talk…"

The sexual intimacy between a man and a woman within the covenant of marriage is a beautiful gift of God. The world unfortunately has different ideas. The Christian sees sex on many levels, including emotional and spiritual where the main ingredients are a lifelong commitment of love, self-sacrifice and loyalty to one partner. The world often reduces sex to an anything-goes physical act that promotes the lie of unending joy, passion and ecstasy.

One view promises a lifetime of lasting pleasure while the other only fulfills short-term appetites that eventually become a recipe for disaster. The latest news from the White House certainly illustrates the potential dangers of unrestrained sexual desire.

How can we share this important truth with our youth? Let's look in Jude (20-23).

1. *Build on the foundation of your holy faith…* It always starts with us. We must set the best possible standard of what sexual intimacy can really mean.
2. *Pray as you are directed by the Holy Spirit…* A disciplined life of prayer acts as a reminder of Who is really in control. Our prayer life can give us direction in dealing with the world.
3. *Live in such a way that God's love can bless you…* Another reminder to practice what we preach. There is nothing worse than a pious phony.
4. *Show mercy to those whose faith is wavering…* Take a stand on the issues, but offer the hand of love and forgiveness to those who struggle.
5. *Rescue others from the flames of judgment…* When someone is in trouble, look for ways to help… not judge.

6. *Be careful that you aren't contaminated…* Prevent this by returning
    to step 1.

The passage ends with this promise as you live a life of faith… God will
*keep you from stumbling, and will bring you into his glorious presence
innocent of sin and with great joy.* There are no easy answers to teaching
our youth moral values, only good examples which come from our own
honest struggle to keep the faith while resisting the temptations of an often-
immoral world.

After discovering Mary in bed with a boyfriend, her family and church
began to really reach out to their troubled daughter. They helped her realize how much God loved her and wanted the very best for her. One day,
Mary told her boyfriend that she wouldn't sleep with him any more.

He said, "But Mary, I love you. I just want to show you how much I
care."

She turned to look at him; "Can you show how much you care by waiting? We are wrong and God would not want me to have sex with anyone
unless that love was pure and committed to me for a lifetime in marriage.
Do you love and respect me that much?"

At first, her boyfriend walked away… but later he returned. The following Sunday, he joined Mary's family in church. There will be more struggles; more questions but Mary's family and God will be with her every step
of the way. Maybe this is what the church is really all about.

Suicide, Choices & 'The Dance'

Mother's Day will always be lousy for my children!
Several years ago, the shrill harsh ring of the phone pierced the late-
night silence of our house. The digital display on our clock read 10:30 PM.
My mother was on the line with tragic news. Christine, my ex-wife, who
had left the kids and me nearly ten years ago to start a new life, had now
ended her existence. Earlier that day she had driven her car inside the
garage and let the carbon monoxide do its deadly work. In her note she
wrote, "I can no longer pretend to be happy."

For me it was sad news but I had happily remarried years ago and was
no longer involved in her life. For my children, their mother's death would
be devastating. Stephen, the oldest was away at college and Lisa, nearing
graduation from high school was spending the night with a friend.
"How do you tell your children that Mom committed suicide?"
Early the next morning, I picked up Lisa, gathered the belongings and

214

hustled her to the car. As we drove away, sensing that something terrible had happened, she kept asking: "What's wrong, Daddy!" A few minutes later the car engine muffled the sound of her screams and heaving sobs as she heard the awful news. Her probing question still disturbs me: "Why, Daddy... why!"

That same morning, Lisa and I drove to Stephen's college. He looked confused as we entered the dormitory room and asked everyone to please leave. I will never be able to erase the image of Stephen's contorted look of shock and horror when he found out why we were there. In anger, he yelled: "It's not fair! It's just not fair! Why would she do that to herself?"

The next day, we drove to Virginia Beach where both grandparents lived and immediately received a call from the funeral home. Because Stephen was the oldest member of the family, all of the decisions about the service and the burial arrangements of their mother, legally needed to be made by him. What an awful task for a nineteen-year-old. While at the funeral home both children were presented sealed envelopes. We left and found a place where Stephen and Lisa could be left alone to read their mother's final words and then... cry and cry and cry some more!

Why am I writing this? According to recent estimates, every fifteen minutes someone in America commits suicide. That works out to approximately ninety-six people a day and at least thirty-five thousand per year. Actually it gets worse because suicides are often falsely or mistakenly reported as automobile wrecks, household accidents and homicides. Also, for every death by suicide there are at least ten attempts made. My prayer is that this story will help someone considering suicide... STOP and think about the horrible consequences of your actions.

Stephen and Lisa's mother killed herself because she could "no longer pretend to be happy." It was said at her funeral that Christine had two distinct personalities: One was bright, witty and cheerful while the other was brooding and often unsatisfied with herself or others. Depression had stalked her for years and treatments had proven only moderately successful.

Although depression often plays an underlying factor usually it's something more specific that leads to suicide. Common causes are: retirement, family problems, feeling unappealing as a person, being widowed, business failure and rejection either by a person or group. Loneliness for whatever reason can be a significant factor in committing suicide. There are no simple answers.

But there is another choice... another option.

And I, I'm glad I didn't know
The way it all would end
The way it all would go.
Our lives are better left to chance
I could have missed the pain
But I'd have had to miss the dance.

I have always enjoyed Garth Brooks, "The Dance," but the song has new meaning now because it plays a small part in a special story of human tragedy and courage.

"I'm going to die!" were the first words of a young man, barely thirty who met me at the church. He had a rare form of cancer that along with other medical complications would make it impossible for him to survive more than a year... one year to live.

I didn't know what to say? What mere words could possibly ease the pain and suffering this young man faced? For a while there was only silence amidst a backdrop of soft weeping.

His next statement sent a frosty chill down my spine. *"I don't know if I can face what is going to happen over the next few months. Maybe I should just end it all now!"*

What would you say? What sort of advice would you give? Would it be so bad to allow this young man and others like him to prematurely end their life of suffering? Is it so terrible to permit a woman suffering with depression and facing enormous difficulties throw in the towel? *Is suicide really such an awful option?*

Emotionally, it's tempting to say, *"Yes, suicide may be okay, but read on."*

The debate on "mercy-killing" and suicide is an intense one and should be continued, but a certain young man crying in a small church did not want to hear a discussion on the merits of suicide. He wanted some honest answers on how to face an extraordinary tragedy.

As a pastor, I've been asked, *"Will God forgive someone who commits suicide."* Personally, I believe God can forgive anything but scripture itself says very little specifically about suicide probably because it wasn't much of an issue in those days. It certainly is an issue today.

216

The prophet Isaiah writes: *"If I walk in darkness without one ray of light..."* (Isaiah 50:10)

Does walking in darkness without one ray of light describe this young man's experience? Could it illustrate how my children's mother felt? Darkness without a single ray of light anywhere? Could this be a signal that it may actually be tolerable to end it all?

Absolutely not! Read the rest of the verse: *"If I walk in darkness without one ray of light...* ***let me trust the Lord, let me rely upon God."*** There is the key toward understanding God's answer.

Suicide is never the right choice because it is the final denial of our trust in God. Yes, this young man faced the darkness of a cancer with no known cure. Yes, my children's mother faced a darkness of personal difficulties combined with depression. But wait, life is not over yet! God is not through. Trusting the Lord and relying upon God may not be an easy answer but it does provide the definitive assurance of hope. Ultimately, hope is what we seek and fervently require.

"If I walk in darkness without one ray of light..." This story concerns two people, two choices and their consequences. One person chose to end her life's journey at this point. What are the sad consequences of that decision?

Christine will miss seeing her daughter go to the Senior Prom and graduate from High School. She will never enjoy watching her son finish college. A mother will never witness a child's wedding or the birth of a grandchild. Her suicide left a permanent injury in the hearts of her beloved children and all of her relatives and friends: A gaping wound that will never totally heal.

"If I walk in darkness without one ray of light..." Again, the same two choices but our young man dying of cancer found supernatural courage and chose to continue his life's journey by trusting the Lord and relying upon God. What were the consequences of that choice?

- He put his affairs in order, took a vacation and spent loads of time with his children.
- The family pulled together to help him deal with the crisis.
- The church and the community began visiting and offering assistance of every kind.
- He began reading his Bible and came to know God, to really know God as few of us do.

This man really changed and as he changed, his courage became a witness for the family, for the church and for the community. One Sunday morning during one of our worship services we all had the opportunity to celebrate and cry when he and seven members of his family came to our church to be baptized. Over the next few months, his life became a testimony of courage and faith in the midst of catastrophe.

It was a difficult year, but the medical profession was able to control his pain and provide a hospice program to help him spend his final months with dignity. He died surrounded by his wife, his children and his closest friends. The funeral was attended by hundreds of people all over the county who had been touched by his courage. When the service concluded we bowed our heads and listened to "The Dance" by Garth Brooks. The final words still burn in my heart:

"I could have missed the pain, but I'd have had to miss the dance."

"If I walk in darkness without one ray of light," describes an experience you will likely undergo at some point in your life. The question to answer is during those inevitable dark periods… what choices will you make? Will you choose to miss the pain and end your life's journey never knowing how the dance will end? Do you have the courage to choose enduring the temporary darkness by putting your trust in a God who promises to restore you to everlasting light?

The choice is always yours. If you know someone who seems depressed and talks about suicide… believe what you are hearing and seek help. If you are thinking of taking your own life… STOP and think again.

Think about two children without their mother on Mother's Day. Think about a young man who set an enduring example of courage and faith.

Then cling tightly to the lifeline extended by God's answer: *"If I walk in darkness without one ray of light…* **let me trust the Lord, let me rely upon God."**

Suicide and Janice

Her first email sent cold chills down my spine: "Please pray. I know God is my Savior. I know nothing is impossible without Him but I am overwhelmed and knowing just isn't enough right now. I know suicide is a sin but I hope that God will know my heart and forgive me. I hold the pill bottle in my hand knowing it is wrong but not having the strength or courage to live. I have a good husband and a teenage son who need me but right now that isn't enough. I just want to die and go home to my Savior. Please pray God will forgive me and take me home." She gave me her name: Janice (changed) but no address.

The second email arrived minutes after the first, again from Janice: "I know I just sent in a prayer request but I am scared. I am not afraid to die. I am afraid to live!"

I responded immediately telling her about the suicide that had occurred within my own family and how much we were all devastated by the tragedy. Later that evening Janice sent me a reply:

"I know the devastation I will leave behind. I know my child; husband and friends may never forgive me. I just can't put into words the pain inside: Both emotional and physical. I have seen God use me even in my darkest moments. I have felt the blessing that he would choose someone as unworthy as myself to reach someone in need. But I am just so tired. I cannot find the hope that once gave me the will to trust in God. To really believe he will take care of me. My life and self-esteem are scattered in pieces and I cannot find the strength or courage to let God finish what was started. I am tired and alone and I just don't want to die without knowing people will pray for my husband and child. I have a wonderful counselor who has been with me through these dark nights of my soul. He promises to stay with me until God finishes but I have taken so much and given nothing back. I am so broken. It hurts so deep inside and all hope is buried in darkness. I wrote this poem but I can't seem to finish it. It describes what it feels like inside:"

It's in the silence of the night that I hear my heart cry. When I wish the days of life would just pass me by. I don't know what I'm feeling... just emptiness inside. The place where lies of darkness go to run and hide. It's a sadness that comes over, a fear of things unknown. I pray to God my Father "Let Your light be shown!"

Yet the darkness all around me, the shadows of the night
Overtake the truths I know in my mind to be right
My intense desire to live... to continue to try
Is now overpowered by a longing to die
Can I trust in You completely to carry me along
Can I believe what You say "In You I am strong"
I'm so afraid to believe that You are standing right there
With Your arms stretched out saying "My child I care!"

That kind of love my empty heart just can't begin to hold
I'm told that I'm unlovable, broken and cold
I long to wrap my arms around you, climb up upon Your knee
To find the strength within to say that I am free.

I want to finish saying I can give God all of me, give him my life, that I trust Him, that I am worthy of His love but I feel none of these. I just feel dark and empty. I want to take the pills. I'm tired. I want to finish and go home. I don't understand why this is a battle. Why can't I just die? It's like I can't even do this right. Please help me. Pray for me. Pray with me.

A real person seeking real help wrote these letters and there are thousands of people around the world who feel the same way. As Christians… what should do? How can we help? What should we say?

Suicide & Janice – Conclusion

"I know I just sent in a prayer request but I am scared. I am not afraid to die. I am afraid to live!" According to recent estimates, ninety-six people a day or thirty-five thousand a year in America commit suicide. Actually it gets worse because suicides are often falsely or mistakenly reported as automobile wrecks, household accidents and homicides. Also, for every death by suicide there are at least ten attempts made. As Christians… what should we say or do?

There had been a suicide in my family so I was confident that I knew the right answer to help her. I was wrong… so wrong! My mistake was in relying on my experience instead of God. I said a prayer for Janice but I neglected the most important part of all… listening for an answer.

Don't worry about anything; instead, pray about everything. Tell God what you need, and thank him for all he has done. If you do this, you will experience God's peace, which is far more wonderful than the human mind can understand. (Phil. 4:6-7)

The message was crystal clear. If I really wanted to help Janice, then I needed to spend more time listening to God's response and less time worrying about my own. So I finally slowed down and began to pray… and listen. During those quiet peaceful moments I finally realized God's answer. Share Janice's story and allow a community of faith to pray and be used by God to reach out to her.

Within minutes, copies of Janice's letter were forwarded over the Internet to hundreds of people who promised to pray for anyone in need.

The response was rapid and incredible. Many began to pray immediately. Soon, Janice received dozens of email letters and a few phone calls from people who shared their own struggle with pain and depression and how God guided their recovery. For example:

✞ After my brother gave up his own life, I wondered if I should do the same, I even stared at my gas oven for a while. However, I know that GOD HAS A PLAN for my life (and yours), and that we are here for a reason. I am not a professional counselor, but I have been praying for you... that we would seek God's wisdom and allow His spirit to work in your life and mine.

✞ I remember VIVIDLY what my struggle was like. I encourage you to hang on. God has heard the cries of your heart. You are important! You are unique. You are deeply loved, fully forgiven, and completely accepted. You might want to repeat those words. I had a "tape" running in my head, "It's hopeless, why keep trying?" We need a new message of hope. Remember John 3:16. "For God so loved the world..." Well, the world includes you and me.

✞ I was touched by Janice's story and felt the need to give her my phone number. She called once and we talked for several hours ... I don't know if I helped her or not but I did feel the need to reach out to her. Please let me know how she is doing.

✞ I felt compelled to respond and send encouragement. I'm only 18 years old, but I've struggled with depression before. Everything was wrong with me, nothing was right. Someone told me... "When you are sad, Jesus is sad too. When you cry, so does He." They told of God's amazing love for me, how NOTHING can separate me from His love (Romans 8:38-39). It was what I needed to hear. Here's my prayer for you.... Father, I come today with a special person on my heart. I pray your love will surround and fill her heart. I pray that her hurts, sadness, feelings of unworthiness be taken away. May Your blessings be poured upon her and may her heart be touched with grace and mercy. Amen. You are special...don't ever forget it.

Janice feels alone and abandoned. I responded to her plea... alone. In many ways, Janice and I needed to hear the same message from God: You are important but you are never alone. You are a unique and vital part of a vibrant community of faith. Learn to replace your worries with prayer and you will experience God's peace, which is far more wonderful than the human mind can understand.

Later, Janice wrote: "I wish I could say your prayers are a success and I have won this battle. I wish I could tell you I feel joy and hope again. But I just can't, so I continue to pray for God to help me and He does by keeping me alive another day: one minute at a time. Thank you for your support and prayers."

Love to all… Janice

Following God, the Mid-East and Dealing with Depression

"Visiting Israel changed my life but not in the way you think," a retiring professor said at a ceremony honoring his years of service. "Because of terrorist threats, there were very few tourists in the area, so I found myself virtually alone on a bus in Jerusalem with a young Palestinian tour guide."

"Obviously bitter, the guide decided to unload all of his people's problems on me. At one point the bus turned down a small side street, he pointed and said, 'that home once belonged to my family. We lived there for many years, until the Jews came. We were thrown out and put into a refugee camp. Promises of compensation never materialized. Our family received nothing.'"

"As the tour continued our guide pointed to other houses and business once occupied by Palestinians, now owned and operated by Jews. 'They took our land, our homes, our businesses and even our self-respect. We have been stripped of everything and no one seems to care.'"

"For the first time," the retiring professor said, "I began to realize that the Jews were not the only ones being oppressed. The Palestinian people have legitimate problems of their own that are crying for recognition. As a university professor, I was in a position of influence. Maybe God was calling me for such a time as this."

"So, I have spent the last sixteen years writing letters and articles explaining the plight of the Palestinian people and urging the necessity of looking at both sides of this difficult situation."

After a long pause, the professor continued, "I must confess that in this task, I have failed completely. I worked hard to deal with a difficult worldwide problem and accomplished nothing. I believe we are all called as Christians for a special task and in that task we will usually be unsuccessful, therefore, we will become depressed and depression is the darkness that often accompanies serving God."

The retiring professor was depressed and by the time he finished speaking, we were depressed. But the amazing part is that he was right… sort of.

222

We likely will not take part in resolving problems between the Jews and the Arabs or any other global events. When we die the world will probably be the same dangerous place it is right now. If you think about it, a little depression seems warranted.

Maybe it's best to not think about it. We should simply do our work, raise our family, watch the news, take our vacations, enjoy a few pleasures and not take any of this other stuff too seriously. Who am I to think that I can actually impact society? After all, how much can one person or one organization do?

"The world is so big and I am so small. What can I possibly accomplish as a follower of God? Are we called by God for a mission... only to fail?"

Are you getting depressed yet? You are not alone. For generations, others have asked the same question. "What can I do?" 1 John is a beautiful letter in the Bible written for a church once filled to overflowing with the enthusiasm of serving Jesus Christ but now becoming discouraged and beginning to ask serious questions about their ultimate mission and even about the identity of God.

"The one who existed from the beginning is the one we have heard and seen. We saw him with our own eyes and touched him with our own hands. He is Jesus Christ, the Word of life. This one who is life from God was shown to us and we have seen him."   (1 John 1:1-2)

This is so important! John, the letter writer, proclaims that God is alive and extraordinarily aware of what is happening in the world and with His church. How does he know? "We saw him with our own eyes and touched him with our own hands." In other words, if God is alive and still in control then our lives have purpose and meaning. We really are called by God for a mission... if only we truly knew and understood what that mission was?

Following God, the Mid-East and
Dealing with Depression – Part 2

The professor concluded saying: *"I worked hard to affect a meaningful ministry in the Middle East and accomplished nothing. I believe we are all called and within that call we will usually be unsuccessful, therefore we will become depressed and depression is the darkness that accompanies serving God."*

Are you getting depressed yet? If so, you are not alone. For generations, others have asked the same question: ***"Am I called by God for a mission… only to fail?"*** 1 John is a beautiful letter in the Bible written to offer encouragement to a church once filled with enthusiasm but now discouraged. *"The one who existed from the beginning is the one we have heard and seen."* (1 John 1:1) God is alive and extraordinarily aware of what is happening in the world and we are a crucial part of God's plan.

John answers the question very simply: *"Dear friends, let us continue to love one another, for love comes from God."* (4:7) That's it? *"Love one another?"* It sounds like something from the old hippie generation in San Francisco: *"Happiness is to love everybody!"* (Give me a break, Larry!) It does sound kind of corny… doesn't it? Maybe it all depends on how you define the word love.

Most of us tend to use "love" to define an intense feeling. *"I love my spouse. I love to watch football. I love chocolate ice cream. I love my church."* Love based on feelings makes a good romance but any marriage with too much emphasis on feelings alone is a one-way ticket to divorce court because feelings tend to rise and fall. People who love a church based on feelings, change churches every two or three years because feelings alone don't quite capture the meaning of… love, as defined by God.

Is God saying love one another like we are supposed to have feelings of love for everyone? I have a confession to make. There are a few, (only a few?) hopefully very few people that I don't feel much love toward. Actually, I don't like their attitude or their personality. In fact, I don't love them at all. But as a preacher, shouldn't I love everyone? I felt so guilty. What does God mean by *"love one another?"*

"God showed how much he loved us by sending his only Son into the world so that we might have eternal life through him. This is real love. It is not that we loved God but that he loved us and sent his Son as a sacrifice to take away our sins." (1 John 4:9-10) God's love goes way beyond feelings and becomes a covenant, a divine commitment and an atoning sacrifice. In a word, it is also called grace.

- ✟ Love is… an act of faith that enables the world to see God through you.
- ✟ Love is… an attitude of grace towards those you would normally dislike.
- ✟ Love is… a commitment to stick together when feelings are no longer enough.

✝ Love is… a discipline requiring a consistent willingness to be obedient to God's will.

✝ Love is… often a sacrifice, willfully putting someone else's needs before your wants.

"Dear friends, since God loved us that much, we surely ought to love each other. No one has ever seen God. But if we love each other, God lives in us and his love has been brought to full expression through us." (4:11-12) As we learn to love God… God's love is expressed through us toward others.

Larry, this is profound but being a loving person offers no help to the depressed professor who could not resolve the Middle East crisis. How can God call us to a mission only to experience failure?

But, did the professor really fail? In love, he offered an act of faith that enabled us to see the world with different eyes. He displayed grace toward a forgotten people. He made a commitment to stick by his promise. The professor consistently wrote letters and articles about the crisis. He often sacrificed his time and energy. I left his presence changed. For me and others, his mission was a total success.

What about you? Are you seeing yourself as a failure when God has other ideas? After all, God never called us to change the world. That is His job! We are simply to be obedient by offering others the same wonderful gift of love God has given us. A word of kindness or a deed of compassion may not solve the world's problems but it could change a life and it's the best way I know to serve God. We have no reason to be depressed or discouraged. *"I write this… so that you may know…"* (5:13)

Pianos, Rats and Born Again

The musicians at the nightclub were complaining about an old piano. The keys would often stick and the sound was truly hideous. After months of listening to the grumbling and whining the owner finally decided to do something about it…. he had the piano painted.

Painted? What good would that do? That's my point. It's all too easy to play Christian without actually being one. We seek comfort… instead of a challenge. You want rest… not responsibility. I all too readily accept peace… and surrender my passion. As followers of God, we are often satisfied to simply paint the old piano when what we desperately need is a full tune-up.

Nicodemus had been painting his piano for years before meeting Jesus. A high-ranking religious leader, Nicodemus could be the preacher of your church (Uh-Oh... this is getting personal) but something was missing. He played it safe and came by cover of night so his minister friends wouldn't see him. But Jesus would have none of it. He looked deep into Nicodemus' heart and said: *"I assure you unless you are born again you can never see the kingdom of God."* (John 3:3)

I thought being "born again" was for others, not me! I don't want to change, too much. A minister wrote, *"I love Jesus but want to hold on to my own friends, to my own independence, to the respect of my profession-al colleagues, to my own writing plans."*

We would rather just paint our piano but Jesus says, *"For God so loved the world that he gave his only Son, so that everyone who believes in Him will not perish but have eternal life."* (John 3:16) God paid the ultimate price so we would inherit a promise and a purpose. The promise is: **"God will never abandon you."** Our purpose is to offer that same astonishing promise to others.

Yet, when it comes to offering the promise of God to others... we have a lot to learn.

Sue Bates is a missionary in Romania working with street kids and orphans. She wrote about a worker who takes clothing and medicine to the streets every few months but doesn't really get too involved. He was try-ing to witness to a 12-year-old boy who lived underground, but was getting nowhere. The boy was sniffing "aurolac"...the cheap inhalant of the streets and not paying attention. So, he asked the boy, *"Why, why oh why, can't you believe in a God of love?"*

The boy thought for a second and then asked the missionary, *"Why do the rats scream at night?"*

The worker said *"See, I tried to talk to him about God and it was like talking to a wall...he wasn't even listening and started talking about rats. Those street kids are hopeless."*

Yet, it was really the missionary who wasn't listening. He had a nice car, a full belly, nice clothes, a comfortable bed, a family, money to spend, etc. The street kid had almost nothing: a filthy "bed" in a stinking hell-hole underground that had roaches, lice, fleas... and rats that screamed at night. The boy's message was plain and to the point. *"You asked why I can't believe in a God of love? Tell me why rats scream at night. Then maybe you can figure why I struggle to believe."*

Jesus came down into our dark world and became "one of us." Christ became flesh in order to *"learn obedience by the things that He suffered."* (Hebrews 5:8) Are we willing to learn by Christ's example? Perhaps, too often we want the best of both worlds. How can we have compassion and understanding for others, if we refuse to allow God to help us regularly become "born again?"

Is your piano sounding a bit out of tune: A little beat up inside? You could simply repaint it...

Or you could expose yourself to the penetrating and healing light of Christ. Sue Bates ends her story, *"I didn't know rats screamed at night. Did you?"* Hmm. Maybe my piano needs tuning too.

A Christian Response to Divorce

Sherry was married at sixteen and is now the mother of two children under twelve. Abandoned by her husband, she must work outside the home for the first time. She is hurt, financially strapped, depressed, overworked and desperately needs help.

"I hate divorce..." (Malachi 2:16) is God's response to divorce. But I constantly find it necessary to remind the people who attend our divorce recovery workshops: "God hates divorce, but still loves divorced people!" That message needs to be heard. The price for marital breakup is always high.

John's wife left him after 11 years of marriage and took the two children to another state. He cannot see them but once every few months when he makes the thousand mile drive. He is angry with her, with the system, and even God for allowing this to happen.

The statistics are cold and clear.

- Fifty percent of those who marry today will divorce.
- On the stress scale, divorce and separation are ranked 2nd and 3rd. Only the death of a spouse is rated higher.
- More than 80 percent of those who are divorced will remarry with in three years and 65 percent of those marriages will fail again.
- More than a million children each year are involved in divorce and more than 13 million children under 18 live with one parent so that single parent families are growing at a rate twenty times faster than two parent families.

Phyllis was trapped for 24 years with an alcoholic and abusive husband. She struggled for years trying to decide what to do. Years ago, she went to her pastor who advised her to "stick with it." Now she is divorced, estranged from the church and doesn't know how to get on with her life.

Divorce profoundly affects children, in-laws, friends, businesses, churches and even society itself. The stories of tragedy are numerous. The pain is real. What should be our response?

A recent Gallup poll seems to indicate that people who experience divorce often draw closer to God by praying and reading the Bible more frequently. However, the same poll also found that those who are separated and divorced feel alienated from their church. The common complaint is that churches are focusing on the needs of intact families and ignoring the divorced.

So many divorced people find a stronger faith in God, yet so few belong to the church. Look at your own church. Of those who have experienced divorce, how many are still active? As a divorced and remarried pastor, I have seen this to be tragically realistic for two reasons.

1. We have simply not learned how to offer ministry to those going through the emotional, financial and physical pain of divorce.
2. Those experiencing divorce often mistakenly assume the church will only judge them and therefore avoid any contact with their church family.

The Gallup poll goes on to say, *"From the standpoint of the church, divorced people are an intriguing and challenging group to try to serve. Their lack of church involvement may make them appear to be alienated or hostile to religion in general. But their private religious practices — frequent Bible reading, regular religious television and radio exposure and dedication to prayer — show that they are far from being a lost cause."*

With so many people experiencing divorce… isn't there something we can do to help?

1. Offer Forgiving Love! When someone dies, we know what to do. It is one of our rituals. We visit, send cards and bring food. There is a visitation where everyone has a chance to say good-bye and finally a funeral service where the deceased is remembered and the family is comforted.

When a couple separates we really do not know what to do. There is no ritual. We don't visit for fear of taking sides. Divorced people receive few cards and little food. There is no visitation or funeral. There is only silence and our silence condemns us!

During my divorce, a neighbor came over and quietly listened while I talked, cried, yelled and talked some more. I don't remember his words, but I will never forget his presence. The children and I received phone calls, food, offers to baby-sit and most of all prayers. It's often the simplest gestures that offer the most reassurance. We can extend our forgiving love.

2. Offer Understanding Patience! Most experts list four basic stages of recovery for divorce:

- **Survival:** There are more responsibilities but less income: more demands but less energy. The pace is often frantic and filled with the anxieties of learning to cope. One person must now fix the car, balance the checkbook, do the laundry and prepare the meals.
- **Grief:** A precious relationship has died and divorced people must grieve. We can't sleep. We lose weight. It is often difficult to concentrate. An old song on the radio often brings tears.
- **Identity:** This is also known as the crazy stage. It could be as subtle as redecorating the house to buying a new car, jumping out of an airplane, going back to school or diving into a new relationship. It can be an exciting but dangerous time of discovery.
- **Directions:** We are becoming more comfortable with who we are as single adults and beginning to think about our future.

All of these stages take time and it is so important for us to be patient and ready to offer help.

3. Offer Continuing Guidance! Divorce is clearly a sin against God and the sacred covenant of marriage, but it is **not** an **unforgivable** sin. Your church has a unique opportunity to become a source of healing and encouragement for the separated and divorced. Many churches sponsor divorce recovery workshops each year. I don't completely understand why the workshops work so well, but I am certain God is wonderfully present amidst the stories of intense loneliness and suffering providing comfort, strength and much needed hope for the future.

Jesus said to the crowd: *"If you had one hundred sheep, and one of them strayed away and was lost in the wilderness, wouldn't you leave the ninety-nine others to go and search for the lost one until you found it? And then you would joyfully carry it home on your shoulders. When you arrived, you would call together your friends and neighbors to rejoice with you because your lost sheep was found. In the same way, heaven will be happier over one lost...*

From a Pile of Ashes... Be Cleansed

From a pile of ashes... While the children slept with friends, we spent the last night of our marriage senselessly arguing over who would get the furniture, the photographs and the dishes. I even remember hiding a plastic coffee carafe under the kitchen sink. Why? I'm not sure but we often do dumb things when our lives are falling apart. By the time she drove off in a borrowed pick-up truck, the house was an empty shell of blank walls, half-empty rooms and shattered lives.

In the Bible, Job described his pain this way: *"And now my heart is broken. Depression haunts my days. My weary nights are filled with pain as though something were relentlessly gnawing at my bones. With a strong hand, God grabs my garment. He grips me by the collar of my tunic. He has thrown me into the mud. I have become as dust and ashes."*

(Job 30:16-19)

Like Job, my lowest point was yet to come... At precisely 8:00 AM, the next morning my doorbell rang. On the front porch stood hand-in-hand, a smiling young couple ready to meet with their minister for pre-marriage counseling. Their bright smiles soon disappeared as I walked them through the wreckage of my house towards the office. I explained what happened and assured them that I would understand if they asked another minister to handle the marriage service.

The book of Job is about tragedy and finding answers to why we suffer. Sadly, there is no reasonable explanation for Job's pain as he cries out to God: *"I cry to you, O God, but you don't answer me. I stand before you and you don't bother to look."* (Job 30:20)

"What advice could a recently separated pastor possibly tell this young couple that would enable them to prepare for a holy marriage? The answer? None! I could say nothing! At that point, I no longer felt qualified or able to give advice! All I had left was God... All I had left was God!"

At that precise moment the lowest point of my life quietly became a momentous turning point because at that instant, I utterly and completely put my dependence upon God.

Then the Lord answered Job from the whirlwind: Who is this that questions my wisdom with such ignorant words? Brace yourself, because I have some questions for you and you must answer them. Where were you when I laid the foundations of the earth?" (38:1-4) Job replied: *"I had heard about you before, but now I have seen you with my own eyes. I take back everything I said and I sit in dust and ashes to show my repentance."* (42:5-6)

In the old days, ashes were sometimes combined with other ingredients to make soap. Isn't it amazing that something as dirty as ashes can be used to cleanse our body? Even more amazing is that our sinful ashes combined with repentance and the power of God can cleanse our soul!

What about your pile of ashes? We all have them you know. It could be alcohol, marriage problems, job difficulties, addictions or abuse. It does not matter what happened or who is to blame. The only thing that matters is what you do next. Who will you turn to? Where will you go?

When Job had nothing left… God appeared out of a whirlwind. At my lowest point, God taught me the true meaning of dependence. Are you ready for God's amazing grace to transform the dirty ashes of your life into a powerful soap that will cleanse your soul? The decision is entirely yours.

More than a decade has come and gone. The young couple had a beautiful wedding, I remained their minister and God has continued to bless their marriage. I have remarried and continue to deeply appreciate Mell's loving companionship. My children have matured and dad is extremely proud. Both now attend college. I continue to serve as a minister and yes, I still offer pre-marriage counseling but with a renewed sense of God-given humility. Oh, by the way… I lost the coffee carafe. Figures!

A Different Look at Father's Day

Father's Day is a second-class holiday! Someone on Mother's Day probably said, *"We really should remember dear old Dad."* The local hardware store owner hearing the "cha-ching" of the cash register, loved the idea and put up the first sign: FATHER'S DAY SALE. Many communities honor a Christmas Mother every year to help needy children but do they ever honor a Christmas Dad? ***"Not!"*** Mothers have M.O.P.S. (Mothers of Pre-Schoolers) What do dads have… D.O.P.S. or maybe F.O.P.S.?

We are often described and stereotyped in the media as:

- ***Workaholics:*** We pay the bills but avoid day-to-day family issues such as changing diapers, disciplining kids or cooking meals. We are heard saying: *"I do the important stuff while the little woman takes care of the kiddos."* (Give me a break!)

231

- **Deadbeats:** If divorced it is assumed that dads are deadbeats on the run from child support. In fact most are very responsible and maintain regular contact with their children.
- **Abusers:** Child abuse can be physical or mental and there are certainly abusers out there but few fathers would dream of doing anything that would harm their children.
- **Macho Men:** He is more famous for exploits on the ball field than for any ability or desire to manage and care for the children. Favorite line: *"But honey... The team needs me!"* Actually community activities involving just men have declined as more dads spend free time at home.

These stereotypes certainly exist but most dads take their responsibilities seriously. Since both parents usually continue their careers, both must look for creative ways to share the duties as well as the pleasures of raising their children. It's exciting to watch young couples grow into their roles.

More dads are now becoming single parents. I chose to raise our children when their mother left. It was difficult at first. Local churchwomen sometimes brought meals figuring no "man" cooks but we survived on a simple menu of hot dogs, hamburgers and frozen pizza. I learned to clean the house, give the children baths and even buy their clothing. I never did learn how to fix Lisa's hair but every Sunday a kind soul would offer help. It wasn't easy but we managed just like every other single parent.

I am happily remarried now and deeply appreciate Mell's contribution to our family, but I have also learned that my role as a father is a vital link in the continued good health of our family.

My son, Stephen, wrote this poem in fifth grade titled appropriately... "Mr. Mom."

> *While my mom was gone,*
> *Dad had to handle things from now on.*
> *So we called him Mr. Mom.*
> *He did the laundry,*
> *Cleaned every dish,*
> *He cleaned up the bedrooms,*
> *Fed every fish.*
> *Now that mom is gone,*
> *Dad handles things from now on.*
> *We call him, Mr. Mom.*

So this is my tribute to the many Dads who struggle to be good parents and good providers for their families. Whether you are married or single if you actively share the parenting role or bear sole responsibility in raising the children... God will bless you, Dad. Paul wrote about us in the Bible: *"Fathers, do not exasperate your children; instead, bring them up in the training and instruction of the Lord."* (Ephesians 6:4) A warning to concentrate our parental energy on what is truly important.

If you are this kind of Dad, I honor you. If you are not... change. It could be the best gift any child could ever receive from you. As for Father's Day...give your dad more than a tie or a tool. Give him your time, your prayers, your forgiveness and most of all your love. As for Christmas Mother programs: honor a Dad this year. By the way, our church M.O.P.S. program will also include... P.O.P.S.

Divorce: When It Strikes Your Pastor

"Pastor Kills Wife and Himself!" was the shocking headline of a newspaper article. *"A pastor fatally shot his estranged wife yesterday before turning the gun on himself, authorities said."* The article mentioned frequent arguments and the pastor's unwillingness to accept the divorce. I noticed one comment by a church member: *"They were such good people. I don't know what went wrong."*

No one is immune to the tragedy of marital distress and divorce... not even the men and women who devote their livelihood to serving God. The same pastor who is depended upon to provide God's loving grace during a crisis often has no place to turn when the family experiencing calamity is his/her own. This is especially true when the predicament involves separation or divorce. I know! I've been there!

"I'm leaving you. I don't like this town or this life and I don't love you!" The conversation took longer but it was what she meant. Within a few days, my wife of fifteen years had packed her clothes, half of our furniture and many of our memories in a borrowed pickup truck and moved away to start over. Left behind were two crying children, an emotionally wrecked husband and a confused church community.

So many questions come to mind during an experience like this and I remember asking them all. *"Why is she leaving me? Am I really that hard to live with? How will I care for my children? Will she come back? What if I lost weight? What if I changed my attitude? Oh Lord... why me?"*

I also had to deal with questions about my career. *"How can I stand in front of my congregation and admit being a failure? Will they let me con-*

tinue as their pastor? Do I even want to continue? Is this what God had in mind when I changed careers to serve the church? Again, Oh Lord... why me?"

A *Newsweek* article states: *"In recent years the divorce rate for protestant clergy has risen to match the general population."* In other words, clergy and their families are not immune to the human tragedies that infect us all. The Bible explicitly describes how pastors should treat their families: *"You must manage your own family well, with children who respect and obey you. For if you cannot manage your own household, how can you take care of God's church?"* (1 Timothy 3:4-5) Good question!

Keith Madsen examines the problem in: "Fallen Images: Experiencing Divorce in the Ministry". *"One view is that a minister cannot show any major flaw or failure. The minister has to project the image of a person who has been strong enough to resist the evils with which others struggle."* Perfection is an impossible image to live up to and attempts can lead to serious trouble.

Divorce explodes the perfect pastoral image. In addition to the excruciating personal pain of a marital break-up there is also the public humiliation of having your leadership abilities challenged before the church and community. So clergy divorce becomes a dual tragedy, personally and professionally, causing severe emotional damage to the pastor and his/her family.

What about the former husband or wife of a pastor? Because most ministers live in church housing the spouse is always forced to move. What happens to the children? Where do they go? Who do they turn too? The church that was once a source of emotional and financial support is now unavailable.

And the news gets worse... clergy divorce also divides the church. Some members will rally around the pastor offering sympathy and encouragement. Others will demand an investigation and maybe a resignation. Most church members will quietly grieve for the family. Some will say, *"I told you so!"* Meanwhile, much of the ministry and work of the church grinds to a screeching halt.

God says it best, "For I hate divorce..." (Malachi 2:16)

What should the church do? Consider clergy divorce a private matter and quietly offer family counseling? Should church authorities automatically require divorcing pastors to resign?

I'll try to give you reasonable and Biblical answers. Meanwhile, let your pastor know how much you love him or her and offer support and prayers. They really need it. Don't we all?

Divorce: When It Strikes Your Pastor — Part 2

After writing about the heartbreak of clergy divorce I encouraged your comments and received many…

✞ When God selects us to a full time ministry it doesn't mean we are perfect, it only means we are obedient to the call. As a matter of fact it is because we acknowledge our vast imperfections. Yet too often we forget that we have to be obedient daily in our walk with Christ. It is the job and responsibility of the Church to hold the Pastor and his family up in prayer.

✞ When those who lead us, go through spiritual trials, whether they are self-inflicted or not, they deserve the same spiritual support given any other member of the flock. A pastor is still a member of the flock only with special responsibilities. I was very impressed by the support and love your congregation gave you. I heard horror stories but it seems to me your congregation got it right.

✞ It would be hard to counsel someone else's marriage when yours failed… Imagine going to the mechanic whose own car is barely running, or asking for a loan from a bank that has just declared bankruptcy. It seems foolish, doesn't it!

✞ I personally know how devastating divorce is. I was planning to be married FOR LIFE! It just didn't work out that way. I learned not to judge others in this matter, for it happened to ME! My prayer is simply to love and encourage those around me and ask God for strength and wisdom. Perhaps with that kind of a spirit and hope, there is yet a great hope for this generation.

✞ Your past experiences are a powerful witness to those of us struggling every day with similar situations. Can a priest REALLY counsel on marriage and sex related problems when he has never been there or done that? Life experiences, though often painful are what we use to learn and relay a personal more intimate look at ourselves. The fact that you have been through it makes you a more compassionate, understanding, and informed Pastor and teacher.

✞ I appreciate you being willing to open this door especially when I'm sure it still hurts. I know a young minister whose wife walked out on him several years ago. He had several children. She had an affair with someone and when the church found out about it, they dismissed him.

✝ I was married to a pastor for 17 years. During this time, I supported his ministry as much as I could. I was abused by him every way but physically. He was arrested for indecent exposure and we eventually got a divorce. He moved in with a girlfriend and eventually married. They are now divorced and he is married for a third time. I was raised not to believe in divorce either but I know that my life and that of my children is better, although I wonder if I will ever learn to love again. I could not have made it without God's help.

✝ I too would be shocked to hear of a divorce in the clergy of our local church. But I discovered not long ago that my wife and I were the only ones in our church family to ever invite the pastor to our home for supper and a time of fellowship.

✝ I believe in my marriage vows and don't believe in divorce but there are just some cases that just can't be helped. I in no way pass judgment on anyone because Jesus said: "Let him without sin cast the first stone," and believe me, I am not perfect. My heart goes out to all who are hurting. That's why I will do just about anything to make my marriage work and boy does it take work!!

✝ Sadly, being "set apart" for ministry isn't always a shared commitment. My spouse supports me but doesn't always understand the time pressures. My two daughters think I've lost my mind...

God says it best, "For I hate divorce..." (Malachi2: 16)

Divorce: When it Strikes Your Pastor – Part 3

I've done my best to describe the heartbreak of clergy divorce. In addition to the excruciating personal pain of a marital break-up there is also the public humiliation of having your leadership skills and even your spirituality challenged before the church and community. Recent statistics show the divorce rate for clergy has risen to match that of the general population. It's a serious problem. What should we do? Nothing? Ask the pastor to resign? What about the spouse... the children?

The Bible explicitly describes how pastors should treat their families: *"You must manage your own family well, with children who respect and obey you. For if you cannot manage your own household, how can you take care of God's church?"* (1 Timothy 3:4-5) Good question? What should we do?

Offer Love – Not Silence: Within a few hours after my wife of fifteen years walked out, I was surrounded by friends, church members, other pastors and relatives. No one knew what to say but it didn't matter. They quietly brought food and offered reassurance that I was loved. Their gestures touched me in ways I still cherish. A neighbor came over late one night and sat quietly while I talked and cried and rambled and even cursed. He lovingly allowed me the opportunity to be angry... to say stupid things... to be human... to release years of pent-up frustration... to grieve. Thank you my friend!

This sounds so simple but hundreds of divorced people said the only response they received from friends and even from their church was... silence: no phone calls, no food, no compassionate listening ear... just numbing cold silence. Why? There is a fear of what to say: A fear of taking sides between two fighting friends. But for those experiencing divorce the silence is interpreted as rejection. It hurts!

Investigate Quickly and Respond Openly: Within days, I met with three ministerial supervisors to investigate the circumstances involved in my potential divorce. For two hours they questioned and prodded and offered possible options for saving my marriage. They concluded I was doing all that could be done and even if it ended in divorce I should learn from my experience and continue my role as minister of the church. A committee at church soon agreed: A needed boost to my self-esteem.

A quick and responsible investigation is vital for the pastor as well as the church. For a minister it could mean the difference between growing stronger or leaving the ministry in disgrace. For the church it could mean the difference between being in compassionate ministry to a fallen leader or becoming involved in a disastrous church split. An investigation clears the air and squelches gossip.

What if the pastor is guilty of adultery, abuse or forcing the divorce? This also needs to be handled quickly and openly. Without revealing details, church officials can help the pastor face the consequences of his or her wrongdoing. An attitude of love and forgiveness from the congregation is important but a minister should resign or at least take a leave of absence for the sake of the church.

Because most ministers live in church owned housing: What happens to the spouse and the children? In the midst of the dilemma surrounding the pastor, their physical and emotional needs are often ignored. It is so important that authorities and church members remember and reach out to them.

Look for Signs of Growth: Over the next few months, I was encouraged to seek out others facing similar difficulties. Eventually we formed a divorce support group and began meeting twice a month. We all needed a chance to talk freely in the company of those who understood the unique problems of separation and divorce. One session would be about anger, then a Bible study on divorce or possibly a discussion on how to raise children as single parents. I soon began writing about those experiences.

As I became involved in helping the divorced renew their relationship with God, my faith strengthened. *"God comforts us in all our troubles so that we can comfort others."* (2 Cor. 1:4) The love, patience and gentle guidance given by a church family enabled my recovery and helped me discover a new ministry. Does this mean I make it easier for other couples to get a divorce? Absolutely not! Divorce is a horrible tragedy and a sin to the sacredness of marriage. Yet it was in the midst of my sin that I discovered God's truly amazing grace. As a renewed Christian and pastor, I am ever thankful.

Diets, Oprah Winfrey & Faith

Spring is the time to get out your bathing suit, but not me. There have been too many covered dish suppers and too few fasts: too many trips to the local fast food joint and too few trips to the treadmill: too much… oh, you get the picture. I've put on a little weight and now it's time to do something.

Buy a book. (Please don't laugh, some of us really think this way!) How about these titles: *"Potatoes Not Prozac"*, *"Good Food for Bad Stomachs"*, *"Weight Training for Dummies"*, *"Can a Gluten-Free Diet Help? How?"*, *"I Wish I Were Thin… I Wish I Were Fat"*, *"The 5-Day Miracle Diet"*, *"From Fatigued to Fantastic"*, *"Eat to Win"* … and on and on.

All of them probably offer good advice, but in the end, I turned to Oprah. She along with Bob Greene wrote, *"Make the Connection: Ten Steps to A Better Body — And A Better Life"*, which combines diet with exercise and a healthy attitude. No one shares the frustration of being overweight and out of control better than Oprah Winfrey. She writes: *"The most important part to understand that it's not as much about the weight as it is about making the connection. That means looking after yourself every day and put-*

ting forth your best effort to love yourself enough to do what's best for you."

Here are Oprah's Ten Steps to A Better Body and A Better Life:

1. Exercise aerobically, five to seven days each week (preferably in the morning).
2. Exercise in the zone. (Keep it challenging for your body.)
3. Exercise for 20 to 60 minutes each session.
4. Eat a low-fat, balanced diet each day.
5. Eat three meals and two snacks each day.
6. Limit or eliminate alcohol.
7. Stop eating two to three hours before bedtime.
8. Drink six to eight glasses of water each day.
9. Have at least two servings of fruit and three servings of vegetables each day.
10. Renew your commitment to healthy living each day (Daily Renewal).

There is an important connection between physical and spiritual exercise. Both require diligence and discipline but they also promise to help you work harder, feel better and have a more fulfilling relationship with God. **When I am out of shape physically, I am also out of shape spiritually.** Paul stresses this in a letter to Timothy: *Spend your time and energy in training yourself for spiritual fitness. Physical exercise has some value, but spiritual exercise is much more important, for it promises a reward in both this life and the next.* (1 Timothy 4:7-8)

So in honor of Oprah and Bob Greene here are Larry's ten steps to a more healthy spirituality:

1. Exercise spiritually, five to seven days each week (preferably in the morning).
2. Exercise in the zone. Challenge yourself.
3. Exercise for 20 to 60 minutes each session. Five minutes just won't do. Stretch yourself.
4. Consume a low-fat, balanced diet of inspirational material each day.
5. Replace drive time radio with Christian tapes or music.
6. Take control of your TV habits and look for healthy substitutes.
7. Ask God for help in overcoming the bad habits that inhibit your spiritual growth.
8. Look for six to eight opportunities to offer a quick prayer to God.

9. Offer at least two hugs and three compliments each day as a part of your witness.
10. Renew your commitment to healthy spiritual living each day (Daily Renewal).

Oprah said it best: *"The biggest change I've made is a spiritual one. It comes from the realization that taking care of my body and my health is really one of the greatest kinds of love I can give myself. Every Day I put forth the effort to take care of myself. And there's no question I'm living a better life."*

Now, if only this pastor can practice what he preaches.

Homosexuality: Judgment or Ministry?

For me, this story begins and ends with a funeral. Let me explain: Jim (name changed) was the son of a successful businessman who never wanted to follow in dad's footsteps. Looking to make a new and different life for himself, he moved to San Francisco. Shortly after becoming a minister, I received a call. Jim had AIDS and was coming home to die!

Suddenly, homosexuality was no longer simply a theological issue. It was the tragedy of a young man who made a poor lifestyle choice and was now paying a horrible price.

Yes, the Bible is crystal-clear. Homosexuality is a sin. Marriage is intended to be a bond between a man and a woman that culminates in an emotional, spiritual and sexual union. Sexual relationships outside the marriage covenant, homosexual or otherwise are sins.

Yes, it is also true that science is discovering that homosexuality could be an inherited trait. In other words you could be born with a tendency to become homosexual. So, if God made some of us with homosexual desires: Is it okay to act upon them? It sounds like a valid argument.

No, it's not! In truth, we are all born with inherited deficiencies commonly labeled sin. I call it simply being human. Since we all have character flaws our task is not to give in to our desires but rather to learn how to defeat them by relying exclusively upon God. **Read this statement carefully. We all sin! Everyone!**

We are made right in God's sight when we trust in Jesus Christ to take away our sins. And we all can be saved in this same way, no matter who we are or what we have done. For all have sinned; all fall short of God's glorious standard. Yet now God in his gracious kindness declares us not

240

guilty. He has done this through Christ Jesus, who has freed us...

Romans 3:22-25

In other words, we are all struggling sinners looking for grace from almighty God. If we can truly see ourselves that way... God will work miracles. We don't have to be homosexuals to struggle against sin.

As the church, our task seems to be twofold: 1. Stand firm against the sin of homosexuality. 2. Help those who are homosexual discover God's healing grace. We are not to judge or condemn in any way because we too are sinners looking for God's grace and guidance.

Unfortunately, there is also a political agenda with homosexuality. One side is pushing for its acceptance as a lifestyle choice. Every major church denomination is regularly petitioned by a vocal minority to promote homosexuality as an acceptable behavior. Recently, a minister made headlines performing a wedding ceremony between two homosexuals. His Bishop suspended him; a church trial could not find just cause to remove him but a later ruling by a higher denominational court finally supported the Bishop. In an area where the church should be clear, there is confusion.

Another side is pushing equally hard to condemn. Philip Yancey, a famous evangelical author visited a Gay rally not because he was gay but to support a friend. Philip watched a group of homosexuals protest peacefully while across the way religious protestors were waving signs and shouting occasional profanities. Isn't there something wrong with this picture? Who is the Christian?

Several years ago, I spent five months training to be a hospital chaplain. One of my assigned areas included the Aid's ward; easily the quietest place in the entire hospital. No visitors were laughing or crying in the halls... just cold silence. Twice, I was called in the middle of the night to be with a dying patient in the ward. Both times, I was the only person with the patient. **Where were the parents, friends... his church?**

Thankfully, this did not happen to Jim. A loving family and friends surrounded him to the very end. Jim became closer to God and read the entire Bible. He called me occasionally to ask questions and share his struggles.

Jim's funeral was packed with friends and relatives, gay and straight who all sat together in order share their love and fond memories of a dear and precious friend. For me, it was an example of how the church should and could be. Offering loving ministry in the midst of a difficult issue accompanied by God's amazing and all-consuming grace.

Letters, Questions and Frustrations: God's Church

It all started when I wrote about a diet book by Oprah Winfrey. Letters came from all over. Some expressing anger that I would criticize a wonderful personality who has helped so many. Others criticized me for not holding her more accountable for her lifestyle. Actually, I made no comments about Oprah, herself. I just liked her book.

Another group of letters came in response to my column on homosexuality. Some asked questions: "I have a close friend who's gay. He grew up in the church and has professed to being a Christian since he was very young. Can he be? I've heard people say that you can't be gay and be a Christian. I know he's living in sin, but aren't we all to some extent? When he told his parents he was gay, he said that as far back as his memory went, back to first grade or even kindergarten, he had always had the feeling that he was "different" from other boys. He is a wonderful, kind, loving, gentle, person. I know that doesn't excuse his lifestyle. Can he be gay and be a Christian? How could he have this inclination at such a young age?"

As I said before, the Bible is clear. Homosexuality is a sin. It is also true that you could be born with a tendency to become homosexual. So, if God made some of us with homosexual desires: Is it okay to act upon them? It sounds valid.

Again, **No, it's not!** We all have inherited deficiencies labeled sin. I call it simply being human. Since we all have character flaws, our task is not to give in to our desires but rather defeat them by relying exclusively upon God. Our challenge is to work through the power of the Holy Spirit to defeat the sin, while offering a forgiving hand to all just as God willingly forgave us.

I would answer the letter above by remembering Jesus words to the woman accused of adultery. Rather than condemn her, Christ said: *"Go and sin no more."* (John 8:11) Protecting her from the stones of the accusers and offering a gesture of compassion and love. Can we do no less?

I received other letters on this subject: "Yet Mr. Davies is hardly alone in failing to use his pulpit to speak the truth. I have never noticed that any of our community's abundant clergy has ever published a sound Biblical stand on the issue. The truth angers lots of people. Are these men afraid to take the heat? Are they too busy with their own churches to be lights in the community? Or possibly many of our preachers have taken strong Biblical stands and I've just missed it."

Perhaps you have missed it. One pastor has taken a lot of heat for his stand against abortion. Another serves on the school board and has played a crucial role in easing racial tensions in the area. One retired pastor has helped Promise Keepers bring the word of Christ to men in our community. Another minister spends several hours each week in a local nursing home simply because he cares. Another serves on the local literacy board. As a writer, I have stuck my neck out and taken a Biblical stand on virtually every controversial issue we face as Christians.

I would answer this letter with Jesus words to the crowd accusing the woman of adultery: *"All right, stone her. But let those who have never sinned throw the first stones!"* (John 8:7) Never once did anyone think that Jesus was condoning adultery. Instead, Jesus changed our mission from judgment to compassion. God will do the judging. Our task is to teach God's word, extend God's love and offer God's grace. In other words, God is firmly in control, not us.

It's interesting that both letters share a deep frustration with the church. One writer is concerned because someone she cares for is going down the wrong path and asks for help. The other writer sees a world growing dark and is appalled that God's church seems unwilling or unable to boldly provide the light of God's truth. In many ways these letters express a frustration we all feel.

Can the church offer help for those on the wrong path and still boldly provide the light of God's truth to a dark world? You better believe we can.

Answer to Letters of Frustration: Sowing Seeds of Faith

Can today's church offer loving opportunities to change directions to those on the wrong path and still boldly shine the light of God's truth exposing the darkness of sin? You better believe we can.

Jesus had just begun his ministry and chosen twelve disciples. Church leaders and even family were beginning to take a critical look at what Christ was saying and doing: *"He's out of his mind,"* they said. (Mark 3:21) How did Jesus respond to the criticism? He began to teach by telling a simple story that would forever define our mission as individuals and as the church.

"Listen! A farmer went out to plant some seed." (From Mark 4) Wait a minute, Larry. Is that it? Plant seeds? What about helping someone change directions? What about boldly shining the light of God's truth? No wonder

they said Jesus was out of his mind. Consider this example:

"Larry… are you nuts," she asked? "You want me to leave a busy law practice and two young children to attend a single adult spiritual retreat? I'm sorry, but there is just no way!"

"Just pray about it…" I said not really believing it. "If you are supposed to go, God will find a way!"

"As the farmer scattered it across his field…

✞ *… some seed fell on a footpath, and the birds came and ate it.*
✞ *…Other seed fell on shallow soil with underlying rock. The plant sprang up quickly, but it soon wilted beneath the hot sun and died…*
✞ *… Other seed fell among thorns that shot up and choked out the tender blades…"*

Occasionally, scattering seeds yields immediate results but not often, so discouraged and frustrated we stop sowing and give up. *"It's no use! I was never meant to be a farmer anyway!"*

A woman I wanted to go to a single adult spiritual retreat could not find the time, a babysitter or the money to attend. Discouraged and frustrated, I was ready to give up. It was then that another farmer stepped in and planted a few seeds of her own. *"I'll take care of the kids and some of us will pay your expenses, if you will go."*

What else could she say? She went. At the retreat, she discovered the power of God's grace and the seeds planted in her began to produce a mighty crop. This busy single parent returned, inspired to start her own ministry to single adults. Within six months she gathered a mailing list of 250 churches and individuals and began offering the love to others, she was so graciously given.

"Still other seed fell on fertile soil and produced a crop that was thirty, sixty, and even a hundred times as much as had been planted."

✞ You can help someone change directions? Plant seeds and trust God for the crop! Isn't that what faith in God is all about?

✞ You can boldly shine the light of God's truth? You can keep planting and keep trusting. You can make a stand against sin and still offer seeds of love and grace to the sinner.

Could it really be that simple? Yes it can. Sowing seeds of faith… challenges me as a pastor, a writer and a Christian to do my best using the tools God provides, namely prayer, Bible study and my sincere willingness to be a witness. But the final crop totally belongs to God!

Then Jesus said, "Anyone who is willing to hear should listen and understand!"

Racism, Alcoholism, Divorce and Gossip

Just as the worship service was beginning, a middle-aged, African-American man, neatly dressed in a black suit, entered the sanctuary and quietly took a seat near the door. He smiled but did not speak to anyone during the service. When the final hymn was sung, he slipped quietly out. An usher said his name was Walter and his breath reeked of alcohol.

Week after week, the story was the same. Walter would enter just as the service began wearing the same suit, the same smile and the same odor of alcohol. Several church members began to complain. One woman stopped attending. *"Deep down, I know it's wrong,"* she said. *"But I just can't bear to see what is happening to our little church!"* More people complained. *"He's a drunk!"* they said. *"We can't have alcoholics fouling up our church service!"*

"What about John?" the minister said. John, the son of a prominent member also attended regularly, was also an alcoholic and was Anglo-Saxon. *"That's different!"* they quietly but firmly stated. Meanwhile, unaware of the controversy swirling around him, Walter continued attending, saying little and as the final hymn was sung, silently slipping out the side door.

What would you do? What should the church do? What would Jesus do?

1. Politely ask him to leave. His presence is disruptive and a bad influence on the children.
2. Do nothing. Leave him alone. He's doing no harm and may leave soon.
3. Get involved and look for ways to offer help. But how?

Jesus teaches: *"You are the salt of the earth."* (Matt. 5:13) The salt represents our willingness as God's witness to add flavor and zest to the world around us. Jesus is also very blunt on how we judge others: *"Stop judging others and you will not be judged...*

And why worry about a speck in your friend's eye when you have a log in your own?" (Matt. 7:1,3) So, if you are to be salt of the earth and not judge others... how could you be a witness for Walter?

Here is another story. Bill and Linda Smith have been members of the same church most of their lives. Bill was head of the governing board and Jane sang in the choir. As a couple, they were an indispensable part of the church. Anyone who needed help often received it from the Smith's. Friends assumed their marriage was as strong as their faith… rock solid.

One Sunday morning, Bill and Linda were not in church and no one knew why. During the week, rumors began to circulate among the church busybodies. *"Bill left home and was living with another woman. Money had been stolen from the business Bill managed."* It was also said, *"Linda was so depressed that she sat at home with the lights out and the shades drawn… crying, drinking and popping pills."* (Most of these rumors were later found to be wrong!)

The next Sunday, Bill and Linda Smith were still gone. Another Sunday passed with no change.

What would you do? What should the church do? What would Jesus do?

Send Bill and Linda a letter asking them to resign from all of their church positions.

Do nothing. Leave them alone. After all, it's their problem. Let them work it out.

Get involved and look for ways to offer help. But how?

Jesus also teaches us to be the *"light of the world."* (Mat. 5:14) The light represents our willingness to witness with our good deeds not just our talk. In Bill and Linda's example there has been too much "talk" and too few "good deeds." So, if you are to be a light to the world and not a spreader of idle talk… how could you be a witness for Bill & Linda?

Racism, Alcoholism, Divorce, Gossip
and Jesus' Sermon!

Walter, a black man who also struggles with alcoholism enters a small all-white church during the worship service. He doesn't make a scene or disturb anyone but as his visits continue others begin to complain. Bill and Jane Smith, a regular part of every church function suddenly stop coming. The gossip is as thick as molasses with talk of adultery, alcoholism and even drug abuse but so far no one seems to know what really happened.

What would you do? What should the church do? How would Jesus respond?

Jesus' Sermon on the Mount (Matthew Chapters 5-7) offers sound spiritual guidance. Most of us readily recognize parts of the sermon, but until recently I never noticed how those parts fit together into one provocative message. Chapters 5 and 6 can be summed up this way:

1. Points out how we should behave: attitude and witness — salt and light.
2. Jesus fulfills God's law, shows clearly our faults' reminding how much we need God's grace.
3. We receive spiritual tools to help us develop a closer relationship with God.
4. Seeking God first strengthens our faith and helps us overcome our worries.

At first, Chapter 7 just seems to be a collection of sayings with no real relationship to each other but actually Jesus is showing us how to apply what's already been learned to real world situations similar to the two stories you have already read. Let's put it together and see what we get:

✝... Do not judge. (v.1) ***Don't judge others on outward appearances.***

✝... Do not give what is holy to dogs. (v.6) ***Be realistic. Listen first and then act.***

✝... Ask and it will be given you; (v.7) ***Seek God's will before getting involved.***

✝... do to others as you would have them do to you. (v.12) ***Treat others with godly respect.***

✝... Enter through the narrow gate; (13) ***Getting involved always means sacrifice.***

✝... you will know them by their fruits. (v.20) ***God will honor your willingness to try.***

Okay Larry... so how do we apply these lessons to help Walter?

✝***Don't judge..*** Welcome Walter to the church just like anyone else. Can we justify doing less?

✝***Be realistic...*** Walter is reaching out. Offering acceptance gives us opportunities to really help.

✝***Seek God's will...*** Help us look past our racist tendencies and see Walter as Your precious child.

✝***Godly respect...*** Treat Walter with the same respect you would want someone else to give you.

✝***Sacrifice...*** Be honest. This is a tremendous challenge and only a few will have the faith and courage to meet it. Are you one of them?

✝ *Fruit...* God will honor your honest efforts. The actual results are between Walter and God.

What should we do to help Bill and Linda Smith?

✝ *Don't judge...* Bill and Linda are going through a crisis. Don't gossip. Visit. Offer real help.

✝ *Be realistic...* Offer God's love instead of cheap advice combined with a willingness to listen.

✝ *Seek God's will...* Pray for Bill and Linda... really pray for ways to get involved.

✝ *Godly respect...* Active church members often feel an extra load of guilt. But, the truth is marital problems happen to everyone. Treat Bill and Linda with the respect God requires.

✝ *Sacrifice...* It's difficult to really spend time with someone in a crisis. Only a few will try. Will you?

✝ *Fruit...* God will honor your sacrifice. Leave the rest to the Smith's and God.

These answers are only meant to stimulate your own prayers and thoughts which is why Jesus ends His sermon with a promise. If we listen and obey, it will be like the wise man who built his house on solid rock. The storms may come, but the house will not collapse. It is the foolish person who takes the easy way and builds on the sand. When the inevitable storms come the house will fall with a mighty crash. There is racism, alcoholism, divorce and gossip in every congregation. The question is... **"How will you and your church respond?"**

Why Talk About Money?

The preacher says: "So, if you really love God... get out your checkbooks, use your Visa card and bestow generously, because the more you give God... the more you will receive!"

The cynic in me hears: "I just bought a new Cadillac and the Jacuzzi payment is due, so if you suckers will just reach deep into your hard earned life savings, I will continue living an extravagant lifestyle you never dreamed of."

Don't you hate it? Churches and evangelists have a reputation of always asking for funds. For many years, like you, I have sat in the pew and complained. Which is why I've hesitated to ask for money myself. It also doesn't help that my former occupation has a reputation for being cash crazy. Talking about our money is a delicate issue, but like it or not, it is one we all must hear.

248

"Why?" Because giving habits say a lot about what kind of person you are. It's not necessarily the amount you give. While some give thousands without a thought, others will be straining to hand over $10. What really matters is: *"Are you following God's will in planning your giving habits?"*

"Why so much emphasis on money?" After all, there are other ways to give. True, but experience has taught that if you are generous with your currency, you are also generous with your time, talents and prayers. Unfortunately, the reverse is also true. Have you ever heard this old saying? *"If God could look inside your checkbook, what would He discover?"* Personally, that scares me.

Several years ago, my preacher spoke in relation to this scripture: *"Bring all the tithes into the storehouse so there will be enough food in my Temple. If you do,"* says the Lord Almighty. *"I will open the windows of heaven for you. I will pour out a blessing so great you won't have enough room to take it in! Try it! Let me prove it to you!"* (Malachi 3:10-11) A tithe means… a tenth.

"Give A tenth?! Are you crazy?!" Usually, when the offering plate was passed, I would stick in a dollar or five dollars or when times were good… twenty. A tithe? I was making a good income, but like most folks I still lived from paycheck to paycheck. *"If I were to give ten per cent back to God, why that would be… a lot of money! No WAY!"* But I couldn't get that scriptural challenge directly from God out of my mind. ***"Try it! Let me prove it to you!"***

Over the next few months, I resolved to first give a smaller percentage and see if I could work up to a tithe. Let's just say, I tried it… reluctantly and hesitantly. Within six months though, I was enthusiastically tithing. Over the next two years, my giving went up dramatically, yet my finances got better! The only real change I noticed was not eating out as frequently. Bills were paid. Credit card debts were actually reduced. Here's the fun part. I was becoming happier and more content.

The lesson for me is this: God does not *need* your money, but wants to *use* your money to teach us the power of faith and trust. Paul said it in 2 Corinthians: *"Remember this—a farmer who plants only a few seeds will get a small crop. But the one who plants generously will get a generous crop. You must each make up your own mind as to how much you should give."* (9:6-7)

Some lessons: 1) Plan all of your giving carefully and prayerfully. You

249

may not be able to tithe yet, but do the best you can. 2) Give joyfully. Have some fun and be creative with your giving. 3) Give anonymously. Don't brag. 4) Trust God. Despite occasional shysters and money goofs, have faith that God is ultimately in control. 5) Follow up your giving with volunteerism and prayer. Each year, everyone in our church receives $5 and is challenged to use it for God. Later, we have a worship service and hear the stories. I am always amazed at the creativity and enthusiasm of everyone who responds. If we can do that with just $5, just think what God can do with your tithe. More important, think what God can do with you. Remember: *"Try it! Let me prove it to you!"*

Three Suicide Letters

Away from home and heavily involved in a series of meetings, I only planned to quickly scan the prayer requests emailed from our Sowing Seeds Ministry website. But my heart skipped a beat as I read the following three letters. All arrived within hours of each other their intent very clear. Names have been removed to protect their identity and the stories have been shortened somewhat but you are reading their very real pleas for help... their cries of anguish... their desperate need for hope.

Letter #1: "I'm not sure why I'm writing this. I went online to look up information on suicide: statistics, methods and all that stuff. I was raised in a family where I went to church every Sunday and was taught the importance of faith and God in our lives. It doesn't matter. It doesn't help me. I got hurt.... bad... when I was a child. I was hurt in a way that no person, no little child should be hurt. I think about suicide on a daily basis... sometimes it's all that I can think about. I've been hospitalized for attempts before. I've been put on medications to help the depression... the mental disorders that doctors are so quick to diagnose. I'm sick of it all. Why should I bother trying anymore? I'm not even afraid of dying. I'm not afraid of pain. I just want to leave this world. Please pray for me. I'm tired of trying."

Letter #2: "I am writing this letter because soon I will hear what I have not wanted to hear. I wrote you a letter about my son who is charged with capital murder of his father. Well, I found out two days ago that his case is going to the circuit court. He is charged with both robbery and capital murder. Before I see my son get the death sentence I will take my own life. I can no longer go through this any more. I keep trying but can't hold on any longer. I am hurting inside deeply… I am all alone, since nobody has ever cared for me. I no longer want to live in this world full of hate and hurt. It is me that has to watch my son and I would rather shoot myself. Like I told my counselor today, I don't want to live anymore."

Letter #3: "As I read your story on suicide, I think it is so easy to sit and judge those that do kill themselves... I know how bad I feel and totally hopeless and that I am not doing my kids any good… so why not commit suicide? I guess I am writing for prayers because I know I shouldn't kill myself but I just cannot get the strength to go on anymore. I read the verse you had (*"If I walk in darkness without one ray of light let me trust the Lord, let me rely upon God."* Isaiah 50:10) but I also believe that God would not give us more then we can handle and I have more than I can handle."

I carefully wrote a reply to all three writers pleading for time to forward their message to other members of our prayer team. To each, I offered no answers but promised to begin praying for them immediately. After clicking "Send Mail" and seeing the last reply leave the computer and head toward the recipient, I poured a fresh cup of coffee to calm my nerves and earnestly began to pray.

More than 32,000 Americans commit suicide every year and over a million suicides occur worldwide or one person every 40 seconds. Attempts are estimated at over ten times that amount. The Sowing Seeds Ministry website articles on suicide regularly receive more than five hundred visitors a month and our worldwide prayer ministry website processes several letters each week contemplating suicide.

What motivates someone to consider the ultimate act of desperation? Other letters offer a few clues:

- I was suicidal all of my life. I had a tape playing in my head that said "I want to die".

- My husband left after 31 years and I really reached bottom.

- I was physically abused by my parents as a young child. So when the man next door started doing things to me when I was four, I didn't trust my parents to tell.

- I'm 22 years old. I don't trust anyone. I am diagnosed with borderline personality disorder, major depressive disorder, and post traumatic stress disorder. I rely on medication to keep me happy enough to stay alive. I forgot to pray. I haven't prayed in a year.

- Why would God want to hear from a wasted miserable loser like me? When I was a child, I used to pray to be allowed to die. It didn't happen.

Hours later, I was still fervently praying for three miracles yet I had no idea what to do or how to begin. This was a life and death situation with no "safe" answers. Throughout the evening I continued praying and worrying. Later, I discovered God provided those three precious miracles.

Three Suicide Letters: Reader Response

The story of three almost suicides brought a flood of e-mail. Before I reveal the story's ending, read a sampling of how others responded.

I too thought of Suicide and have the marks on my arms to prove it. I never felt loved. I was sexually abused. When I was six years old; my teacher saw me with a piece of fruit and said I had taken it off her desk. I told her my brother gave it to me but the teacher wrote my mom a note telling her I stole the fruit. Mom took my clothes off and beat me so hard I can still feel the pain. The worst part was when she pointed her finger at me and said: "If I ever hear of you touching anything that don't belong to you again I will cut your fingers off!" Just think of a six-year-old child hearing that. It stayed in my mind. I went back to school and the teacher walked up and said, "I made a mistake. I left my tangerine on the dinning room table so I brought you another one." As she walked off I threw it in the trashcan and to this day I will not touch a tangerine. Priscilla

I am a 25-year-old male who grew up in a mediocre Christian home. I began a struggle of lusting after guys because of a hurt with a girl. Sure, I knew it was wrong but I was in such pain. One day, I thought this is the day I am going to end it all but you know what? Nothing transpired, God intervened, and I don't believe this happens to just one person. Chad

I had a period where I almost lost my hope. Quite frankly, it was the flicker of hope that I had in Christ and the constant encouragement of my closest friends and family that kept me going. Some people don't have even that much, and as a result, many people DO take their own lives. That is tragic. I'd like you to do something today. Undoubtedly, someone you know is discouraged. Drop what you are doing and reach out in love to them. You may not solve their problems but let them know that you care. Pray for strength and ask God to give you what is needed. Brian

Your devotion struck a deep chord in me. So often in Christianity, suicide is "looked down on." People courageous enough to ask for help when considering suicide are shamed. I am in seminary now, and part of what I am studying is how to help people who have grown up with abuse. I have been abused and I have felt the desire to end my own life. If you know of any way my experience can help those you have received prayers from, please let me know. Kriss

Three years ago, I married a man with emotional problems. Later we had a heated discussion. He stepped outside and I called my pastor to set up a counseling session. He came back in, took off his class ring and looked at me kind of strange then went back outside. He returned and asked me to come outside so he could show me something. I was with the pastor and could not hang up. He went back outside. Later, I went out to look for him. I went to his truck and he was inside. I opened the door and asked if he was coming in. Getting no response I nudged him and he fell over on me. They later found a gun in his truck. If I had not been on the phone, I would have went outside when he wanted to show me something. To this day I don't know if he wanted me to talk him out of it, make me watch him do it or take my life also. Beverly

My father committed suicide 23 years ago next week. I used to wish I were dead all the time, but never had enough nerve to commit suicide. I try to pray and do what I am supposed to but sometimes I think there is no reason for me to be here. I know many folks much worse off than myself so I keep going. I know God loves me, but I sometimes wonder. I do not like myself. I never have! Margaret

I was a college junior five hours away from home and mother wanted to divorce my dad. The next time I went home, I found out dad tried to commit suicide and was hospitalized. That fall was just the beginning of a terrible darkness that lasted for years. I honestly don't know how many times dad attempted suicide. I couldn't fix what was wrong with him. I struggled with how I could give him some of my will to live. My dad believed that he was no good to his kids, that he couldn't do anything right. Everyday, I prayed God would keep him breathing. God answered my prayer. It took four years but he did get better. Don't presume to know what your children believe or what your worth to them is. Just keep breathing, one day at a time. Michael

Three Suicide Letters: Conclusion

1. I'm sick of it all. Why should I bother trying anymore? I'm not even afraid of dying.

2. I can no longer go through this any longer. I will take my own life.

3. I guess I'm writing for prayers because I know I shouldn't kill myself but...

Three e-mails crying out desperately for understanding and hope. I was fervently praying for three miracles yet I had no idea what to do or how to begin. This problem was too big for one person.

Bianca Tate of the Trauma Resource Network wrote: *People consider suicide because they don't know or believe God loves them. There are so many lonely people in the world today clinging to everything but God. People who are suicidal need the love of God... for once you know and feel His love, you will never be incomplete again! Everyone's life is valuable for it was worth the blood of Christ. Just see the cross! It's all there.* Bianca

Later that same night, I sent an email to our Sowing Seeds Ministry subscribers: *Here are three prayer requests that need your closest attention. Each person is seriously considering suicide and urgently needs your prayers and possibly an email offering encouragement. Will you bow your heads for a moment? "Dear God, we need a miracle for three precious lives. Show us the way to get involved and let us trust in your love and power. Amen."* The response was immediate and effective...

I went online to write my final farewells. Imagine my surprise when I found 60 emails from people I'd never met before. The tears flowed as I read the words of encouragement for me... someone I didn't think mattered. Do you know how long it's been since I cried? I can't remember the last time.

Sixty e-mails! Can you imagine receiving that many letters offering encouragement and love? One example: "We haven't met but I offer this prayer: May Our Lord bless you. May Our Lord hold you tight. May a Host of Angels hasten to your side. May your heart slowly open to good things? May your pain decrease as your amazing grace increases. May you be surprised with tiny bits of joy. May you look at a mirror and smile at the precious image. May you picture yourself wrapped in a Heavenly Blanket of Love, Calmness, Gentleness, Understanding, Peace, Patience, STRENGTH and Openness to better days ahead. May you embrace the prayers that are being said on your behalf. May you go forth with renewed faith. May you remind yourself that you are SPECIAL. May your tears wash your soul clean. May your happiness sneak around the corner and pop up when you least expect it."

Guess what? I have decided not to commit suicide. Everything was planned and I wanted to end it all, but after all the many, many emails and words of encouragement received by literally hundreds of praying friends, I decided to give life another shot. I know it won't be easy but I am willing to try. I have a lot of hurt and problems to sort out but praise God; I know they will come out right. I didn't know God and so many others cared about me! Please keep praying and don't stop those encouraging e-mails!

Other letters shared their own tragic stories: "I understand how it feels to be at the bottom of a deep dark well with no hope of getting out. My grandma passed away and I went through a heartbreaking split. I was lost and felt so alone. I was ready to die. When a roommate found me, I was unresponsive. They did not expect me to live through the night. I wondered why I was still alive and tried to accept the struggles ahead. I heard Michael W. Smith sing *"this is your time."* The words struck and I fell on my knees and prayed God would forgive me. I have now fully recovered and given my life back to the Lord. An 18 year old friend of mine was contemplating taking her life and came for help. We spoke for hours, talking and crying. She called me two days ago so that we could go shopping. Shopping!"

Larry there is no way to express how opening your note today touched me. I have felt SO alone in this struggle. I can't lean on those around me because they all look to me for their strength. NOTHING compares to the feeling of knowing there are prayer warriors out there on my behalf.

How do we help someone who may be considering suicide? 1. Watch for signs. If someone speaks of ending it… they are usually serious. 2. Pray for guidance. 3. Get involved and offer encouragement. 4. Ask for help. 5. Continue to pray and follow up. 6. Whatever happens… don't blame yourself.

"God comforts us in all our troubles so that we can comfort others." (2 Corinthians 1:4) Is this God's answer for getting involved? "Maybe there is a purpose for all my suffering... maybe someday I will help someone else. I would certainly like to try. It seems the only time I'm happy is when I help others."

Hi Larry... just wanted to let you know I'm still around... still praying.

Things are still hard, but hey, God never said it would be easy... only that it would be worth it.

Breaking The Peanut Butter Habit . . .

Following God's Recipe For A Wonderful Life.

Chapter 7

Seasonal Food: Fall, Christmas & Winter

Confessions of a Potato-Race Cheater

I only came to the church Halloween party as a gesture of support for the people who were working there, but nooooo... they also made me play in those silly youth games.

First, I was blindfolded and told to smell, feel and taste various gross objects such as smelly socks, sour pickle juice and a weird pudding. Ecch! The youth enjoyed the thrill of having a minister at their mercy. In return, I got a sour taste in my mouth and a piece of candy... It wasn't worth it.

The next game, however, got me in serious trouble. Russell Yancey, another youth leader and I were asked to get on our hands and knees and see who could push a potato from one end of the room to the other the fastest. Did I mention the only part of our body, which could touch the potato, was the nose? Can you picture in your mind how this race must look? Oh, the shame of it all.

Russell described what happened in Sunday school several days later where I was forced to publicly face the consequences of my sinful actions. He said: "I was putting my nose to the spud-stone, so to speak working my nostrils off trying to win the race. Blood was spurting on the floor, but I didn't mind because it was all for our youth. The next thing I knew a potato went flying past me straight to the finish line. No mortal nose could send a spud flying with such velocity. It was obvious to me what happened. Larry cheated and threw the potato."

Three witnesses in the Sunday school class agreed that I indeed maliciously and without any sense of shame picked up the potato with my hand and threw it over the finish line.

"Holy French Fries, you've got me dead to rights," I cried out. "I confess! I confess! The frustration and shame of Russell beating me by a nose was too much to bear. I plead guilty to the shameful crime of illegal potato throwing. Please forgive me!"

After the laughter died down our Sunday school class began to talk about the real sins we commit from potato-race fibs to mass murders. The truth is, we all make mistakes, so how does God want us to atone for our sins? Psalm 32 gives some encouraging answers:

"Blessed is the one whose transgressions are forgiven...When I kept silent, my bones wasted away through groaning all day long. For day and night your hand was heavy upon me..." (1,3,4)

• Don't keep silent about your sins. It's not what you did as much as what you do next.

"Then I acknowledged my sin to you and did not cover up my iniquity. I said, 'I will confess my transgressions to the Lord' — and you forgave the guilt of my sin." (5)

• Confess, knowing God will forgive. This is the cornerstone of our faith.

"Therefore let everyone who is godly pray to you while you may be found." (6)

• Seeking God begins the process of overcoming sins vicious hold on you.

"...But the Lord's unfailing love surrounds the one who trusts in Him." (10)

• Trust in God to love and protect you through difficult times.

I still throw potatoes occasionally along with other sins, but it is comforting to know that if I am willing to face my mistakes, confess and seek God's help there will be a promise of love and encouragement to see me through. You can bet the whole spud ranch on that one!

Even on Halloween it's possible to find something of God, if you are willing to look for it. But let me give you a warning. Beware the youth and their games...

Christmas, Suitcases & Stress

Here is a unique way to have fun! Line up ten suitcases and attempt to carry them all at the same time. "Let's see, I can jam this one under my arm. This one can go on top of my head, while this one goes between my legs!" Now, just to keep things exciting, invite an audience to watch as you struggle. I attempted this interesting but stupid feat at a church service and actually succeeded in picking up nine of the suitcases (or was it eight) but as I tried to swing the last one over my shoulder... the rest of my body followed and I was soon lying amidst a heap of luggage on the floor. (Stop laughing, please!)

Now what? Obviously, I cannot carry but so many suitcases without falling.

So, sheepishly, I asked someone in the audience for help. Immediately someone picked up four or five of the suitcases while I retrieved the others and in just a few moments we had easily accomplished together what I absolutely could not do alone.

Once I asked for and accepted help, an impossible task became manageable.

The stress and burdens of living often become a long line of real-life suitcases. We can carry two or three, maybe even six or seven but as stress and burdens increase… our capacity to carry the load diminishes. Eventually, we must ask for help. Christmas can bring additional stress and burdens to an already full load. For example:

- A grieving family prepares for their first Christmas without a loved-one.
- Students trying to finish the end-of-semester rush of papers and exams.
- Workers dealing with the added stress of holiday business.
- Single parents facing too many bills, too many needs, too little income and too little time.
- Christmas parties, gift buying, baking and the frantic pace of preparing for the big day.
- Families just managing to get by are now faced with the additional burden of purchasing gifts.
- Abused or neglected children pretending to enjoy a holiday that only promises more of the same.

The stress and burdens continue to lie heavily upon our sagging shoulders year after year eventually causing us to stumble, fall and lie helplessly among the pile. No matter how strong you may be, the load cannot be carried alone. It is impossible! Recently, I discovered sound Scriptural guidance:

"So I tell you, don't worry about everyday life—whether you have enough food, drink, and clothes. Doesn't life consist of more than food and clothing? Look at the birds. They don't need to plant or harvest or put food in barns because your heavenly father feeds them. And you are far more valuable to him than they are. Can all your worries add a single moment to your life? Of course not… You have so little faith… Why be like the pagans who are so deeply concerned about these things? Your heavenly Father already knows all your needs, and he will give you all you need from day to day if you live for him and make the Kingdom of God your primary concern. So don't worry about tomorrow, for tomorrow will bring it's own worries. Today's trouble is enough for today." Parts of Matthew 6:25-34

This is more than a simplistic "do not worry" speech. Instead we are reminded:

●Replace worry with faith. Go back to the basics of working on your relationship with God. Resolve this Christmas to spend more time in prayer. Share your burdens with a trusted friend.

●Faith will eventually lead to trust in a God who will lovingly guide you during difficult times. Take a quiet moment to sit and read one of the Gospels. Listen to your favorite Christmas music.

●Be content with looking for God's help today. Tomorrow will bring it's own worries. Attend worship at your local church. Become involved in a Sunday school class or Bible study.

Your faith in God can provide the needed help turning impossible tasks into manageable ones... even during Christmas. No matter what stress or burdens you may be facing, there is help available, if you are willing to ask. God's promise is to be there, ready to help. Christmas was never meant to be an additional burden. Replace your worries with faith and let God help you carry the load.

Now, if only someone will help me get these suitcases back to my house!

The Story of 'Christmas Parents'

It always happens just before Christmas. I receive calls like this one: "I'm sorry to bother you but I don't know what else to do!"

"How can we help you?"

"My husband's been laid off and we have no savings." or "I'm a single parent and everything I make goes toward paying the bills." Or "My daughter has a drug problem and I'm raising her children and doing every-thing I can but there is no money." They all end their plea saying: "Is there anything you can do to help our children have a better Christmas?"

Our church, like others, will do what we can. Several families receive food and a few gifts for the kids, but it never seems to be enough. Two questions keep haunting me:

1. "How many more people are in desperate need of our help but never ask?"

2. "How do you tell a child that Christmas is for others... but not for them?"

261

Let's face facts. For a child, Christmas is about Santa Claus and presents: some giving and whole lot of receiving. You can say it's about family and friends. "Yeah, right!" Hopefully you will try to remember the celebration of Christ's birth. (Watch their eyes turn glassy.) But if you turn on the television, visit a department store or pick up a bulky newspaper full of toy ads, the ugly truth screams it's horrific message. Christmas is about gifts and lots of them!

Unfortunately, for some children, Christmas and Santa Claus represents an all too visible and miserable reminder of who we are and who they quite honestly, are not!

It was never meant to be. Jesus, himself, was born in a barn with only farm animals and a few shepherds as witnesses. He grew up the son of a blue-collar worker in a land occupied by Rome. Throughout his earthly life, Jesus had few if any material possessions. How did we get everything so mixed-up? More important… How can we recapture the Christ in Christmas?

We start by remembering the children. Jesus never forgot: The disciples had been arguing over which of them was the greatest. Jesus sat down and… put a little child among them. Taking the child in his arms, he said to them, "Anyone who welcomes a little child like this on my behalf welcomes me…"   (Mark 9:34-37)

Christmas presents were meant to be symbolic of Christ's gift of eternal life to us. In other words, what Christ has given to us… we pass on to others. Giving a gift should be our way of saying; "I love you in the name of Christ!" If we only give to our friends and family, where is the love of Christ? The challenge is to broaden our horizons and give to those truly in need.

Three years ago, religious and community leaders in our area met to talk about providing a better Christmas for all of our children. The result was "Christmas Parents". Last year, we were able to distribute gifts to 993 children. However, more important than the statistics are the stories. One grandmother found a stuffed bear her grandchild had wanted at our toyshop. Other parents made it clear there would have been no gifts for their children without the help of Christmas Parents.

✤ Every community has an organization like Christmas parents. Volunteer your help.

✤ Teach your own children about giving by going out to buy gifts.

Then donate them.

- ✝ Take a child to a service or a special Christmas program.
- ✝ Read the Christmas story from the Bible to a child.
- ✝ Join a group of children and sing Christmas carols.

And speaking of Christmas carols… look at the third verse from "Away in a Manger." "Be near me, Lord Jesus, I ask thee to stay, close by me forever, and love me, I pray; bless all the dear children in thy tender care, and fit us for heaven to live with thee there." Put Christ in your Christmas this year by helping a child. God will bless you for it. Have a Merry Christmas.

I'm Just A Businessman!

I've been running a profitable business in town for years. There have been no tax problems, no accusations of fraud so why am I so upset and confused? Something inside me has changed.

It all started several weeks ago on a cold, dark night. My little hotel-restaurant was packed with out-of-town customers. The mood of the crowd at first was dark with talk of rebellion. After all, no one likes being forced to travel just for a census. Time, a few drinks and the opportunity to renew friendships soon lifted traveler's spirits and the atmosphere became more festive.

Business was good — almost too good. All my rooms and others were filled so people were sleeping in the streets. Our supplies of food and drink were getting low but my pockets were filled to the brim… with cash.

Later that night, two travelers, a young man and his obviously pregnant wife astride a donkey, approached my front gate. They both looked exhausted from the long journey. "Please sir, we have come a long way and need a room. Can you help us?"

I had turned away other people with no qualms but the look of panic in the man's eyes and the young girl's condition made me pause. "There must be somewhere I can put them," I thought. Sadly, there were no rooms available. "I'm sorry. There is no room in the inn."

Something in the young woman's eyes made me pause… she looked so calm and serene. "Wait a minute…" I blurted out. "There's a stable around back with an empty stall. I can add a little fresh straw and you will at least have shelter." What is wrong with me? Why am I concerned about the welfare of this young couple? After preparing their area, I didn't even ask for payment.

"And while they were there, the time came for her baby to be born. She gave birth to her first child, a son. She wrapped him snugly in strips of cloth and laid him in a manger, because there was no room for them in the village inn." (Luke 2:6-7)

The frantic banging on the front door began just as I was finally falling asleep. One of the shepherds in a nearby field said, "You must come at once to see the child. She has sent for you."

"It's just a baby." I said. "I've seen babies before." But I hurriedly dressed and rushed to the stable. Only a few animals and shepherds surrounded Mary and Joseph. "Where did the shepherds come from?" I wondered. Then I noticed the child. What a beautiful child! He wasn't crying... just quietly smiling and looking... at me. His eyes seemed able to see clear through my very soul. How could this newborn baby affect me so?

Something happened to me that night. Don't get me wrong, I'm still a businessman. I didn't run off and become a preacher but seeing that child changed me, forever. Over the last few weeks I've done a lot of thinking and praying about where my life is going. With God's help, this is what I hope to do:

- Become more generous in my giving and look for opportunities to really help those in need.
- Treat my employees with more respect and pay what they earn, not whatever minimum wage I can get away with.
- Maintain a stricter accounting of the books and be honest with my customers.
- Spend more time at home with my wife and children.
- Start going to church and look for ways to become more involved in the ministry.
- Be in prayer for my family, for my business, for others, for my pastor.

What about you? How will seeing the Christ-child affect you this year? Peter said: "As we know Jesus better, his divine power gives us everything we need for living a godly life. He has called us to receive his own glory and goodness!" (2 Peter 1:3)

Seeing the Christ-child changed this innkeeper forever. I pray this Christmas you too will gaze into the eyes of the Christ-child and be transformed! May God richly bless your journey of faith.

Torture, Forgiveness & Advent?

"For if you forgive others their trespasses, your heavenly Father will also forgive you, but if you do not forgive others, neither will your Father forgive your trespasses."
(Matthew 6:14-15)

It sounds so simple and fair. Forgive others and you will be forgiven. Later, Jesus tells of a servant who is forgiven a huge debt by the king, but when presented a similar opportunity to forgive someone else a pittance the servant chooses punishment instead. The king finds out and is outraged. "You wicked servant! I forgave you all that debt because you pleaded with me. Should you not have had mercy on your fellow slave, as I had mercy on you?" And in anger his lord handed him over to be tortured...
(Mat 18:32-34)

Someone forgiven of millions in debt promptly rushes out to bash someone's head in over five bucks. This is a no-brainer, Jesus! Of course the idiot should be tortured... right? But... the last verse sneaks up on you. "So my heavenly Father will also do to every one of you, if you do not forgive from your heart."

Wait a minute Jesus! Surely you can't be talking about me? You don't know how much I've been hurt! My spouse abandoned me... I was abused as a child... My business partner skipped town with all the profits... My employer has been an unmerciful tyrant... Surely you're not suggesting that I could be tortured for not offering forgiveness?

Perhaps your torture has already begun. There is a stark reality to life we must all face. People get hurt. People hurt others. Your attitude in dealing with your pain can be a critical factor in your healing. Forgiveness is a process for healing the victim not necessarily freeing the oppressor. The word 'forgiveness' is mentioned more than 90 times in the Bible so it must be important. A psychiatrist told me she would lose nearly 70% of her patients if they could simply learn how to forgive and let go.

At a recent singles ministry gathering, a father told one of our small groups how his son was murdered less than a year ago and the man who killed him would be going on trial in just a few days. With tearful eyes, he described the struggle he would face, day after day sitting in that courtroom listening to the gruesome testimony and watching the legal maneuvering to protect the murderer, the man who cruelly took away the life of his son.

The father's group leader stood and asked us all to pray for God to give this man Holy courage during the trial. We prayed for justice. We prayed for grace both for the father and the murderer.

Several months later, the father wrote, "Before that prayer meeting, I was trapped within my own hatred. Just being able to share my concerns with all of you and knowing that your prayers and God's love would be with me somehow helped to ease my suffering. It will take a long time to completely forgive and heal but I'm off to a good beginning."

The word Advent simply refers to a time of preparation before the birth of Christ. How? Nothing is emphasized in the Bible more often than forgiving love. It's all part of a Christmas present called God's grace. Is forgiveness ever easy? Of course not, but it is a vital part of learning to put our complete faith and trust in One who so graciously forgives us. Here is the best part: As you learn to forgive others… you will begin to heal.

The alternative to forgiveness is torture!

This kind of Christmas preparation applies to all of us, from preachers to pew-sitters to sleep-in-forget-about-church-believers. It may be the most important preparation you ever attempt. The "Good News" is that with this kind of preparation you will really appreciate the birth of the Christ Child. Have a Merry Christmas.

Christmas 2000: Memories

Some things change while others stay the same but Christmas? Well, Christmas is forever! For that simple promise, I am grateful. Why? Because in the midst of worldly chaos, it is comforting to know Christmas continues to show God's love through Jesus' birth. Here are my 2000 Christmas Memories.

Tacky Lights: For me, Christmas always starts with lights… lots of lights. What can I say? I grew up in Virginia Beach, home base of the original "Tacky Light" tour. I have an interesting theory: Brighter lights on the outside mean brighter, happier families inside. If true… our family is very happy!

Who will be President? For thirty-seven days a nation waited breathlessly. In the end, the majority ruled five to four: judges rather than voters. As frustrating as the whole process seemed, it could have been much worse. Maybe Al Gore said it best: "I don't agree with the court's decision but I accept it!"

Christmas Parties: I learned a new tradition called "Dirty Santa." The tackiest gifts imaginable were opened and traded. My wife received a backscratcher. I got a can of body spray. We also sang a new version of 12 Days of Christmas with a salute to Florida: "12 lawyers filing, 11 judges judging, 10 legal rulings, 9 reporters guessing, 8 spokesmen whining, 7 politicians babbling, 6 disenfranchised voters..."

International Ministry Starts over Breakfast: Thanks to the enthusiasm of a young Korean pastor named Peter Jung and his family, several representatives gathered to pray and combine resources to reach out for God to a rapidly growing international population. They came from various nationalities, churches and groups who as Peter said: "God is working among us and guiding us to His melting pot."

Children's Pageant: What is Christmas without children in bathrobes proclaiming, "I bring you good news of great joy for everyone! The Savior – yes the Messiah, the Lord has been born tonight in Bethlehem..." Meanwhile two angels are shoving over who stands in front, baby Jesus is passed over everyone's head to a waiting mother with a fresh diaper and a shepherd wanders from the group.

Death on a Bridge: Two teenagers died when they were bumped from a railroad trestle by a Norfolk Southern freight train. Miraculously, another survived thanks to a dramatic rescue. "I wish we could have saved the others," a rescuer said. "Now there are two families without their kids for Christmas."

"A Night at the Inn:" We were greeted at the door by young waiters and seated at our table. On stage were musicians and jugglers along with the innkeeper's family and several guests. In between food servings we sang Christmas carols and watched the drama of Christ's birth unfold as if we were there.

Divorce Recovery Group Graduates: Several months ago, they were brokenhearted individuals who shared the tragedy of divorce. As each one told their stories, God's Holy Spirit began to stir within the room and a miracle of healing began. Tonight, they were a group of friends, laughing and celebrating their graduation with a Christmas party. Next week, they are all going out to eat together. After that...

Christmas Cantata: Music can be the gateway to the soul but not always at rehearsals. For some reason, Cantata's seldom sound right until the proper time. Is it because God's Holy Spirit takes over turning an ordi-

267

nary performance into inspired worship? I like that answer. Speaking of taking over, one choir member was taken over by the flu, turned green and was led away. There is always something…

Something else happened during our Christmas events. People attended who had not been to church in long while. Why? Maybe some had simply been too busy… Some didn't think church was very important… A few were angry at the church or the preacher or God… Some were struggling with serious faith issues… Yet during Christmas, they came back. Whether looking for answers or seeking comfort, people often come back. Such is the power of Christmas.

Some things change while others stay the same but Christmas? Christmas is forever! Praise God! May your Christmas be filled with precious memories. May Christmas strengthen your relationship with God. After all, Jesus is the reason for the season. Merry Christmas!

Christmas, A Victim and Opportunities

The Victim: It was a cold, December night as Judy finished working late shift at the restaurant. The supervisor warned the employees not to walk through the parking lot alone, but she was in a hurry. Nearing the car Judy felt rather than heard the presence rushing toward her. Before she could react a rough hand grabbed her by the neck jerking back hard. Both feet left the ground as she felt herself lifted high as if she were no heavier than a child's rag doll. Then there was the too brief sensation of free falling through the air as she was flung to the hard pavement. Dazed and in pain, Judy noticed the foul odor of stale cigarettes and cheap wine as the attacker began to loosen the strap of her purse. Before there was time to scream, she saw his evil scowl and the flash of his knife...

Opportunity One: Ed, a pastor in the area was driving home from a long and frustrating meeting at the church when his headlights picked up the attacker who upon seeing Ed's car left Judy and ran. "Somebody needs help," thought Ed and he paused before resuming his driving. "But it is so late and violent crime happens a lot in our area. I could get hurt. But something needs to be done about the violence in this community. I should hold a prayer vigil at the church or write the mayor…"

Judy had no idea how many times she had been slashed and stabbed but sensed that somehow she must find help or die. Slowly and painfully, Judy began to crawl toward the nearby street desperate for any passing motorist to see her. Struggling to her feet, in pain and nearly blind from the blood in her eyes, Judy began to stagger down the roadway…

Opportunity Two: Phyllis was feeling good about the songs her choir was singing in the Christmas Cantata. The music was on cassette so she could practice while driving. "Joy to the World, the Lord is Come," she sang in perfect harmony with the accompanying voices of the tape. So intent on singing, Phyllis almost hit Judy staggering across the roadway. Swerving the car and honking the horn, Phyllis still managed to yell out, "Lousy drunk…why don't you get a job!" After a moment she calmed down and resumed singing, "Let every heart prepare Him room…"

As the car raced by, Judy cried out: "Oh God! Somebody please help me!" collapsed and passed out.

Opportunity Three: The next few hours were a blur in Judy's memory, but through the haze she remembered hearing a soft whisper, "It's okay. You are going to be all right!" As she regained consciousness she noticed the hospital surroundings. A nurse was looking at several monitors. Then Judy realized the tubes and wires from the machines were attached to her. "What happened?"

The nurse looked her way, smiled and said, "You are a very fortunate young woman. You were beaten and stabbed repeatedly and apparently left for dead."

"How did I get here?" Judy asked.

The nurse smiled and replied, "You were rescued by our hospital custodian, Ed Harris. On the way home he saw you, called the rescue squad and stayed with you until just a few moments ago."

Three different people were given opportunities to offer help. After a similar story, Jesus asked, "Which of these three do you think was a neighbor to the one who was robbed and beaten?"   (Luke 10:36)

The expert in the law replied, "The one who had mercy."

Jesus then said, "Go and do likewise."

Your opportunities to help someone may or may not be this dramatic. It makes no difference. What matters is how you respond. This Christmas, be alert for the opportunities God gives you.

Did you know that Jesus never said, "Take up your cross and join the church?" He actually said, "Take up your cross and follow me." May Jesus be the reason for your Christmas season.

Seven Dollars and Forty-Three Cents

The checkout at the local grocery store was long and I was in a hurry. Seeing another line nearly empty, I walked over and stood behind the only customer still to make a purchase. A young twenty-something woman was holding a small basket with fifteen to twenty jars of baby food. There was nothing else in the basket: just baby food.

"This is great," I thought. *"She'll only be a minute and I can be on my way."*

The clerk took the woman's check for seven dollars and forty-three cents and efficiently typed in the numbers and slid it into the proper slot on the register. At this point the cash drawer was supposed to open while a receipt was printed, but not this time. A light began to blink: *"See Manager."* The clerk called on the intercom for the supervisor while running the check through again on her register. The same sign kept flashing: *"See Manager."*

"Oh no!" I thought. *"Not another delay. I'm in a hurry and don't need for the cash register to break down."*

When the supervisor arrived, however, he didn't even look at the cash register, but instead picked up the check and began to talk to the customer. I could feel the muscles in my stomach tighten as the reality of what was happening struck me.

The check for seven dollars and forty-three cents was no good and the manager was quietly saying she could not buy her baby food here. The clerk quickly set the groceries aside, closed her account and began to ring up my purchase.

"She should manage her money better!" I tried to convince myself while leaving the store. *"She's probably an alcoholic or a drug addict."* But my flimsy excuses would not erase the picture in my mind of a grocery basket filled with jars of baby food.

Jesus teaches: *"You are the light of the world...we don't light a lamp and put it under a bowl. Instead we put it on a stand and it gives light to everyone in the house. In the same way, let your light shine so they may see your good deeds and praise your Father in heaven."* (Mat. 5:14-16)

Every day, all of us receive opportunities to help someone in need. Our light shines when we use those God-given opportunities to witness our faith by reaching out and getting involved. There is nothing dramatic about these day-to-day encounters, but they emphatically tell the world what kind of Christians we really are.

At this point, I want to finish the story by writing how I approached the manager and offered to pay for the purchase of the baby food. It was the right thing to do. I don't have much money, but I can afford seven dollars and forty-three cents. Instead, hiding my light under a bowl, I turned my head and walked away. There are no acceptable excuses. I had a great opportunity to help someone and walked away.

Next time, I will do better. God has taught me a valuable lesson today. What we believe as Christians only works if we turn our faith into action. How about you? How many opportunities have you missed to let your light shine and instead hid it under a bowl?

The next time you are in a check-out line at your local grocery store. Instead of worrying about your schedule, look around you. Maybe God will give you the opportunity to help someone who needs seven dollars and forty-three cents to buy some baby food. Please, in the name of God, let your light shine and give them a helping hand.

$7.43 X 100 = A Lesson in Ministry!

Tom Riddle was a tough, but fair boss who always knew how to get the best out of me. Over the years, he has also become a close personal friend. On a recent trip to Virginia Beach, my old home town, I decided to stop in and visit Mr. Riddle to talk about old times and talk about one of my books.

The surprise however was on me. Instead of a simple visit, Mr. Riddle taught me a unique lesson on giving and ministry.

At one point, he said: *"I enjoyed your book so much, I read it all in one night. One of my favorite stories, was titled "$7.43."*

"$7.43" was about my visit to a local supermarket where a young lady, just in front of me, tried to buy several jars of baby food which happened to total $7.43. Her check was no good and the store manager asked her to leave. I made excuses, but I could not get the image of the baby food out of my mind. I should have given the lady $7.43, but actually did... nothing. As a result, I learned a valuable lesson and promised to do better next time.

Mr. Riddle then said: *"Well, Larry, what have you done since then?"* I tried to think of something smart to say, but for once no words came.

"I've got an idea," he said and picked up the phone and instructed his secretary to bring him a check for $743.00. *"I want you to take this money and put it into one hundred different envelopes and give it to 100 people in need."*

As I took the check and began to thank him, Mr. Riddle asked me another question. *"Larry, this is my gift. What will you do?*

Again, I did not know what to say, but knew he expected me to do something. Mr. Riddle had given something of value and it was now my turn. But how could a preacher give a gift that would make a real difference?

Peter wrote in 1 Peter: *"Each one should use whatever gift they have received to serve others, faithfully administering God's grace in its various forms."* The message is that all of us have something to give of great value. We simply need to find it and use it. A soft voice inside me kept saying: *"The best gift you can give is your book."*

"But Lord," I said. *"I haven't even paid the printing bill yet!"*

Several nights later, at a Christmas gathering, I shared the story of Mr. Riddle's gift and passed out 50 of the envelopes along with fifty copies of my book. The instructions were to give one envelope and one book to someone in need and tell the story of $7.43. On the following Sunday morning, fifty people in our church were given the same opportunity.

Two weeks later, Mr. Riddle was our church's guest and heard the stories of the lives that were touched by his special gift.

- One woman experiencing a divorce used the money to take the kids to a local restaurant and then read the book for continued devotional support.
- Another gift was sent to a man in prison who used the money to send home for his daughter's Christmas present and then passed the book around to fellow inmates.
- A third gift was given to a family struggling through a recent job layoff.

One church member after another stood and spoke of the lives that were touched and how they felt led to become even more involved with the person who received the gift. They also spoke of the joy they felt being able to offer something encouraging to a person in need.

In addition to helping at least 100 people, Mr. Riddle taught me a valuable lesson on the importance and the joy of giving. **All for $7.43.** Try it for yourself and watch God make it grow!

Competitive to the Extreme: King Herod

Christmas has come and gone… now what? How should we respond as the New Year begins? For answers we look to the story of the wise men. "About that time some wise men from eastern lands arrived in Jerusalem asking, 'Where is the newborn king of the Jews? We have seen his star as it arose and we have come to worship him.' Herod was deeply disturbed by their question…" (Mat 2:1-3)

Why was Herod so "deeply disturbed" by the questions of the wise men? Why did he feel so threatened? Answer: Herod was fiercely competitive… to the extreme.

For the first twelve years, Herod competed to establish his reign by eliminating hundreds of potential opponents including his wife and her two sons. During the next dozen years, he would rebuild the cities and towns and establish himself as one of Israel's greatest kings. But it was the final nine years when Herod was at his worst. Hundreds, maybe thousands of people were executed including his brother. It was here that Herod received the wise men announcing the Messiah's birth. Shortly after that visit Herod sent soldiers to Bethlehem to murder every boy in the community under two years old.

Confession time: I am also competitive… too competitive. My sister and I spent a lot of time together playing board games such as Monopoly, Scrabble and Life. It took her awhile to catch on to why her big brother was winning so frequently. Eventually she realized, the rules were subtly changing from one game to the next. (Larry, that is so low! I know. I know!) Whatever it took: I wanted to win. Ouch!

A competitive personality can be an asset of course. Competition fosters harder work and greater creativity. The success of our economy is driven by our competitive nature. The most exciting sporting events are those where the competitive rivalry between opponents is at its highest. Our democratic political system is based on at least two competitive office seekers slugging it out before voting day.

A competitive personality can also be treacherous. When you twist the rules, use unethical business tactics, deliberately injure an opponent or slander a rival you are being competitive to the extreme. At this point you cross a fine line that separates aggressiveness from brutality. If you feel compelled to lie, cheat or steal to get to the top of the heap… to stay at the top your brutality will only get worse.

Of course, none of us would ever be this competitive or feel this threatened… would we?

When a new employee is hired and they display extraordinary enthusiasm for their job do you rush to learn from him or encourage her? (Get real,

Larry!) I doubt it. More likely, you feel threatened. You may even find yourself in a few back room discussions to find ways bring him/her back down to size. When a new member joins the church and suggests ways the church can improve or shows interest and talent in the area of the church you serve, do you look for ways to be supportive? Do you pull them aside and tell them we don't do things that way around here? Do you talk behind their back?

Before I sound too smug, I attended a local pastors meeting recently and one particularly gifted new minister was enthusiastically sharing ideas for church growth. I remember leaning over and whispering to one of the other old fogy's… oops, I mean ministers and whispering, "He'll burn out in ninety days."

Let's be honest. We are all competitive to a degree. We occasionally feel threatened by new talent and fresh ideas. We all possess a little bit of apprehension that our position will be eliminated and we will no longer be needed. It is natural and very human to feel this way but competition taken to the extreme is a form of paranoia and is still very, very wrong. There is a little bit of King Herod in all of us.

The Christ child was born and soon the family was forced to flee to avoid Herod's competitive fear. How many talented people do companies lose because other employees refuse to offer support? How many churches lose their young and gifted because long-time members refuse to adjust to new ideas?

The question is: What should we do next? How can you learn from Herod's tragic mistakes? What will enable me to be more supportive of new people and ideas?

Competitive to the Extreme: King Herod – Conclusion

"After the interview with Herod the wise men went their way. *Once again the star appeared to them, guiding them to Bethlehem. It went ahead of them and stopped over the place where the child was. When they saw the star, they were filled with joy! They entered the house where the child and his mother Mary were and they fell down before him and worshipped him. Then they opened their treasure chests and gave him gifts of gold, frankincense and myrrh."*   (Mat. 2:9-11)

Herod saw the Christ child as competition and a threat to his rule. His reaction was to crush whatever stood in his way.

The wise men however had a different response:

☆ They saw the star... Everyone could see it. Why were foreigners the only ones who understood the significance? Why not a Jewish priest? Why not anyone already in Israel? Maybe they weren't looking. What about you? Are you looking for the star?

☆ They followed... They dropped everything to follow a star. Some historians predict that it might have taken months to make this kind of long, arduous journey. Why did they do it? Because they sensed God's will. Was it easy? Of course not but they followed with faith. Will you?

☆ They were filled with joy... The wise men kept looking and following until reaching their destination. At times they must have been tempted to turn back... to simply go home. Yet they kept pressing on. Their reward at the end of the road was an unspeakable joy.

☆ They fell down and worshipped... Others only saw a baby but the wise men saw God and responded with humility and adoration. What was it like to look into the eyes of God? Yet, you have the opportunity each day. Are you willing to bow down and worship God?

☆ They gave their best gifts... The wise men were called from afar to witness Christ's birth. They responded by giving the very best of what they had. Think about it. You are offered the awesome opportunity to be in relationship with almighty God. Will you respond with your best?

I thought the story of the 'wise men' was simply a children's story. I was so wrong. There are precious gifts of wisdom for us all if we are willing to learn. For this upcoming year, if you want to become more of a 'Wise Man' than a 'Herod' there are questions we should ponder as individuals and as a church:

1. Do you have a plan for personal spiritual growth? When you are busy focusing on your relationship with God, you are not as likely to feel threatened by the actions of others.

2. Does your church have a plan for spiritual growth? Have they made a commitment before God to help others grow stronger in their faith?

3. Are you willing to change jobs to better serve God? Would you be open to moving? Would you give up your church position to give someone else an opportunity to serve?

4. Is your church willing to listen to new ideas? Will they make adjustments in order to facilitate the needs and potential contributions of new people?

5. Is your life an example for others to follow? Will they see in you the wise man following God's star wherever it may lead? No one expects perfection but are you willing to try?

6. Does your church support leaders who have a vision for growth and inspire enthusiasm for the future? Will you support that leadership or better yet... be a part?

Christmas has come and gone... now what? How should you respond to the birth of the King of kings?

Will you be 'deeply disturbed' like Herod because of the inevitable changes a commitment to Christ requires?

Will you be 'filled with joy' like the wise men because they made a commitment to follow the star and found the 'precious babe lying in a manger?'

The star beckons...

Caught In the Christmas Eve Storm

Christmas Eve began like any other day for me. During the last several weeks our church had been involved in a flurry of activities from special Christmas programs to mission projects offering toys and coats to needy children. Our candlelight worship service tonight would be the last big event. My wife, Mell and I were looking forward to a few days of rest and visits with family.   At 6:30 AM, we were sharing a cup of coffee when the lights began to first flicker then go out. "No electricity? Oh well, a few hours inconvenience," we thought as we continued our normal routine. The weather reports had mentioned a possibility of ice and snow, but nothing major.

How could I know that we were in the middle of a freak ice storm that would blacken nearly 400,000 homes across Virginia? Throughout the long day ice and sleet continued to fall.

By 4:00 PM, I reluctantly joined hundreds of other churches and cancelled Christmas Eve services. Wanting to escape the inconvenience of no power and still not realizing the seriousness of the storm, we decided to visit relatives in Virginia Beach. Bad decision! Wrecks were all over the highway. Trees and large branches littered the road and occasionally fell just in front of us. A normal three-hour drive turned into six hours of terror. There were no lights on the road to guide us and no gas stations or restaurants open to offer respite from the storm. Everything was closed.

The next morning, Christmas Day, we assumed power would return soon and decided to go home to see what could be done to help others caught in the storm. Another bad decision! The weather was deceptively calm and the trees glistened like crystal chandeliers on the long drive back. The only evidence of the massive damage was the piles of limbs stacked beside the road. Driving through town was like the aftermath of a hurricane with trees and debris everywhere.

Our house still had no power and no alternative source of heat. I came home with noble intentions of helping others but with a sickening feeling soon realized that the one who would need help first would be me. There were no emergency shelters available so I had to first figure out how to survive. During the next four days and long nights we were forced to live day-by-day and only through the generous help of friends and neighbors did we survive. Along the way, I received some hard-learned lessons.

Lesson 1: Be Prepared! The old boy scout motto certainly counts here. I had given no thought to how we would manage without electricity. Could we obtain other sources of heat? Did we have candles, flashlights and batteries for light? Could we get enough food and water? By not being adequately prepared, I was forced to ask for help rather than offer help to others. In our spiritual lives, good preparation can also mean the difference between seeking aid and aiding others.

Lesson 2: Aggressively Share! We desperately needed help, but hesitated to ask for it. One friend called and delivered a kerosene heater. Several neighbors offered shelter. A local hotel offered rooms to the community for hot showers. A retreat center offered free rooms. As electricity was restored, some folks looked out of cold dark windows and saw houses brightly lit and obviously warm. It was especially appreciated when they opened their doors and generously offered us aid. In our spiritual lives, those of us who are fortunate to know God's light and warmth should aggressively share with those who are still feeling left out in the cold and darkness.

The real hero's of the storm were the hundred's of workers who left their families during Christmas holidays to labor sixteen and eighteen hour days restoring our power. A local nursing home was without heat for two days and in serious trouble. When a local lineman found out, he summoned a crew and immediately went to restore their power, possibly saving several lives. Our community can never thank them enough for their hard work and sacrifice.

As the lights return, the clean up begins and the Christmas Eve storm fades into memory. But I will never forget the generosity and kindness of others. It's a simple gesture really, but maybe that is what being a follower of Jesus Christ is really all about.

I Love M&M's

I love M & M's!

You know: "The candy that melts in your mouth, not in your hands." I have a bag full in front of me. I don't want to keep you in suspense. I'm reaching in and taking out a handful and setting each M & M on my desk. Do you mind if I eat while I write? Of course you don't.

Do you have a favorite color? Is it Green? Let me eat one you. Oh yes, green is good!

By the way, one of my New Year's Resolutions for 2001 is to share more freely with others. John the Baptist in Luke 3:11 says, "The one with two tunics should share with one who has none, and the one who has food should do the same." I think we should all be willing to share. Don't you?

How about brown? Do you like brown M & M's? Uhm, that's good too!

In the Bible there is a verse from James 3:15 that says, "Suppose a brother or sister is without clothes and daily food. If one of you says, 'Go I wish you well; keep warm and well fed,' but does nothing about his physical needs, what good is it?" That is so important! Don't you think so?

Have you tried red? Oh, heavenly morsels! Red is delicious!

Sharing is a New Year's Resolution all of us should make. Jesus said, "When you give to someone, don't tell your left hand what your right hand is doing. Give your gifts in secret and your Father, who knows all secrets will reward you." (Matthew 6:3-4) Isn't that a great attitude to have when you give? Remember, you are never more like Christ than when you share of yourself and your possessions.

Have you tried one of the new colors? How about blue? Oh my, what a treat! Blue is good!

"Wait a minute! What are you thinking? You don't expect me to share my M & Ms? Do You?"

Paul said in a letter to the Romans: "Share with God's people who are in need. Practice hospitality." (12:13) Sharing with hospitality must be accompanied by personal compassion. Not only are we to give but give with a warm smile and a willingness to become personally involved.

Wouldn't you agree?

"But nowhere in scripture does it say, 'Thou must share your M & M's.' Does it? I'm in deep trouble." Sharing means:

✢ Individuals: Sharing freely of what you own rather than what is convenient. It means becoming involved in the giving process and treating those who receive with love and respect.

✢ Business: Giving back part of the profits to help others but also creatively looking for ways to share your ideas, skills, training and resources with the community.

✢ Churches: Sharing starts with a food basket or donated clothes but continues with a willingness to listen and include those we are helping in the life and activities of the church.

✢ Government: While recognizing that a program will not eliminate poverty an attitude of concern and a willingness to look for real solutions can offer genuine hope to those who are suffering.

✢ For me this means genuine sharing... (Oh this hurts) even my M & M's and more importantly giving with enthusiasm and a smile on my face. (Now I've gone from preachin' to meddlin'!)

As our world economy struggles, a willingness to freely share will become ever more critical. So, will you join me in forming a New Year's Resolution to share with hospitality?

New Year's Resolutions like this are essential but impossible to keep without help, which is why my other resolutions will include prayer, more prayer and even more prayer. May God bless each of you during the next twelve months and may you have a healthy, prosperous new year.

By the way, after writing this, my next New Year's Resolution will be to lose 15 pounds. I really do love M & M's! Pray for me.

Hospitals & God's Comfort

Anne was brought to the hospital with an infection in her knees and hips so severe; she had not been able to get out of bed for nearly a year. At the young age of forty-two, this poor woman was facing extensive surgery plus a mountain of personal problems including drug abuse, family squabbles and a stack of unpaid bills. Anne was in big trouble.

I was approaching the end of a long three months of chaplain training required to become a pastor in my denomination. I began as a brash young pastor who thought he could change the world and left the hospital a little older and wiser focusing more on changing me and leaving the "world changing" to God. I also learned to deeply respect and admire the hard work, tough training and dedication of those in the medical field. But even with all the training and the skills there is only so much healing, human beings can provide. The rest is up to the patient and God.

Routine blood tests revealed an additional problem for our forty-two-year old sufferer. Anne was HIV positive and would likely develop full-blown symptoms of Aids soon. Can you imagine that? She was already suffering from so much… now AIDS! What a catastrophe! The doctor wisely called for the chaplain to accompany her, which in this case was me. I wanted to help but how? What could I possibly say or do that would help to resolve Anne's dilemma or ease her suffering?

At one of our early meetings as trainees, the former business manager in me noticed some inefficiency in our visiting schedule and made the brash comment we could see more patients if we didn't take so many breaks. The supervisor gave a knowing smile and said, "you will understand soon enough." She was right! All too many patients like our 42-year-old woman soon helped me understand the real meaning of the word… break: a rest between two tragedies.

After the doctor explained the meaning of HIV positive and the ramifications, she left. For nearly an hour Anne alternately talked and cried. She had been horribly abused much of her life and sought escape in the only way available hoping a local gang would satisfy her longing for friendship and love. Anne could not have been more wrong but by the time she realized her mistake, it was too late. The years of beatings, brutal sexual abuse and drugs took their toll.

One requirement of chaplain training was "night shift" in the emergency room. Since this hospital was located in the poorest part of the city the emergency room resembled a M.A.S.H. unit in the middle of a war zone: accidents, fights and gunshot wounds. Often, after a shooting our duty could best be described as "riot control." Friends and family would gather to offer support but often articulated it as rage: at the shooter, at society and occasionally even the hospital itself.

At one point, Anne, too was filled with rage: at her family who abused her, her so-called friends who used her and even God for seemingly abandoning her. I had no answers. Soon she would face excruciating surgery followed by a long, painful recovery only to cope with aids. What could any mere human being possibly say? "Would you like to receive communion?" She looked at me for the longest time… and with a tear beginning to run down her cheek, Anne nodded: yes!

Later, that night, amidst the busyness and noise of a large metropolitan hospital a struggling student chaplain and a deeply troubled woman discovered the words of comfort only God can give:

Merciful God, we confess that we have not loved you…
…in the name of Jesus Christ you are forgiven.
The body of Christ, given for you. Amen.
The blood of Christ shed for you. Amen.

A hospital chaplain who thought he could do it all and a struggling woman who seemingly lost it all both discovered the greatest gift of all… the all encompassing comfort of God.

Several days later, following her knee and hip surgery, I was summoned to Anne's room for a different purpose. "I sensed the presence of God in the room that night during communion and for the first time in my life I felt truly loved. Thank you! Now, I have a surprise for you!" She stood up triumphantly and asked me to escort her on the first real walk she had taken in two years: down the length of the hospital hall and back. This time it was my turn to cry.

Responding to Tragedy: The Church

There has been a tragedy in our household.

How should the people who know and love us respond? As a pastor, I know what to do and have written about possible responses many times, but now I was on the other side. My family was suffering and desperately needed compassionate, loving ministry. How would the church help us?

You notice acts of caring. I was amazed at how little gestures meant so much to us. We received cards and letters from people who suffered a similar tragedy in their own family. Their willingness and courage to share their experiences was a tremendous help for us. We took delicious delight each morning simply going to the mailbox and reading the many cards and letters offering prayers and support. Our home looks like a florist shop. One kind soul sent money to cover travel and meals. A plate of cookies always seemed to come at the right time.

You also notice the silence. I was surprised at how many friends never said a word. Even among fellow professional caregivers, people who were leaders in my field, ministers who knew better, who helped others so well were either too busy or simply didn't know what to say. Instead, they chose to say nothing and their silence was the cruelest blow of all.

Then the dreadful truth hit me between the eyes. At times, I have offered loving gestures of compassion and support. At other times, I have also been guilty of the unimaginable act of callousness by saying or doing… nothing. "Forgive me Lord and help me do better!"

The Apostle Paul gave this advice to us: "But just as you excel in everything – in faith, in speech, in knowledge, in complete earnestness and in your love for us – see that you also excel in this grace of giving." (2 Corinthians 8:7) I'm beginning to learn the hard way that we are judged, not by our church attendance, Bible study, hymn singing, or even by how much money we place in the offering plate. They are certainly good disciplines, which help us, become better Christians but we will be judged by how we utilize those same disciplines to respond to the world around us.

It is often the simple gestures of tenderness and care that says to the grieving heart… I love you and God loves you! I'm beginning to deeply understand how much they benefit our healing.

So, what did I learn from this experience?

✝ **We are not alone.** It' a comforting thought even in the midst of heartbreak. The church offers love and compassion from a human perspective and a grace that can only come from God.

✝ **Some of us are hurting.** I am aware that some have not experienced the same grace and compassion, loving people of God should offer. As a church we should do better.

✝ **Simple gestures of love and support are noticed and appreciated.** Don't put off writing that card or making a phone call to someone in need. Bake a cake or send some cookies if you are able. Look around and do a needed chore such as cutting the grass or cleaning the house. It sounds simple enough but those gestures are so deeply appreciated.

✝ **I need you.** As a pastor, I try to look and act independent but truthfully I need you.

✝ **I need God!** Just when I start to give myself all the credit, God sends a poignant reminder. The events of the past few days drove me to my knees because there was nothing else to do.

✝**Tragedy can strengthen our faith.** It's true, you know. God may not cause catastrophe, but it can be the catalyst God uses to help us strengthen our faith, if we will allow it.

Maybe this is why I love God's church. Where else can you feel such love? Is it perfect? Of course not! But we need continuing support from each other and from God. Even pastors need to be occasionally reminded of that all-important lesson. My prayer is that you too will receive loving comfort when you need it most.

Breaking The Peanut Butter Habit . . .

Following God's Recipe For A Wonderful Life.

Chapter 8

Seasonal Food: Easter & Spring

Spring, Arnold Palmer and Humility!

Spring is in the air. Can you feel it? Birds are singing. Flowers are blooming. Honeybees are buzzing and stinging. Ouch! The house needs spring-cleaning and the grass needs cutting. (*To capture the mood, go outside, take off your shoes, put on a straw hat and read this aloud, while leaping wildly in the air, and gaily flinging dried flower petals.*) Yes, spring has arrived, the season for romance, long walks, pollen induced allergy attacks, barbecue grills and golf. (Pause) Why golf?

I don't want to brag or anything, (*Yes, I do!*) but did you know that I once played eighteen holes of golf with the one and only, Arnold Palmer and won by three strokes? (No, *not a golf klutz with the same name. No, I did not cheat. No, I can't afford to bribe him! Yes, his health is good!*)

We played at Harbourtown in Hilton Head Island, South Carolina. It's a beautiful golf course if you stay in the fairway, but full of water hazards, huge sand traps and thickets if you mess up. Can you imagine how intimidating it is to stand on the first tee with one of the great legends of golf? Yet, Arnie (his friends call him Arnie, I call him… sir) was kind and gracious but he was also determined to win.

For the first 13 holes it was nip and tuck as we struggled to a tie score. He would win one hole with a spectacular birdie then I would win with another. But on the 14th hole, I sunk a 35-foot putt to go ahead by one stroke. Am I good or what? On the 17th hole, I made another birdie. And finally on the 18th, Arnie went for broke on a long putt and missed. Victory was mine. Let the celebration begin!

"*Yahoo! I beat Arnie!*" I shouted while pumping fists into the air and performing a version of the funky chicken! (*Wouldn't you like to see that?*) Hey, it's not every day you beat Arnold Palmer!!!

Are you getting sick and tired of my arrogant boasting yet? Of course you are even if this crazy story is true and it is… sort of. But here is the point. When you hear someone sound off like this… do you have an urge to hug him… or do you want to slug her? No one enjoys the company of a bragger or a famous namedropper. Yet, could a little of this obnoxious tendency be in all of us?

When Jesus noticed that all who had come to the dinner were trying to sit near the head of the table, he gave them this advice: "If you are invited to a wedding feast, don't always head for the best seat. What if someone more respected than you has also been invited? The host will say, 'Let this person sit here instead.' Then you will be embarrassed and will have to take whatever seat is left at the foot of the table! "Do this instead—sit at the foot of the table. Then when your host sees you, he will come and say, 'Friend, we have a better place than this for you!' Then you will be honored in front of all the other guests. **For the proud will be humbled, but the humble will be honored."** (Luke14: 7-11)

Jesus is talking about more than good table manners, isn't he? The most important people at a wedding feast are, of course, the bride and groom. Not you! What would a wedding be without them? By maneuvering to get the best seat you detract from the couple's happy moment and look like an insensitive jerk or worse. We see it in others, but do we notice it in ourselves? Not always.

By trying so hard to beat Arnold Palmer, I missed the opportunity to enjoy his company and admire his unique abilities. Likewise, our arrogant attitude detracts from the God we all claim to serve and prevents us from appreciating and learning from the immensely talented people who surround us.

Our society applauds a "win at any cost" mentality and expects us to revel in the victory. Yet, Jesus clearly demonstrates another answer. It is in our humility not our boasting that we truly discover God.

Now Larry, what is the truth about that celebrity golf match? (Pause) Did you know that it is simply amazing what computers can do? They can simulate almost anything... even a game of golf. Yes, I did play Arnold Palmer at Harbourtown, but from the comfort of my office and computer screen. Sorry!

Just think, in one story, I've been exposed as arrogant, boasting and slightly deceitful. At one time or another haven't we all? Maybe this is why we need God and from the sound of my bragging? Yes, I need God too.

Spring, Snakes and Psalm 23

"Whew, spring!" It's a beautiful time of year but it also means chores, especially outside. We still had sticks and debris from last year's ice storm to pick up. But at long last, the labor was nearly finished so I strolled around the yard to inspect the work and admire the view. On the way back, a sudden movement caught my eye. The longest black snake I had ever

seen was slithering up the steps toward the entrance to our house.

"Now what do I do?" The snake wasn't poisonous but I certainly didn't want to annoy him. Maybe if I just waited he would slink off to hassle someone else. But NOooo…, the snake was obviously after something and whatever it was… was on the other side of our doorway. I had never seen a snake so aggressive or so long. At one point while sliding up the door his head was over the top of the frame while the tail almost touched the bottom making him (*Was it a him? Do you really think I checked*?!) at least six feet long. I definitely had a predicament on my hands.

Quietly and menacingly the snake draped his body over the top of the doorway and waited. Seconds later, my wife, Mell appeared. ***"Don't open that door, Honey!"*** I yelled. She stared at me quizzically, glanced up, saw the snake and gasped. Fortunately, Mell never opened the door but it was pretty close.

Thanks to help of a friendly neighbor, I disposed of the animal and said a quiet prayer of thanks. It was a scary feeling seeing that snake draped over our doorway. Suppose my wife had walked out the door and that huge snake had dropped on her? (*I don't even want to think about it.*) Suppose he had gotten into the house? (*We would have moved! Just kidding. I think?*)

Life can be pretty ordinary most of the time, full of daily chores and routine decisions. Then a sudden movement can catch your eye and out of nowhere comes a slithering snake of dilemmas. You wait, hoping that he'll slink off and hassle someone else but NOooo… this snake is more aggressive. He's perched over the doorway waiting for an unsuspecting soul to pass underneath.

"Now what do you do?"

- You receive a call from the doctor's office. They want to see you right away.
- A sleepy driver misses a stop sign right in front of your car.
- 6,000 people went to an ordinary day of work at the New York City World Trade Center never knowing that September 11, 2001 would be their last.

Do you remember this part of Psalm 23? *"You prepare a table before me in the presence of my enemies. You anoint my head with oil."* I always assumed this passage was about a dinner table. David is talking about preparing us for snakes.

In a mountainous region, a "table" is a flat section of land. Before entering a new "table," a good shepherd inspects the ground for holes, which are potential hiding places for poisonous brown snakes. In each hole he will pour thick oil and then with the same oil "anoint" the sheep's nose and mouth making the surface too slippery to bite. A loving shepherd does that.

We are never promised that snakes don't exist or that they won't occasionally bite. Instead God offers to inspect the "tables" before you, providing safety. When the occasional snake does get through the first layer of protection you are anointed with a second layer of oil called God's comfort protecting you from the poison.

Are there snakes perched on your doorway ready to strike? Have they soured your disposition and challenged your faith? Get out a Bible and read Psalm 23 again. Read the words slowly and think about what it would be like for you to personally receive the Good Shepherd's anointing oil of protection and comfort. I feel safer already. Do you?

A Prayer for Lent

- Lord, at the beginning of this Lenten season, I sense my need of you; yet, I am not quite sure how to reach you.
- I heard someone say, '*Read your Bible.*' But too often the words are like bullets that ricochet off my brain.
- I heard someone say, '*Pray.*' But my prayers, hurled heaven ward, fall back to earth like lifeless stones.
- I heard someone say, '*Meditate.*' But my wandering mind was lost in a desert of random thoughts.

Could this prayer by Robin Van Cleef describe your spiritual life at times? Trust me, you are not alone! I tend to look at a computer screen or newspaper instead of God's Holy Word. Not good! Sometimes reading the Bible is a stimulating journey of fresh discoveries while other times I honestly struggle to turn every page. It's sad but true. Forgive me Lord!

Do you ever pray and wonder if anyone is listening? I do. Prayer can be a daily delight where you feel bathed in the very presence of God. But prayer can also be a desperate plea for a rope to help you climb from the deep dark depths. But the rope does not always seem to be there. Prayer can be a cry for answers… sometimes there is only silence. "Where are you God?"

Meditation seems too slow for my hectic lifestyle. I tend to seek stimulation rather than meditation… a comfortable conversation instead of lonely contemplation… entertainment rather than education. "Meditation? Me?

I'm too busy right now Lord but after I retire and sit in the rocking chair…"

Spiritual growth seldom happens naturally. Lent is a time of preparation for Easter: A time to remember the life and death of Jesus before we celebrate the resurrection of Christ. Lent is an opportunity to renew and deepen our relationship with God. Read your Bible. Join a Bible study. Look for fresh opportunities to pray. Ask your friends if you can pray with them. Find a quiet place and read something you find spiritually inspiring. Then, sit back, be still and quietly… meditate.

Over this particular Lenten season, God wants to reach out and touch you, embrace you and love you. But we must be willing to do our part. Is it easy? Of course not. Will it be worthwhile? With patience and perseverance… always!

> ▷ Don't be impatient for the Lord to act! Travel steadily along His path. He will honor you…   (Psalm 38:34)
> ▷ So think clearly and exercise self-control. Look forward to the special blessings that will come…   (1 Peter 2:13)
> ▷ One day soon afterward Jesus went to a mountain to pray and he prayed to God all night. At daybreak, He chose…   (Luke 6:12)
> ▷ Pray at all times and on every occasion in the power of the Holy Spirit. Stay alert and be persistent…   (Ephesians 6:18)

Did you notice God emphasizing patience, steady travel, self-control and persistence? Did you also detect God's promises? God will honor you. You may look forward to special blessings. You will discover guidance for making difficult choices. You will receive the power of God's Holy Spirit!

The prayer at the beginning by Robin Van Cleef admits three areas of struggle but then he continues…

> ✞ Lord, speak to me through your **Word** and let it penetrate my mind and my heart.
> ✞ Lord, speak to me through **Prayer**, and turn the lifeless stones to bread.
> ✞ Lord, speak to me in my **Meditation**, that I may see, amid life's wilderness: The way, the truth and the life.

Wow! The only word I can think to add is… Amen.

Palm Sunday: Jesus Christ… Superstar!

Palm Sunday: Many worship services will celebrate with masses of children walking happily down the aisle waving palm branches and singing Hosanna's. As the church, we try to remember what happened when Jesus triumphantly entered Jerusalem. The enthusiastic crowd spread their coats and waved palm branches shouting, *"Bless the King who comes in the name of the Lord! Peace in heaven and glory in the highest heaven!"*

(Luke 19:38)

Palm Sunday marks the beginning of Holy Week when we remember and relive the last few days of Jesus earthly life. Prepare for a roller coaster ride because in one week you will hear about Palm Sunday, Jesus teaching in the Temple, Christ ransacking the market square in the Temple, the plot by the Pharisees to destroy Jesus, the last supper with His disciples, the agonizing hours of prayer in the garden, the arrest, the trial, Peter's denial, the painful crucifixion and finally the glorious resurrection. We hear all of this in just eight short days. Wow! It's too much!

Pick any one of the four Gospels and reread the Biblical account of Jesus' last days. Then stop your busy schedule for a moment and think about what this week means to you. Where would you be right now if these events had not taken place?

Every year at this time I brush the dust off the old record player and listen to a Rock Opera that was famous during my teenage years: "Jesus Christ Superstar." I love the way Jesus is portrayed on Palm Sunday. Some of you older ones can probably sing it with me:

Hosanna, Heysanna, Sanna, Sanna Ho… Sanna Hey Sanna Ho Sanna.
Hey J.C., J.C. you're alright by me… Sanna Ho Sanna Hey Superstar.

Can you feel the excitement? Jesus Christ Superstar is riding into a ticker tape parade. You can feel the enthusiasm of the crowd. They love him. They adore him. They worship Him.

Christ you know I love you. Did you see I waved? I believe in you and God,

So tell me that I'm saved. (Repeat Often)

Every preacher loves big crowds that are excited and enthusiastic. Church attendance is up… Hallelujah! All is right with the world. Jesus is a real success as a minister… or is he? Jesus Christ Superstar goes on to record Jesus' response.

Neither you Simon, nor the fifty thousand, nor the Romans, nor the Jews,

Nor Judas, nor the Twelve, nor the priest, nor the scribes nor doomed Jerusalem itself,

Understand what power is, understand what glory is, understand at all….

…to conquer death you only have to die. You only have to die!

Scripture says it so simply: *"...as they came closer to Jerusalem and Jesus saw the city ahead, he began to cry."* (Luke 20:41)

"...he began to cry." Why?

For three years Jesus tried to teach the meaning of God's Son being on earth but no one understood: the disciples, the crowds, the Romans, the Jews, the religious leaders, none of them. They wanted a great leader: A Messiah who would free the Jews and save Israel. Jesus did not come to only save Israel. Christ came to save the world.

The same crowds that shouted "Hosanna" on Palm Sunday would in a few short days be shouting... ***"Crucify Him! You're not what a respectable Messiah should look and act like. So, Crucify Him!"*** Before the end of the week, Jesus would be arrested, tried, whipped, humiliated, spat upon, cursed at, plotted against, crucified, dead and buried. When Jesus was born there was no room for him in the inn. When He died, there was no room for Him in the world.

So instead of rejoicing on Palm Sunday... Jesus wept!

Maybe we should too!

Crucifixion, Letters and Forgiveness

Jesus prayed, "Father, if you are willing, please take this cup of suffering away from me. Yet I want your will, not mine." Then an angel from heaven appeared and strengthened him. (Luke 22:41-43)

"It has been 15 years since my first abortion. I have recently been coming to terms with my past and it scares me. I remember the first one pretty vividly. I remember the date, sights and sounds and the smell. The other two, I have no memory at all. I need help with forgiveness but it is a daily struggle."

A servant girl noticed Peter in the firelight and began staring at him. Finally she said, "This man was one of Jesus' followers!" Peter denied it. "Woman," he said, "I don't know the man." (Luke 22:55-56)

"I am sitting here with tears streaming down my face, thankful to Jesus after hours of surfing the net and typing in the words 'Christian & Divorce' over and over again. I've been reading endless opinions (mostly condemnation and hopelessness) feeling that perhaps my best bet would be to drive my car over a bridge rather then face the rest of my life as a divorced Christian woman who left her 20 year marriage to a Christian man. I came across 'From Ashes to Soap' about your divorce recovery and God caused

a tiny glimmer of hope to rise up in me. I love the Lord with all my heart. When I originally left my husband of 20 years I was not thinking of divorce but things have escalated to a point of no return and the divorce is now final. I can't go back but emotionally, I can't go forward either. I am hurting so badly because like many Christians, I never believed this would happen to me. Larry, I can relate to ashes. I see ashes all around me and I just need to know that Jesus can take the ashes of my life and restore me. I want to believe that the grace of God can extend to even me. I have always taught others of this grace but now I question it for myself. Please pray for me."

Jesus said on the cross, "Father, forgive these people, because they don't know what they are doing." (Luke 23:34)

"I am the 33 year-old Kindergarten teacher who stumbled upon your website as I continued my struggle to develop my faith in God and Jesus. I asked you to pray that I would find my way to God and let Jesus into my heart. I told you of my struggles and conflicting thoughts and feelings and asked for help through prayer. Thanks to your website, I received at least a dozen responses. I never expected to have people write and try to help me. The support and advice given to me by complete strangers was nothing short of miraculous. When I sent my prayer request to you, my faith in God and mankind was at an all time low. Being a Kindergarten teacher, when everyday I try to instill positive moral values and beliefs in my kids and teach them the importance of being kind and polite to each other… you can imagine the torment my soul was in. I am learning the value of "praying without ceasing," and I am slowly beginning to develop a relationship with God and Jesus. Thank you."

One of the criminals hanging beside Jesus, scoffed, "So you're the Messiah are you? Prove it by saving yourself – and us, too, while you're at it!" But the other criminal protested, "Don't you fear God even when you are dying? We deserve to die for our evil deeds, but this man hasn't done anything wrong." Then he said, "Jesus remember me when you come into your Kingdom." Jesus replied, "I assure you, today you will be with me in paradise."

"I asked for you to pray because I thought I had done things that could not be forgiven. Well, I want to thank every one of you that took the time to pray. I went to church and accepted Jesus as my personal Savior. Guess what: He forgave me. I feel so wonderful now. I went to church not even

293

thinking about getting saved. We were in the middle of praise and worship and I cannot even tell you the song we were singing. It was like the room got quiet and I was sitting there arguing with myself. Then the most wonderful thing happened. I said one last time: 'He will not forgive me.' Then I heard a voice that said, 'Yes I will.' I never felt so light headed in all my life."

Then Jesus shouted, "Father, I entrust my spirit into your hands!" And with those words he breathed his last.   (Luke 23:46)

Dreams & Spectators: Making A Choice

Several years ago, I had an eerie dream after reading about a luxury cruise liner. In the dream, I was a member of the crew. Standing on the deck near the bridge, you could see the passengers through the ornate glass doorways as they danced and ate to their hearts content. I watched my shipmates on the bridge as they scurried about.

Something, however, seemed strangely wrong. The talk circulating among the crew was about radio messages warning of possible icebergs. "The ship was moving dangerously fast," one crew member remarked. The captain, partying with the passengers, wasn't too concerned. Disaster loomed, but what could I do? I was just a member of the crew? The dream ended with a sign over the bridge naming the ship… "Titanic." Ouch! What a nightmare.

Here is another scene. Imagine coming to Jerusalem for the Passover celebration. It is supposed to be a party but nobody seems to be having any fun! A prophet named Jesus triumphantly entered town last week at the head of a parade, but just a few days ago he was executed.

Everyone is in a foul mood. Rumors are circulating that Jesus body was stolen to make it look like a resurrection. Others claim to have seen Christ alive. The debate is hot and intense. Is Jesus the Messiah? What do you say? What do you do? Who can you believe?

Here is a more modern nightmare to consider. Violent crime is at an all time high. Drug and alcohol abuse, spousal abuse, child abuse, teenage suicides and violence of every kind loom like icebergs directly in the path of common decency. Morality and ethics are discarded in our eager pursuit of success and pleasure.

Three tragic dramas unfold before you. Here is the question: Are you merely a helpless spectator watching to see what happens next or is there another choice?

Paul laid out our responsibilities very clearly in a letter to Timothy, *"I solemnly urge you... Preach the word of God. Be persistent, whether the time is favorable or not. Patiently correct, rebuke, and encourage your people with good teaching."* (2 Tim. 4:1-2) In other words:

- Don't watch the Titanic go down. Help someone to a lifeboat. Comfort the frightened. Be a witness to the fact that God is with us even in tragedy.

- Don't watch Jesus' disciples as they enthusiastically tell the crowds, *"Jesus is alive!"* Join them as a witness to the Good News.

- Don't complain about our modern day lack of morality. Become a witness to our society that clearly says, ***"Christ is alive and offers us another way to live!"***

Before Easter fades into history remember this critical message. God never asked us to be spectators. We are called to preach, be persistent, be willing to gently correct if necessary and most of all encourage others with good teaching.

Take a moment to think about what you've read. Take out a piece of paper and write down some ways to improve your witness within the community. Are there organizations or projects where you can volunteer? Is there a neighbor who could use a kind word or thoughtful deed? Do you know a teenager in need of comfort?

Your willingness to be a witness may not save the "Titanic" but with God's guidance you could help someone to a lifeboat. Well, what are you waiting for... the movie!

Easter Faith

✝ On the Monday following Easter, a business owner will have to lay-off an employee who has been with his company since the beginning. How will Christ's resurrection help him make critical decisions?

✝ On the Monday following Easter, a minister and spouse will be asked to move to a remote country church more than two hours further away from elderly relatives dependent upon their care. How will Jesus' resurrection help them find needed answers?

✝ On the Monday following Easter, you must wake up and wrestle with the unique challenges our world offers. How will Jesus Christ's resurrection help you face life's obstacles?

If celebrating Easter is to mean more than bunnies, brightly colored eggs and wearing new clothes, questions must be answered. The resurrection of Jesus Christ has to be more than just an annual story-time... doesn't it? The sinking of the luxury cruise ship "Titanic" is a compelling story as the recent movie demonstrates, but would you want to relive it every year?

Maybe this is how Jesus followers felt as they removed a lifeless body from the cross and laid it in a borrowed tomb. For three short years their lives had meaning and purpose. Once, they were preparing for a "New Kingdom... a New World" and Jesus Christ would be their Messiah. Now, they were holed up like frightened rabbits, broken dreams lying in the dust at their feet. But soon there would be a dramatic change...

Early on Sunday morning, as the new day was dawning, Mary Magdalene and the other Mary went out to see the tomb. Suddenly there was a great earthquake, because an angel of the Lord came down from heaven and rolled aside the stone and sat on it. His face shone like lightning, and his clothing was as white as snow. The guards shook with fear when they saw him, and they fell into a dead faint. Then the angel spoke to the women. *"Don't be afraid!"* he said. *"I know you are looking for Jesus, who was crucified. He isn't here! He has been raised from the dead, just as he said would happen. Come, see where his body was lying. And now, go quickly and tell his disciples he has been raised from the dead, and he is going ahead of you to Galilee. You will see him there. Remember, I have told you."* (Matthew 28:1-7)

Jesus was alive! The disciples could pick up their broken dreams and joyfully continue their preparations for a "New Kingdom... a New World." Christ was their Messiah after all. No longer frightened rabbits, the followers of Jesus would boldly launch a movement that would change the world. ***"Hear the Good News! Jesus Christ has defeated the forces of death and offers eternal life to all who believe."***

✝ For the business owner, the critical decisions must still be made but the living Christ gives him the compassion and wisdom to provide real help for his employee and friend.

✝ The minister must move, but church members begin visiting his parents offering help and support. Jesus Christ is alive and actively involving the faith community.

✝ You can now wake up on Monday morning in the secure knowledge that you will never again face life's obstacles alone! A risen Jesus will give you much needed hope for the future.

Because Jesus is alive, Easter is no longer simply a story. It is a testimony of faith. Share this column with someone and ask him/her to join you in celebrating the resurrection of Christ on Sunday morning. Remember that Jesus Christ is alive! Bet your eternal life on it!

Doubting Thomas and Resurrection Faith

You must endure darkness before experiencing the dawn. *"Early on Sunday morning, as the new day was dawning, Mary Magdalene and the other Mary went to see the tomb."* (Mat. 28:1)

Anyone could be a Doubting Thomas... even you. Imagine being holed up inside a house, fearful, confused and desperately seeking answers. What happened? Your leader, spiritual guide and closest friend was brutally tortured and executed. The word out on the street says they are searching for you and your friends. As you huddle together, you have to wonder... who will be next?

Eleven frightened disciples followed Jesus faithfully until... the cross. Could there be a Kingdom if the king was dead? Could there be miracles if the miracle worker disappeared? Could you offer sight to the blind, healing to the sick or hope for the poor if the one who made the promises... ceased to exist?

Now Mary Magdalene and the other Mary come running from the tomb to claim they saw him... alive!

"No way!" you say. "I heard his final words. I saw the spear thrust into his body. I saw him die! I won't believe it unless I see the nail wounds for myself and place my hand into the wound on his side!"

Suddenly Jesus was standing there among us! *"Peace be with you,"* he said. As he spoke, he held out his hands for us to see and he showed his side. Most of us were filled with joy when we saw our Lord but not you. Then Jesus walks over and says to you: *"Thomas, put your finger here in my hands. Put your hand into the wound in my side. Don't be faithless any longer. Believe!"*

(from John 20:20-27)

What else can you say? "My Lord and my God! Please forgive me for doubting but I am so afraid!"

Jesus replies: *"You believe because you have seen me. Blessed are those who haven't seen me and believe anyway."* Wow! Jesus is alive! He's reassuring everyone in the room, just like the old days... only different. Something has changed. You can feel it.

Then he said, *"When I was with you before, I told you that everything written about me by Moses and the prophets and in the Psalms must all come true."* Then he opened their minds to understand these many Scriptures.

(Luke 26:44-45)

Finally, you realize that Jesus Christ's death and resurrection had a purpose and was predicted by scripture. After years of confusion while sitting at Christ's feet, the teaching becomes clear. Then Jesus said: *"With my authority, take this message of repentance to all the nations, beginning in Jerusalem: 'there is forgiveness of sins for all who turn to me.' You are witnesses..."*

(Luke 26:47-48)

1. You've just experienced the miracle of knowing Christ is alive! You saw Him alive!
2. You are to take Christ's message of forgiveness to everyone starting here in our community.
3. You can share the message with confidence because we are Christ's living witnesses.

But what about those who are waiting outside? What if others do not believe us? You are so afraid! Will they crucify you just like they did to Jesus? It's one thing to believe... it's another to face fear.

Then Jesus said: *"And now I will send the Holy Spirit, just as my Father promised. But stay here in the city until the Holy Spirit comes and fills you with power from heaven."*

(Luke 26:49)

There is the final answer! Did you catch it? God understands your fear and is sending help...

1. Jesus is alive and you just witnessed it... now believe it!
2. You are to extend Christ's message of faith and hope to others.
3. Do not be afraid for the Holy Spirit will fill you with power from heaven!

Are you a Doubting Thomas... still holed up, fearful, confused and desperately looking for answers and courage? Hear the Good News! Christ was dead! Christ is risen! Christ will come again! Easter is the promise that you will be filled with the power of God's Holy Spirit... do not be afraid! Confidently open your doors and take Christ's message of forgiveness and hope to all the nations. ***Christ is risen! Christ is risen, indeed!***

Did You Forget Something?

"Nice worship service, Larry? Why don't you and your family join us for lunch?"

"Sure, that would be great."

I'm very embarrassed to say that in my rush to gather up my materials and drive to the restaurant, I forgot something… my five-year-old daughter. Can you believe it? Actually, I assumed she was riding with someone else and thought everything was fine until I stood in the buffet line and happened to notice… *"Where's my daughter? Have any of you seen Lisa?"*

"Not since church… she wanted to ride with you? Don't you have her?"

With a lump in my throat and a huge growing knot in my stomach, I ran out of the restaurant, squealed rubber pulling from the parking lot and flew back hoping and praying that my precious little child was okay. Upon reaching the church, I saw her standing by the front door with the saddest look on her face and huge crocodile tears running down both cheeks. Fortunately a kind gentleman had stayed behind assuring Lisa that her forgetful Dad would be back soon.

As I carried her to the car with both little arms clinging tightly to my neck, she was still sobbing. I will never forget her cry of anguish… *"Daddy, how could you drive off and forget me?"*

Let's face it. We can all occasionally become so focused on our urgent activities that we literally *"drive off and forget"* about something much more important but not always urgent such as: our marriage, our family, our friends and especially our God. For example:

- ▶ Will that special someone describe you: "with a loving smile and starry-eyed wonder," "a blank look but hopeful of more to come" or "a sneer displaying venom and frustration?"

- ▶ Would your family portray you as: "busy but compassionate and loving," "occasionally wild and crazy" or "mommy/daddy/ brother/sister… who are they?"

- ▶ Could your circle of friends be defined as: "growing stronger in every way", "occasionally we run into each other" or "we used to be close… a long time ago?"

- ▶ Your relationship with God would be described as: "struggling to deepen day by day", "regular as in every Christmas and Easter" or "dusty as the Bible on the coffee table?"

"Daddy, how could you drive off and forget me?"

Just before dawn on Easter morning, several women came to lovingly prepare a body. *"Mary Magdalene came to the tomb and found that the stone had been rolled away from the entrance. She ran and found Simon Peter and the other disciple whom Jesus loved. She said, 'They have taken the Lord's body out of the tomb, and I don't know where they have put him?'"*

(John 20:1-2)

At Easter sunrise the relatively average lives of a few women, eleven disciples and the entire world would never be the same. In your rush of urgent day-to-day duties have you forgotten the excitement and the significance of that morning? ***"Surprise... Christ is alive! Hallelujah!"***

☦ Easter can restore the starry-eyed wonder in your significant relationship.

☦ Easter can recapture the loving, occasionally crazy aspects of family living.

☦ Easter can redefine your friendships as continually growing stronger.

☦ Easter can renew your struggling connection with a loving, forgiving Father.

It took the love of a little girl saying, *"Daddy, how could you drive off and forget me?"* to remind me yet again of the critical difference between what is urgent and what is really important in life. With God's help I will do better. This Easter, may God help you do better, too.

A Basketball Goal, Cursing & Psalm 51

If you want to discover my very worst flaws, ask my daughter, Lisa. She will be happy to tell all.

Have mercy on me, O God, because of your unfailing love. Because of your great compassion, blot out the stain of my sins. Wash me clean from my guilt. Purify me from my sin. (Psalm 51:1-2)

For months, I had promised to put up a basketball goal behind our house. The equipment was in the shed, so one fall afternoon, under my daughter's watchful eye, I began assembling the goal. The directions said: first, dig a hole and second, attach the goal to the pole then finally, place the entire assembly into the hole. *"Sounds simple enough,"* I thought.

For I recognize my shameful deeds – they haunt me day and night. (v.3)

Everything went fine. The hole was dug. The assembly was attached.

All I needed to do was pick up the basketball goal and place it into the hole… Did I mention that it was extremely windy?

Against you, and you alone, have I sinned; I have done what is evil in your sight. (v.4)

Just as I stood the pole upright, the wind literally ripped the entire assembly out of my hands, carrying it several yards before crashing to the ground smashing the backboard into several pieces. My pastoral dignity was completely forgotten as the curses began to flow. Fortunately, I thought, *"we live in an isolated area and only one person heard me!"* Unfortunately, that one person was my daughter and I was about to learn a hard lesson.

You will be proved right in what you say, and your judgment against me is just. (v.4)

Not much was said until Sunday during worship when prayer requests were asked for in the congregation. I noticed several youth giggling on the back row while my daughter raised her hand. *"I would like the church to pray for my Dad and his temper!"* she said.

But you desire honesty from the heart, so you can teach me to be wise in my inmost being. (v.6)

At that point, I told everyone how their pastor had blown it. Interestingly enough, after my confession, we were all able to laugh and feel better about ourselves and our relationship with God, knowing that we are human and constantly in need of forgiveness.

Purify me from my sins, and I will be clean; wash me and I will be whiter than snow. Oh give me back my joy again; you have broken me – now let me rejoice. (v. 7-8)

The lesson: We must have the humility to ask for forgiveness as well as a willingness to forgive. Then, God promises to turn our bitterness and rage into joy.

Don't keep looking at my sins. Remove the stain of my guilt. Create in me a clean heart, O God. Renew a right spirit within me. (V. 9-10)

We all have the equivalent of basketball goals ripped out of our grasp:

- A businessman loses his temper over a misunderstanding and insults a close friend.
- A wife feels betrayed because of her husband's crude comments about her in front of friends.
- A child who has wanted to play basketball all his life is cut from

the local team. The boy's father angrily confronts the coach during a practice session and begins to curse him.

In the heat of passion, tragic errors of judgment are made... now what! The lesson of Psalm 51 is difficult but clear. We must be willing to ask for and also freely give forgiveness so that God can turn our bitterness into sweet, sweet joy.

Then I will teach your ways to sinners, and they will return to you.... You would not be pleased with sacrifices, or I would bring them...The sacrifice you want is a broken spirit. (V 13,17)

Now if this preacher can only learn to practice what he writes! Maybe that is why we also desperately need prayer.

Precious Memories, Graduation and Lisa

It was my first appointment as the pastor of a church and we were moving from the city to a small town. I was busy unloading furniture so the children were left to entertain themselves. Lisa was five years old at the time and eager to explore her new surroundings. She walked up the street to a neighbor's house and within a few minutes came back full of excitement. *"Daddy... Daddy!"*

"What, sweetie," I replied.

"I already made lots of new friends!"

"That's great!" I said, wondering where she found so many children so quickly. *"Where are they?"*

"Right over there." She was pointing in the general direction of one child.

"I only see one friend. Where are the others?" I asked.

"No Daddy! Look closer! The rest of my friends are dogs!"

You have just met my daughter, Lisa: The little girl who never missed an opportunity to make a friend whether it had two legs or four. Lisa was the child who took the term *"Sleepover"* to mean every day and whose motto was *"have sleeping bag will travel."* My darling little girl, Lisa, turned eighteen this month and is about to graduate from High School. How did she grow up so fast?

Like most parent-child relationships, there have been numerous precious memories and more than a few gray hairs raising Lisa. If there were one word that could best describe her... it would be *"Adventure."* Like the time...she signed up with a friend to go to a weeklong summer camp. Lisa assumed the camp was about trips to the pool and making crafts. She had no clue that her so-called camping experience was actually designed for "woods survival training." Lisa summed up her experience nicely when she said: *"Daddy, there were no bathrooms! Yecchh!"*

Within a few short months, Lisa will ride off to a new "adventure" and play "sleepover" every night of the week as she moves to a college dormitory. As a parent, most of my day-to-day tasks of rearing children will be over. So, what have I tried to teach her as a loving parent?

✝ *"Teach your children to choose the right path and when they are older, they will remain upon it."* (Proverbs 22:6) Lisa, I have done my best as a parent to be a good example for you. Please remember the values I stood for and forgive my many mistakes.

✝ *"Unless the LORD builds a house, the work of the builders is useless."* (Psalm 127:1) Lisa, I pray you will learn the value of working hard but please, never forget God's desire for you to keep your priorities in life focused on God and family.

✝ *"See how very much our heavenly Father loves us, for he allows us to be called his children and we really are!"* (1 John 3:1) Lisa, even through the worst moments of our family crisis, I always knew that God loved me and loved you. Just as you will always be my precious little girl, you are also eternally a special child of God.

I pray that Lisa will continually be comforted knowing dad is extremely proud and lovingly watching as she continues the journey toward becoming a responsible adult. But I also pray that she never loses her sense of *"adventure"* and her eagerness to make new friends.

In a few short months, I hope to receive a phone call: *"Daddy... Daddy!"*

"What sweetie," I'll reply. *"How are you doing?"*

She will say: *"Daddy, I'm doing well and already made lots of new friends and you know what? Some of them are still dogs!"*

Beware of Gorillas Armed with Cracker Jacks

"You are going to have a guest speaker," the principal informed one of her kindergarten teachers early one morning. *"He is an education student who will be demonstrating a sample lesson on storytelling to young children. The session needs to be video taped and your kindergarten class will make a perfect audience. Do you mind helping out?"*

"No, of course not," replied the teacher.

"Oh, by the way, the student will be in some sort of costume, a gorilla or something."

Indeed, later that day a gorilla did visit the kindergarten class and told several stories to the delight of the children, but then something very strange happened. The gorilla approached the teacher, dropped down on one knee and offered her a box of Cracker Jacks, *"Open it, please!"*

The teacher's jaw dropped as she reached into the box and pulled out an engagement ring.

"Will you marry me?"

It's a crazy story... but it's true. Do you want to know how it ends? Hang on! I'm getting to it.

Whether describing a relationship between a husband and wife, close friends or God. Described more than 800 times in the Bible, no verb is mentioned more frequently than *"love."* One of our greatest commandments is to *"love the Lord your God with all your heart, all your soul, all your strength, and all your mind. And 'love your neighbor as yourself.' "*

(Luke 10:27)

To love someone is to offer up your ultimate expression of loyalty, passion and creativity. Love can be described in many ways, but one of them should never include the word... dull! In other words, it's okay to be a little 'gorilla-crazy' when you're in love. Do you need some examples?

- •... David passionately danced before the Lord while bringing in the Ark. (2 Samuel 6:14)
- •... Jesus said, "unless you have the faith of a child, you will never get into the kingdom of God. (Mark 10:15)
- •... the woman who poured expensive oils and perfume on Jesus feet and wiped them with her hair. (John 12:1-8)
- •... Peter seeing that Jesus was alive leapt from the boat and swam to shore. (John 21:7)

Finally there is the warning in Revelation: *"I know all the things you do, that you are neither hot nor cold. I wish you were one or the other! But since you are like lukewarm water, I will spit you out of my mouth!"* (3:15-16)

Are you one-half of a *'lukewarm'* couple? Do you belong to a *'lukewarm'* church? Are some of your friendships *'lukewarm?'* More importantly, could your personal relationship with the God who loves you so passionately be described as (gulp) *'lukewarm'* Maybe it is time to seek forgiveness for your lack of passion and creativity. Then, pray that God will bring out the 'gorilla' inside you.

If you haven't guessed the ending to the story, the kindergarten teacher said yes to the gorilla and kissed him while the children cheered. A few months later her class was given special seating at the wedding. How do I know? Her name is Mell Davies and we've been married for many exciting, amazing years.

Has the love between Mell and I always been this wild? Of course not, but that is where another aspect of a loving relationship becomes important... forgiveness.

Wild Weddings

As a minister, I do weddings... literally hundreds of weddings. Most of them are problem-free ceremonies of worship providing many precious memories for everyone. There have been a few weddings, however, which can only be classified as... *wild!*

One *wild* wedding took place in-between bands performing at the Blue Grass Festival in Amelia, Virginia. (Yes... you heard me right!) The groom had always wanted to be married at the festival, but could not find a woman crazy enough to marry him under those circumstances: But his lifelong wish finally came true and the girl of his dreams said yes on stage as the crowd began to clap and cheer. After the ceremony, there was a standing ovation from the crowd for the couple. I was tempted to turn and bow, but restrained myself.

Another *wild* wedding began innocently enough at a local college chapel. During the ceremony, I asked for the rings and the best man handed me pink plastic "Cracker-Jacks" specials. *"These are pretty cheap looking rings! Is this how the marriage is going to go?"* I asked and everyone laughed...except my wife who thought I had lost my mind. The rings were replaced and the rest of the ceremony went off without a hitch until the couple strolled down the aisle and the groom pulled out a can of spray streamers and covered his family in bright green and yellow string.

But the prize for the *wildest wedding* goes to a couple who each decided to write their own vows as a surprise for their mate. It all happened a few years ago on a wooden boat dock overlooking a beautiful pond out in the country. The bride called me the night before the wedding and asked me to read an additional set of marriage vows she had written for her hus-

305

band. She would give them to me just before the wedding started.

Just before the service, the groom pulled me aside and handed another set of vows this time to be read as a surprise to his new wife. Without looking at the vows, I hurriedly said, *"sure!"* The people were in place and the simple worship service went without a hitch.

Then, as instructed by the bride, I turned to the new husband and asked him to gaze lovingly upon his wife and emphatically respond to the following with: *"I agree!"*

- *Do you agree to cook steak and potato's on Friday?*
- *Do you agree to cut the grass and take out the trash?*
- *Do you agree to keep the truck and the car clean?*
- *Do you agree to have my coffee ready when I awake?*
- *Do you agree to take me shopping once a week without complaining?*

My next instructions from the groom were to have the bride her husband by the hand, look lovingly into his eyes and repeat the vows written for her:

- *I _____ agree to lovingly serve you breakfast in bed every Saturday morning and to learn how to bake homemade pies and cobblers. I will also never insist that you go shopping with me for more than one hour at a time.*

Afterwards, I commented: *"This couple doesn't need a minister. They need a lawyer to abide by these vows."* A proper ending might have been to push both the bride and the groom in the pond and declare them both insane, but after laughing, I discovered an important lesson.

Solomon, the wise sage, said it so well: *"There is a time for everything...a time to weep and a time to laugh, a time to mourn and a time to dance..."* (Ecclesiastes 3:4) Life is so short and God is always reminding us to make the most of it: to keep our priorities in place.

I admire a couple that can play a practical joke in the midst of such a serious commitment. If they can hold on to this ability to laugh and poke fun at each other... maybe there is hope for their marriage. Let's face it; with a better sense of humor, there would be more hope for all of us.

Wedding Vows

Easter, more than anything is about love: a love so enduring that God is willing to make the ultimate sacrifice. *"For God so loved the world that he gave his only Son, so that everyone who believes in him will not perish but have eternal life."* (John 3:16) One way to appreciate the power and influence of love is to watch a couple and their respective families prepare for marriage. Recently, I was involved in two weddings; each offering it's own unique story of love.

The first wedding was a celebration that could have ended in tragedy. The groom had endured divorcing parents and the death of a beloved grandfather. As a teenager, he ran around with the wrong crowd and was heading nowhere fast. Yet, in the last few years, he changed…. really changed. As he repeated the traditional wedding vows you could see the radiant glow of love on his face and the newly mature eyes of a boy who endured the tough trials leading to manhood.

"Will you have her to be your wife, to live together in a holy marriage? Will you love her, comfort her, honor and keep her in sickness and in health and forsaking all other, be faithful to her as long as you both shall live? Will you?" With a smile, he looked at his bride and whispered: *"I will!"*

The bulletin was the clue that the next wedding would be unique. Carefully wrapped with a white linen bow enclosing two symbolic wedding rings, the cover included these words: "Our family is a circle of love and strength. With every birth and every union, the circle grows. Every joy shared adds more love. Every obstacle faced together makes the circle stronger."

For over a year, Katy and Nathan carefully selected music, poems, prayers and Scripture readings. They even wrote their own marriage vows. Fearing a memory loss they gave me a copy during the service for prompting but didn't need it as each looked tenderly into the eyes of their future mate and declared their undying love to one another before us and before God.

"Katy, I pledge to love you from earth to sky from sea to mountain and from sun to storm. I promise to make your joy, my joy: your laughter, my laughter: your dreams, my own. I will listen patiently and try to understand completely what you say while walking hand in hand and side by side throughout life with you. I will try to grow wiser through conflict always knowing that at the end of the day we are eternal. I promise to remember how easily we could have missed each other and marvel at how the hand of fate brought us together. I will remember the harsh lessons I endured to learn the way to your heart and never take for granted the blessings I have found in you. I will love you with laughter, with no secrets and no lies as long as there is breath in my body on earth and forever with my spirit."

"Nathan, I've always been able to express myself. I've been both a writer and an artist. But when it came to telling you how I much you mean to me, it was very hard to put my feelings into words. Here is my attempt: Today, I give my life to the most wonderful person I have ever met. The person who has shown me a love more powerful than anything I have ever felt. My equal, my perfect match and the person I cannot imagine living without. I promise that I will fill your life with happiness and humor, friendship and tenderness, compromise and growth, understanding and trust, respect and balance and most importantly unlimited and unconditional love."

Maybe this is why the Bible occasionally refers to the church as a bride and Jesus Christ as the loving groom: *"For I promised you as a pure bride to one husband, Christ."* (2 Corinthians 11:2) I can almost picture God's pledge of love for me on Easter morning: "Larry, I vow to love you from earth to sky from sea to mountain and from sun to storm…" My response? "God, I've always been able to express myself but when it comes to telling you how much you mean to me, it is so hard. Today, I give my life to a God who has shown me a love more powerful than anything…"

I have to admit, there is one difference between marriage vows and God's love expressed at Easter. At least after it's over, you don't have to watch fourteen hours of video taped memories.

Where Are You God?

It's been an emotionally draining week in our community. The kind that makes you want cry out: ***"Where are you God?"***

- ✝ A young boy is fighting for his life in an intensive care unit after an automobile accident.
- ✝ Another frustrated couple can find solace only in separation.
- ✝ A man facing death is making final preparations.
- ✝ Another young man is struggling with a drinking problem.
- ✝ A woman continues her brave battle against cancer with yet another round of chemotherapy.
- ✝ Another woman is desperately trying to break the pervasive hold of an abusive relationship.
- ✝ Doctors inform someone who has been in severe pain for the last three years, *"there is no cure and it will only progressively get worse."*

Where can someone find God in the midst of this much tragedy? Where is the hope?

Paul, sick and in prison was writing to a church in Corinth that was in the midst of it's own struggle. Yet surrounded by hopelessness, Paul speaks of hope: *We are pressed on every side by troubles, but we are not crushed and broken. We are perplexed, but we don't give up and quit. We are hunted down, but God never abandons us. We get knocked down, but we get up again and keep going.*   (2 Corinthians 4:8-9)

How does Paul do it? How does he maintain his faith? He writes: *That is why we never give up. Though our bodies are dying, our spirits are being renewed every day. For our present troubles are quite small and won't last very long. Yet they produce for us an immeasurably great glory that will last forever! So we don't look at the troubles we can see right now; rather, we look forward to what we have not yet seen. For the troubles we see will soon be over, but the joys to come will last forever.*

(2 Corinthians 4:16-18)

Here is the point:
1. Your body may be dying but with trust and faith, your spirit will only get stronger.
2. The tragedy and suffering you experience now will soon be replaced with God's glory that lasts an eternity.
3. We must learn to look beyond our troubles to the joys God promises us all!

How do we do that? Why do you think God organized the church? It may be filled with imperfect human beings, but it is still the best place I know to receive comfort and hope in the midst of disaster. During this same week, I found some great examples:

❖ One man struggling with career problems finally found a new job with great potential.

❖ The young boy fighting for his life is showing signs of improvement.

❖ Thirteen women graduated from an eight-month intensive Bible study and described times when the group or studied scripture helped them cope.

❖ The woman breaking free from an abusive relationship is now seeing someone who seems to genuinely care about her. Together they are working toward a deeper faith.

❖ A group of our local youth joined 5300 more from around the state to hear a famous Christian rock group and nationally respected leaders share the love and grace of Jesus Christ.

❖ A young man visits our church sharing his dream of starting Boy Scout troops throughout the county. His unique gift is touching the hearts of young boys and offering them God's love.

❖ A young man from a previous church that I served visits to tell how God changed his life. He has opened a Christian bookstore and is actively helping others deepen their spiritual walk.

Where is God? Maybe Paul answered it best: *For the troubles we see will soon be over, but the joys to come will last forever.* If you are looking for God, don't give up, pray, reach out to a friend, look to your church, open your Bible and He will soon find you!

Think of Me...' Remembering David McCraw

When you hear the crack of bat and ball, or hear the umpire bellow out his call of "safe" or "out"...

When you see a ball in lofted flight, or players tangled in the nigh as runner slides and baseman tags...

think of me.

It was supposed to be a great day. Four baseball players returning from a church camp to play in an all-star game. One of them, sixteen-year-old David McCraw was sitting in the back seat listening to the radio and laughing with friends. David's mother was waiting at the ball field with his uniform. Another man who would be charged with reckless driving under the influence ran a stop sign and rammed into the side of the players' car. Three boys were injured. David died on the way to the hospital. Within a matter of seconds a great day became a community tragedy.

When class bells ring and hallways crowd with endless chatter soft and loud of ordered chaos...

When wanton mischief calls and laughter causes sides to split and tears to fall as mirthful mouths grow wide in glee...

think of me.

David McCraw was the son of our organist and grew up in a wonderful little country church near Amelia, Virginia. He played with my daughter and occasionally got bored during long choir practices. But it was David who asked the tough questions about God and showed a real desire to grow stronger in his faith. He also had a knack for making friends everywhere he went.

When music rocks and speakers boom compelling all within the room to

echo lyrics that rap the soul...
  think of me.
David was a talented ball player and a typical teenager who had a tendency to play his music a little loud and move a little fast. In other words, David was normal. That's what makes this story so difficult. David should not have died. We all know that life isn't fair... tragedies happen.

When hands are held and friends embrace with words of comfort,
love and grace to shoulder sorrow and share in joys...
think of me.

We all need God. I could not write these words if I didn't passionately believe that David is safely with God. But now what? When tragedy strikes, how do we respond? How do we go on and keep the memory of David McCraw alive in our hearts?

1. Get angry but don't carry a grudge. Anger is a normal part of the grieving cycle, but carrying a grudge is destructive for you and everyone around you.
2. Look for ways to help the family. Donate to David's Memorial fund. Visit the family, share stories and have a good cry. Make a scrapbook of memories and present it to the family.
3. Join the crusade against Drunken Driving. Something needs to be done. There are organizations for adults and youth. Get involved.
4. Ask some hard questions about your faith in God. Where is God when tragedy strikes? What can you do to deepen your faith? How can God help you cope?
5. Live life to the max! What are your dreams? Follow them with all of your heart and soul. That's what David was doing... What better way to honor his memory? Go for it!

When prayer is short and words too mute to speak the pain
That's taken root deep within the spirit's womb, then...
Think of me

My favorite Bible passage says a lot about who God is and what our ultimate purpose in life is all about. "He is the source of every mercy and the God who comforts us. He comforts us in all our troubles so that we can comfort others. When others are troubled, we will be able to give them the same comfort God has given us." (2 Corinthians 1:3-4)

✟ God provided comfort when the entire community surrounded David's family.

✝ There was comfort when two churches opened their doors to accommodate the large crowd of mourners. One organized and hosted the funeral. Another prepared food for the mourners.

✝ There was comfort when the fellow teachers stood by David's mother and helped her handle the necessary tasks of grieving.

✝ There was comfort when David McCraw's teammates came in uni form to pay their respect and carry his coffin to a final resting-place.

Maybe, this is what being a Christian is all about. Offering comfort during times of tragedy, learning from them and growing stronger in our faith. If we can do that David McCraw's death will not have been in vain.

Think of me for I am there
in every place and face and heart
that beats and every breath that's drawn in life, not death;
my strength, my love, my joy to give, for as you go on,
so shall I live in you, as I also live in God.

("Think of Me" was written especially for David McCraw by Rev. Richard A. Barclay)

Ode to Honey

The doctor carefully shaved the area and applied a clear gel over the smooth skin. As he gently placed the sensor on the spot, a picture appeared on the connected monitor. The ultra-sound machine was accurately showing a diseased heart that was nearly twice its original size.

"She has a bad valve in the left ventricle." I heard him say along with a lot of technical jargon only doctors could possibly understand. His next words are engraved in my memory. *"There is nothing we can do! With proper medication, she will last a few months... maybe a year at most!"*

The next few minutes seemed like hours as the doctor explained the nature of the disease in detailed language we frankly did not care to hear. Then he outlined how to use the various medications being prescribed to help her live as long as possible. Finally the staff quietly presented the bill that, by the way, needed payment immediately.

My wife cried, while I drove home in silence reflecting on the memories and tried to figure how we would deal with this new tragedy in our lives. *"It's just a dog,"* the voice inside of me cried out. *"How can you get so emotional about a dog?"*

Several years ago, I would have laughed at this point and called the author slightly touched in the head, but now I am the one being emotional about "Honey" our eight year old Cocker Spaniel because she has become a part of our family and I love her.

We actually have two dogs and like children they have uniquely different personalities. Honey is our chubby, easy-going dog who will endure almost anything yet still wag her tail and lick your face. No trash container or newspaper is safe with her around. Molly, on the other hand, is the high-strung whiner who will bark at everything. Temperamental is too mild to describe Molly.

Honey now has her own pill container with the days marked to remind us of all the medication, more than most adults consume. One of the pills is a diuretic that helps her get rid of fluids. In other words, she has to go to the bathroom frequently. So, if you see me outside in the middle of the night, I'm walking Honey.

Do you wonder why I'm telling you all of this? Because everyone at one time or another must endure a medical crisis or some other form of bad news, which could involve a beloved pet, a friend or a loved one. We all face these crisis periodically. How do we respond? After years of helping others cope, I have discovered helpful advice.

- **Be Optimistic:** The information could be flawed or the doctors could be wrong. God could intervene with a miracle. Patients who survive terminal illness often possess a positive attitude and a strong belief in God.
- **Be Realistic:** You also must ask yourself, *"If this news is true, what should I take care of?"* Are there final words, or unfinished business?
- **Maintain Trust & Faith in God:** A secure knowledge of Who is in control, even in crisis is a critical factor in learning to cope.

Paul writes to the Philippians: *"The Lord is near. Do not be anxious about anything, but in everything, by prayer and petition, with thanksgiving, present your requests to God. And the peace of God, which transcends all understanding, will guard your hearts and your minds in Christ Jesus."* *(4:5-7)*

Our family crisis with Honey is a reminder to put the final outcome in the hands of a God who will give us all strength and a supernatural peace to endure even to the very end.

Ode to Honey Continued!

No "Sowing Seeds" devotion received more attention than the one about Honey, our nine-year old Cocker Spaniel dying of an incurable heart condition. People would stop me in the street and ask about her. Some would share their own stories of beloved pets and offer heart-felt prayers.

For four months, we fought to keep Honey alive. There were four daily prescriptions: three for her heart and one for her breathing passages. She needed constant care, but Honey never suffered and even seemed to enjoy the extra attention. A few days before Christmas we took pictures of Honey freshly cleaned and clipped with green and red Christmas bows in her ears.

On New Year's Eve, Honey began to noticeably weaken despite all of our efforts and sleepless nights caring for her. Dr. Eliasson who had spent a few late night hours with her also finally had to admit there was nothing more to be done and tearfully administered the final shot. Mell and I took Honey home and buried her beside a recently planted tree behind our house.

"Why am I telling you this?" Because death is something everyone must experience as a part of life. We are all going to lose relatives, spouses, close friends and beloved pets. For our family, Honey's death was nearly as tragic as losing one of our children. The question is: ***"how do we manage the grief that comes when we lose a loved one?"***

Dr. Elizabeth Kubler-Ross in her book "On Death and Dying" mentions six stages of recovery from grief.

- **Denial**: *"Just because Honey died, nothing has really changed."* Grief is very real and must not be denied. It is okay to feel sorrow for the loss of a loved one.
- **Anger**: *"Why did Honey have to leave me? God, why did you let this happen?"* It is only natural to look for someone to blame. It could be the one who died or God or even yourself.
- **Bargaining**: *"I'll serve you forever, if you'll bring Honey back, Lord!"* What has happened to you is beginning to sink in and you are at this point looking for any way to avoid it.
- **Depression**: *"If I can't even be with my dog, why am I struggling so hard? I'll just stay home and watch TV."* The reality of the loss is beginning to sink in, but at this point there seems to be no light at the end of a very long, dark tunnel.
- **Acceptance**: *"Honey is gone and I miss her terribly, but I must live."* Much of the anger and depression is now gone as you begin

to learn new coping skills.

- **Hope**: *"Honey is gone, but God still loves me and I will cherish the memories."* Hope is when you regain your interest in life and are able to look ahead once again.

Jesus said to the disciples, just before his death: ***"I will not leave you desolate; I will come to you."*** God never promised us a world free of pain and misery. God says, "I will not leave you desolate; I will come to you." There is a higher power who will see us through. Count on it!

Some do's and don'ts:

- Don't make any quick major decisions. The temptation is strong to rush out and buy another dog or begin dating again or change jobs or sell your house. Just remember this: **DON'T!**

- Do pray the serenity prayer. *"God grant me the serenity to accept the things I cannot change. God grant me the courage to change the things I can. God grant me the wisdom to know the difference."* **DO PRAY FOR SERENITY!**

Honey is buried by a freshly planted tree, just behind our house. Our family can go out there from time to time and talk about the memories and even laugh about the crazy dog who seemed to fit right in with our wacky household. If you have lost someone recently, my prayer is that this will help you cope with the present and give you hope for the future. May God be with you.

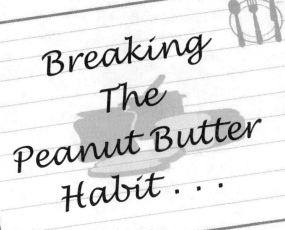

Breaking
The
Peanut Butter
Habit . . .

Following God's Recipe
For A Wonderful Life.

Chapter 9

A Little Dessert
Never Hurt

Turning Points: Computer Crashes, Silence & Renewal

My computer crashed and died on the same day an infamous email virus "love bug" struck throughout the world. Most of my files and 3,000 email addresses were in danger of being lost. So, I reacted like any technologically handicapped person and panicked. I grabbed my precious cargo and raced to the local computer doctor pleading for help. *"Shoot me straight, Doc. I can take it! Is it the love bug?"*

He smiled and looked at me for the longest time. (I hate it when they do that!) *"Did you download any program updates off the Internet recently?"*

"Well, sure." I replied. *"Microsoft has a great automatic update reminder. Several days ago there was a message to download something to improve the Active X... whatever that is."*

A look of horror came across his face and with a look of professional disdain he asked: *"Was anything wrong with your computer? Was it acting up?"*

"No!"

He continued, *"Did you need an improvement so you could become more productive?"*

"No! I don't even know what Active X is?"

"Then why did you do it?"

With a sheepish look I stammered, *"Because Microsoft told me too?"*

After a long pause the doctor quietly asked: *"Do you always do what Microsoft tells you?"*

What could I say? I had been caught red-handed (and red faced) and charged with the crime of being careless and naïve. After a lecture on the importance of backing up your files and avoiding unnecessary downloads the doctor prescribed five days of bed rest and therapy (for the computer).

"Five days! Five days! What would I do with myself for five days? There was important work to do!"

It was at this point... that I realized... there was a problem but it wasn't with the computer!

The Apostle Paul gives this warning to us all: *"Don't copy the behavior and customs of this world, but let God transform you into a new person by changing the way you think. Then you will know what God wants you to do and you will know how good and pleasing his will really is."* (Romans 12:2)

As followers of God we are to be a "light" to others but all too often our light is subtly dimmed and discolored by the worldly passions of life. In my case it was the day-by-day demands of writing, web-site maintenance and ministry. In other words, I was doing the work but I was neglecting something far more valuable: my intimate relationship with God. It all boils down to this: What are your priorities in life? Most likely, it is what takes the majority of your time and energy. So what is dimming your light?

▶ Could it be the pressure to succeed in a highly competitive work environment?

▶ Maybe you're feeling the daily grind of maintaining a household and caring for children.

▶ Are you caught up in the mind-numbing allure of any number of entertainment pleasures?

The first day was tough. Like an addict, I needed a computer fix… bad. *"How do I write my devotion? Where is my schedule? What if I borrowed somebody else's computer? Maybe, I'll buy a new one."* The hours seemed to drag on and on. I was feeling lost and vulnerable… right where God wanted me.

Something happened during those forced periods of solitude. I did a little more reading and a lot more praying. In the midst of a forced withdrawal from my hectic routine, I discovered a gem of Biblical truth.

Turning Points:
Computer Crashes, Silence & Renewal Part 2

After the doctor gave me a lecture on the importance of backing up my files and avoiding unnecessary downloads he prescribed five days of bed rest and therapy (for the computer). *"Five days! What would I do for five days? There was important work to do!"*

It was at this point that I realized… there was a problem but it was not with the computer!

For you the problem may be pressure to succeed at work. Maybe you're feeling the daily grind of raising a family. You may simply be watching too much TV. In other words, whatever is sapping your creative energy and stealing your time is also preventing you from becoming all God planned for you to be. What are your priorities? Unfortunately, mine were out of order and in the shop for repair.

The first day was tough. Like an addict, I needed a computer fix… bad. *"How do I write my devotion? Where is my schedule? What if I borrowed somebody else's computer? Maybe, I'll buy a new one."* The hours seemed to drag on and on. I was feeling lost and vulnerable, right where God wanted me.

"Maybe I should read? Yes, that's good. Read!" A story by Arthur Gordon caught my eye about a doctor's advice for someone going through a bleak period in life. The doctor said: *"Find an isolated area, leave your beeper and telephone behind and take one of these prescriptions every three hours."*

"Sounds easy enough," I thought. "It's late and I can't sleep anyway." The story mentioned four slips of paper each with separate instructions. The first prescription was two words: ***"1) Listen carefully."***

"Listen to what? My telephone's turned off. The beeper is in a drawer! There is no whirring computer in the background. What do you mean?" This was going to be more difficult than I thought. At first, I could only pace the room and fret but slowly… ever so slowly, I began to settle down. Finally something inside me seemed to whisper, "First, read, but don't just read anything. Read Proverbs."

The first chapter of Proverbs hit me like a bowling ball rolling for a perfect strike. *Come here and listen to me! I'll pour out the spirit of wisdom upon you and make you wise.* (1:23) God wasn't interested in my productivity, my writings or even my ministry. Like a wise parent, God was urging me to sit still and listen… really listen. Lately, I had been too busy. Imagine that and I'm a preacher! What about you?

As the hours passed, I was slowly beginning to relax. Reading soon turned to talking and talking led naturally to prayer. No longer in a hurry, I freely shared frustrations and concerns and began to patiently and quietly listen for the comforting voice of God. Inevitably, I would feel a gentle nudge to read Scripture or write a note. As the hours passed, I learned…

- …being quiet and taking the time to listen is seldom a time waster. It's excellent preparation.
- …it's difficult to really understand someone until you first make time to listen to what they say.
- …it's impossible to hear the sweet, soft voice of God until you slow the frantic pace and listen.

Are you feeling the pressure to succeed? Slowing down a few moments each day, listening to your surroundings, listening to your coworkers and most of all, listening to God will calm your nerves and enable you to discover new insights. New insights often become keys to success.

Are you feeling the daily grind of raising a family? Taking the initiative to slow down and really listen could even help you understand your crazy teenager. (Nahh!! But it may give you more patience.)

Are you watching too much TV? Reading too many novels? Spending too much time in the Internet chat room? Maybe you're substituting entertainment for much-needed quiet and contemplation time.

1) Listen carefully." Advice I needed to follow. Maybe you need it too.

Turning Points:
Computer Crashes, Silence & Renewal Part 3

"Shoot me straight, Doc. I can take it! Is it the love bug virus?" No, it wasn't but my computer was still broken and in the shop for at least five days. *"Five days! What would I do for five days?"* I had a problem but it wasn't the computer. While looking to fill the time, I ran across a story by Arthur Gordon about a doctor's advice for overcoming bleak periods. I was to find an isolated spot and follow the instructions on four slips of paper. The first prescription was *"Listen carefully."*

As the hours passed, I slowly began to relax. Listening soon led to prayer and prayer led to a quiet stillness and the comforting presence of God. At times, there would be prompting to read a particular scripture or write a brief note. "Listen carefully" was a reminder that even in this fast-paced environment, God is still very much in control. *"Come here and listen to me! I'll pour out the spirit of wisdom upon you and make you wise."*

(Proverbs 1:23)

By now I was ready to open the doctor's second prescription: *"Try reaching back."*

"Try reaching back? For what?" On the desk is a photo album given by my two children containing a few of their favorite pictures over the years. *"Memories? Is that what I'm supposed to reach back for?"*

I flipped the pages of the album slowly and began to sort through the stories behind each precious photograph. The smile on my face reflected the warmth in my heart as I paused to slowly reflect and remember. There were:

▶ Baby pictures… (my how they have grown).
▶ Loving moments with my spouse… (we don't do this nearly often enough)!

▶ Family vacations, parties… (we all have them you know).

▶ Silly moments… (I try to forget).

▶ Special occasions… (priceless)!

▶ Pets and other things… (always a special part of our family).

Each picture represented a new story to remember and enjoy. Each story represented golden moments to savor and appreciate. Each golden moment became a treasure trove of memories offering reassurance that I am a precious child of God, created for a purpose… and that purpose is realized in the faces and the hearts of those I have had the privilege to love and receive love in return.

At first, I didn't expect much help from the Bible because there were no photographs. Wrong! Each book is full of God's word pictures imploring us… to learn and remember.

☩ Genealogy lists serve as vivid reminders of those people who went before us.

☩ Stories illustrate the struggles of real people valiantly striving to serve God.

☩ Jesus poignant reminder to, *"eat this bread and drink this wine in remembrance of me."*

☩ Chapter 11 of Hebrews represents God's photo album illustrating heroes of our faith.

My son, obey your father's commands and don't neglect your mother's teaching. Keep their words always in your heart… Wherever you walk, their counsel can lead you. When you sleep, they will protect you. When you wake up in the morning, they will advise you. For these commands and this teaching are lamps to light the way ahead of you. (Proverbs 6:20-23)

☩ Reaching back helps you recall the teaching of your family… of God.

☩ Reaching back offers reassurance that your life has meaning and a purpose.

☩ Reaching back can be the spark, the charge that can rekindle your fire.

This week, try reaching back into your own album of precious memories? I pray you will receive a spark to rekindle your fire. Also, read chapter 11 of Hebrews and catch a glimpse of God's photo album of faith.

Turning Points:
Computer Crashes, Silence & Renewal Part 4

The computer was in the shop for five days but I was the one in real need of help. While searching for answers, I ran across a story by Arthur Gordon about a doctor's advice for overcoming a touch of depression. *"Find an isolated spot and follow the instructions on four separate slips of paper."* While reading the four prescriptions I also studied the book of Proverbs. The combination proved invaluable.

1. Listen Carefully. This first prescription was a poignant reminder that in this fast paced world, God is still very much in control. I was the one who needed to pause. *"Come here and listen to me! I'll pour out the spirit of wisdom upon you and make you wise."* (Proverbs 1:23)

2. Try Reaching Back. A photo album represented precious memories and golden moments to savor and appreciate. Each moment became a treasure trove of memories offering reassurance that I am loved and shaped by family and friends. More than that… *"Wherever you walk, their counsel can lead you. When you sleep, they will protect you."* (Proverbs 6:22)

So far, so good! By now, I was eagerly anticipating opening the third prescription. Carefully unfolding the third piece of paper, I read: ***Reexamine Your Motives.***

"Reexamine your motives! Why? There's nothing wrong with my motives. I work hard to be successful and provide for my family. I enjoy being good at what I do. Is there anything wrong with that?"

A quiet authoritative voice seemed to whisper in my ear… *"Maybe? It all depends on **whom** you're working so hard for? What are your real motives?"*

Truthfully, my motives had subtly changed over the years. I enjoyed the adulation and compliments a little success can bring. I yearned to be recognized as an authority among my colleagues. I liked having a little extra money in my checkbook. Is it wrong to desire the fruit of my creative labors?

Did you notice the last paragraph's emphasis on "I" and "my"? In other words… "I" had a problem.

Reexamine your motives. Are you working for something bigger than yourself?

Choose my instruction rather than silver and knowledge over pure gold. For wisdom is far more valuable than rubies. Nothing you desire can be compared with it. (Proverbs 8:10-11)

Until now, I thought this passage was a reminder to spend more time in Bible study. Not really! Actually, God is showing us where to focus our motives. Silver and gold represent the motives of personal status and financial security. Instruction and wisdom represent striving for something beyond personal accomplishments. In the end, God promises: *"Nothing you desire can be compared with it."*

✞ Reexamine your motives… is a call to discover God's purpose for your life and carry it out.

✞ Reexamine your motives… provides the comfort of knowing you are valued for who you are.

✞ Reexamine your motives… requires courage to reach beyond what is comfortable.

✞ Reexamine your motives… demands humility because ultimate success belongs to God.

✞ Reexamine your motives… promises gifts far greater than anything you've ever imagined.

"All who fear the Lord will hate evil. That is why I hate pride, arrogance, corruption and perverted speech. Good advice and success belong to me. Insight and strength are mine… I love all who love me. Those who search for me will surely find me… My gifts are better than the purest gold, my wages better than sterling silver! Those who love me inherit wealth, for I fill their treasuries. (Parts of 8:13-21)

"Reexamine your motives," for me… was a much-needed reminder from God to repent. *"Forgive me Lord. Purify my heart and help me change."* In the quiet of the early morning hours, alone in my study, I began to cry. Embarrassed, I tried to wipe away the tears but they simply would not stop. For several minutes, I was trapped by an overwhelming sense of guilt. Yet, this is exactly where God wanted me. Because without discovering a need to change, I would never understand what happened next.

Turning Points:
Computer Crashes, Silence & Renewal Part 5

It took five days with a busted computer to teach me that I was the one who really needed fixing. While doing some serious soul-searching, I ran across a story by Arthur Gordon sharing a doctor's advice for overcoming difficulties. *"Find an isolated spot and follow the instructions on four slips of paper."* So, I settled down one long night to study each of the four prescriptions along with the book of Proverbs.

1. **Listen Carefully.** A poignant reminder that in this fast paced world, God is still very much in control. I was the one who needed help. *"Come here and listen to me! I'll pour out the spirit of wisdom upon you and make you wise."* (Proverbs 1:23)

2. **Try Reaching Back.** A photo album provided precious memories and golden moments to savor and appreciate. A treasure trove offering reassurance of the love and acceptance of family, friends and God's blessings. *"Wherever you walk, their counsel can lead you. When you sleep, they will protect you."* (Proverbs 6:22)

3. **Reexamine Your Motives.** Are you working for something bigger than yourself? Whether it's a call to discover God's purpose for your life or the comfort of knowing that you are valued for who you are reexamine your motives requires courage and demands humility. *"Those who search for me will surely find me."* (Proverbs 8:17)

My motives had subtly changed over the years and I needed to repent, so in the quiet early morning hours, alone in the study, I began to cry. For several minutes, I was trapped by an overwhelming sense of guilt. Yet, this is exactly where God wanted me. Because without discovering a need to change, I would never understand what would happen next: The fourth prescription.

Carefully, I opened the piece of paper and studied the six words: ***Write your troubles in the sand.***

For a long time... I didn't know how to respond. The idea of standing on a quiet beach and writing my troubles in the sand soon to be washed away by the incoming tide was certainly comforting. More than anything, I needed the reassurance that I could be forgiven and continually loved and nourished.

Could it be that simple? Actually, no! There is something missing. Troubles don't disappear so easily. Melancholy is not so quickly washed away. I didn't find much help in Proverbs either except for this: *"Happy are those who listen to me, watching for me daily at my gates, waiting for me outside my home! For whoever finds me, finds life..."* (Proverbs 8:34-35) Did you catch it?

...listen to Me...watch for Me...wait for Me...if you find Me, you find life.

This verse turned out to be the answer but it I didn't realize it until I noticed a painting by Thomas Kinkade entitled "A Lighthouse in the Storm." At first all you see are waves crashing against the beach poised to destroy all within their path. It would be a bleak picture if not for the lighthouse. Somehow the bright light continuing to shine in the storm looks reassuring… comforting.   You sense that no matter how hard the storm rages, the lighthouse will continue to stand and provide a light for the lost.

Write your troubles in the sand… can only take us so far. The foaming waves still attack the beach. Where will I look to receive strength? The fierce winds still blow you off course. Where will you find a steady light to guide your way? We need a lighthouse to provide direction and stability. God says: *…listen to Me, watch for Me, wait for Me… if you find Me, you find life.* In other words:

1. **Listen carefully.** God is in control… not you. *"Come here and listen to me."*
2. **Try reaching back.** Look to your treasure trove of memories. *"…they will protect you."*
3. **Reexamine your motives.** Serve something bigger than yourself. *"Those who search…"*
4. **Write your troubles in the sand.** God's promise of forgiveness and hope.
5. **Look to the lighthouse.** God's steady light to guide your way. *"If you find me, you find life."*

As the early morning rays slowly crossed the horizon, I realized it had been a long but satisfying night. I lost a computer but gained something far more precious: a restored and renewed relationship with my precious Lord. *"Your Word is a lamp for my feet and a light for my path."* (Psalm 119:105)

Letters

Dear Larry, I thought you might be interested in knowing that your devotions have become "world travelers". I just returned from a mission trip to Venezuela where I was asked to speak at the English speaking Baptist church in Maracaibo. This was a spur of the moment request and I was rescued by your weekly devotionals "Turning Points" entitled Job and One String. The volunteer mission group held devotions each morning, and I had taken my copies of your weekly series to use at that time. What a blessing! By combining the two weeks on Job and expanding the topic a bit, I had a sermon!!! Thank you for your work and your commitment to serving God. It is amazing how God can use our everyday activity to spread the Gospel. Sowing Seeds of Faith is presented in such down-to-earth fashion that it truly reaches people. You don't have to be a theologian to understand the message. Your sister in Christ, Jean

The story of your dog Honey touched my heart. Our Chablis looks just like her and we even have a picture with a birthday hat. Chablis has not been herself for several days now and in my heart I feel her time is coming soon. She lives with my sister and her old spunk was not there. This is hurting. She is 10 now. Thank you for your web site and the wonderful story of Honey. Thanks, J

What a wonderful surprise to get your mail plus all the others from all over the world. Thanks so much for your thoughtfulness and kindness in what you did with regard to setting up the prayer chain for Ryan. I know for sure that the soaking of Ryan in prayer will produce the desired results.

As a start Ryan was discharged from the hospital today. He feels great, is in a little pain, but quite controllable. His faith and his attitude are so positive that he is already planning a bike trip up through Africa to Zanzibar and Kenya. This is awesome for only a week ago he was hospitalized due to unbearable pain and convulsions. Thanks again for your concern and love. Vince

Larry, I wanted to let you know that I appreciate the effort you put into your weekly devotions. I am the Webmaster for my church's online web site, and have started adding a weekly devotion and a newsletter myself, and realize that what you do is not all that easy. In Christ, Casey

Rev. Davies, I need to tell you just how much I appreciate you and your little church. I sent in a prayer request last week because my home life has been turned up side down. My husband of five years told me he didn't love me anymore that he felt trapped in our marriage and wasn't happy... Since I put in the prayer request I have gotten some answers!! My husband wants to continue counseling and come home. I am praying now that with God's help his attitude will turn around. He will realize the good in our lives instead of focusing so much on the bad. I ask that you would continue to pray for us. I thank God for you, your ministry and your congregation. Prayer is an AWSOME thing. Victoria

Dear Larry: Many moons ago, I was fortunate to attend an Emmaus gathering when you gave us one of your books, "Sowing Seeds of Faith...

In a World Gone Bonkers." You included an envelope with $7.43. We were to sow seeds or do a good deed. I kept this and searched for a place to sow. Nothing happened until this November of 1999. I was part of a medical team to Sri Lanka for two weeks. At lunch one day, I had the opportunity to talk with a Catholic nun who goes among the poorest of the poor and brings children to her school to teach them and provide clothing and food. Otherwise they would not have anything, not even a bowl of rice. I visited the school and saw such precious children. They are beautiful. They sang for us about Jesus. At that moment, I knew that I needed to give the sister my $7.43. She is a humble Christian lady. The $7.43 would go to buy crackers or juice for the children – a rare treat. Thank you for sharing $7.43 with a part of the world that is really in need and much of it has really "gone bonkers." May the year 2000 give us many opportunities to share. Peace, Pauline

More Letters

Every year, Sowing Seeds Ministry receives many letters. Here are a few samples from 2001:

The day has arrived and I have decided not to commit suicide. Everything was planned and I just wanted to end it all, but after all the many, many emails and words of encouragement received by literally hundreds of praying friends out there, I decided to try it out and give life another shot. I know it won't be easy but I am willing to try. I have a lot of hurt and problems to sort out but praise God I know they will come out all right. I am starting over and trying to get back on track. Please keep praying and don't stop those encouraging e-mails! It really helps. God bless you for saving my life! — Selwyn.

I stumbled upon your site this morning; I thought quite by accident and found it really spoke to me. It is clear that each life has brokenness and pain and somehow the veil of e-mail encourages people to share. Your presence on the "Web" is as valuable as the neighborhood church of bricks. — Dan

What a wonderful site! I've been sitting for an hour reading your devotions. It is such an inspiration. I started teaching a high school girls Sunday school class and have never done this before. I know this is the Lord's will for I see growth each week. Please pray for me. God Bless your ministry! — Frankie

I really enjoy reading your e-mails each week. I came across your site a few years ago while working on the Religion section of my city's newspaper and was seeking articles to make the section more diverse. I have really enjoyed reading yours… Anyway, you are my only source of "church" each week and wanted to let you know that I find your e-mails inspiring and uplifting. — Joellyn

I was on your website searching for a devotion for tomorrow night at my Stephen ministry meeting and the title of this one (It's Been A Really Bad Day, Lord!) really resonated with me. Over the last few days, I went to the funeral of a friend's sister who died unexpectedly at 28. I had a minor auto accident and I just learned my ex-husband recently remarried. All in all, what you could safely call a "really bad weekend." Anyway, I intend to read this devotion tomorrow night at my Stephen ministry meeting. It's particularly appropriate given that many of our receivers experience "really bad days" which is what drives them to seek support through Stephen ministry. — Laura

Thank you for your prayers and for this website. A friend of mine introduced this site to me after learning what I am going through. I received so many responses to prayer requests and I appreciate that. God is truly moving in my life. The tears haven't stopped falling yet, but I do know that I'm in God's hands and everything will be all right. God bless you. — Unknown

I don't know who writes this but I have to stop and say thank you for whoever built this site. A few months back I was at my end. My wife and soul mate decided to divorce me to be with someone else who was already married. It almost killed me. One day I went looking for some comfort and found Sowing Seeds of Faith. I have since made a ton of online buddies who prayed me through. Thank you Sowing Seeds. Thank you Lord for the people that make the ministry what it is. — Leon "The Link"

I was searching for poetry contests to enter to get me out of financial straits. I stumbled onto Sowing Seeds of Faith, to which I owe God a debt of gratitude. Tears of joy streamed down my face when a couple of my "Thoughts to Ponder" meditations were "in print" on this website. I've always wanted to write and felt God has been calling me to do so. I've turned my pity parties into devotions, prayers and reaching out and praying for others. Thank you Reverend Davies for allowing God to work in your life via the Internet. Two words sum up Sowing Seeds Ministry: Alleluia and Amen. — Salley

What a wonderful and powerful ministry you offer the world. I've grown so much in my Christian walk and become a better person. I look forward to the weekly devotionals and the prayer chain. Just in case I don't thank you enough... THANK YOU. — *Teri*

I write to encourage you today. Your work is changing lives every day... Keep up the great work in Him, because He is using you to bless more than you'll ever know. — Mike

More from Sowing Seeds Ministry

I hope you enjoyed reading, *Breaking the Peanut Butter Habit... Following God's Recipe for a Better Life*. My prayer is for God to inspire you through the stories and improve your walk of faith. Here are the other Sowing Seeds products currently available.

● **Website** – One of the largest devotional sites on the internet: *www.SowingSeedsofFaith.com* offers over three hundred pages of devotions and ministry ideas.

● **E-mail Ministry** – Every Thursday join thousands of subscribers around the world who receive devotions.

● **Prayer Ministry** – Every Tuesday, Wednesday and Friday you can receive prayer requests from around the world. You can even answer the requests by email.

● **Newspaper Ministry** — Weekly devotions can be emailed directly to your hometown newspaper.

● **Bulletin Inserts** — Each insert begins: **A Gift from Our Church to You**. Continuing devotions that can be read and passed on to a friend.

● **Annual Sowing Seeds Writing Contest** – Every July we select the best submitted from around the world of Devotions, Sermons or Poetry.

If you are interested, simply go to the website and you will receive further instructions. *www.SowingSeedsofFaith.com*

Or write:
Sowing Seeds Ministry
Larry E. Davies
47 Greenwell Ct.
Lynchburg, VA 24502